W9-CAT-040

Revitalizing Congregational Life:
A Synagogue 2000 Series

The Self-Renewing Congregation

Organizational Strategies for
Revitalizing Congregational Life

Isa Aron, Ph.D.

Founding Director, the Experiment in Congregational Education (ECE),
a project of the Rhea Hirsch School of Education,
Hebrew Union College–Jewish Institute of Religion

Foreword by

Dr. Ron Wolfson

Co-Developer, Synagogue 2000

JEWISH LIGHTS PUBLISHING

WOODSTOCK, VERMONT

The Self-Renewing Congregation:
Organizational Strategies for Revitalizing Congregational Life

2002 First printing
© 2002 by Isa Aron
Foreword © 2002 by Ron Wolfson

For information regarding permission to reprint material from this book, please mail or fax your request in writing to Jewish Lights Publishing, Permissions Department, at the address/fax number listed below.

Grateful acknowledgement is given for permission to use the following material:

Excerpts from *Leadership without Easy Answers* by Ronald A. Heifetz, pp. 20, 252–253, 258, 268, Cambridge, Mass.: The Belknap Press of Harvard University Press, copyright © 1994 by the President and Fellows of Harvard College.

Excerpts from *Lord's Song in a Strange Land: Music & Identity in Contemporary Jewish Worship* by Jeffrey A. Summit, copyright © 2000 by Oxford University Press, Inc. Used with permission of Oxford University Press, Inc.

Excerpts from *The Jew Within* by Steven Cohen and Arnold Eisen are reprinted by permission of Indiana University Press.

Library of Congress Cataloging-in-Publication Data
Aron, Isa.
The self-renewing congregation : organizational strategies for revitalizing congregational life / Isa Aron ; foreword by Ron Wolfson.
     p.   cm. — (Revitalizing congregational life)
Includes bibliographical references.
ISBN 1-58023-166-7 (pbk.)
1. Synagogues—United States. 2. Jewish way of life. I. Title. II. Series.
BM653 .A76 2002
296.6'5—dc21   2002010333

10 9 8 7 6 5 4 3 2 1

Manufactured in the United States of America

Published by Jewish Lights Publishing
A Division of LongHill Partners, Inc.
Sunset Farm Offices, Route 4, P.O. Box 237
Woodstock, Vermont 05091
Tel: (802) 457-4000   Fax: (802) 457-4004
www.jewishlights.com

To my husband,
Bill Aron,
who has taught me so much about self-renewal

This book is a product of the work done by the Experiment in Congregational Education (ECE), a project of the Rhea Hirsch School of Education, Hebrew Union College–Jewish Institute of Religion, Los Angeles.

Founded in 1992, the ECE's goal is to assist congregations to become both congregations of learners and self-renewing congregations.

KEY TO SYMBOLS USED IN THIS BOOK

 Case Study

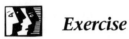 *Exercise*

 Handout

 *Text Study*

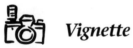 *Vignette*

CONTENTS

FOREWORD

by Dr. Ron Wolfson, Co-Developer, Synagogue 2000;
Director, Whizin Center for the Jewish Future, University of Judaism

For me, the climactic moment of the Shabbat morning prayer service comes when the Torah scroll is returned to the Ark. We have just read from a portion of our most sacred text, distributed honors, celebrated important lifecycle moments, and prayed for those in need of healing. We have paraded the scroll throughout the congregation, so that those in attendance can embrace our "tree of life" with touches and kisses. And, then, as the music swells to a crescendo, we sing the words *Hadesh, hadesh yameinu kekedem!*—"Renew, renew our days as of old!"

The Hebrew word *hadesh* comes from the root *hadash,* meaning "new." *Yameinu* is the plural form of the word *yom*—"day." The prefix *ke* means "as," and the word *kedem* in this tense means "of old." In a different tense, the word *kedem* can mean "to anticipate," "to be in front of." Thus, the plain reading of the text is a call to return to times of old, when things seemingly were better, simpler. But what if we read the statement as a call to action for the future: "Renew, renew our days as we anticipate our future"?

In this important and urgent book, Dr. Isa Aron once again demonstrates her brilliant grasp of what the synagogue must do to become an ever more effective and relevant center for Jewish life. The title says it all:

The Self-Renewing Congregation. The choice of language is crucial. While some have called for "transformation" or "change" of congregations, Dr. Aron calls for "renewal"—renewal of a specific kind. It is a call for renewal from within, not from without—a renewal that begins with institutional self-reflection, proceeds through a process of self-engagement, and ends with self-generated innovations that can deepen the synagogue congregation as sacred community.

The core of the book offers any congregation seeking this path a compelling and realistic roadmap, a vision, and a process that is rooted in applied research and practical experience. In a four-part strategy infused with a combination of organizational dynamics theory, Jewish text study, group exercises, and actual case studies, this valuable volume points the way to congregational renewal that has the maximum chance for success.

The key chapters of the book describe the four steps toward becoming self-renewing. Reminding us of the value of Shabbat as a time of pause, Dr. Aron calls upon busy congregations to literally stop their "busy-ness" to reflect on what it is that drives the vision of the synagogue. But reflection is clearly not enough; congregational leadership is notorious for talking an issue to death and failing to act. Being proactive—linking reflection to action—means anticipating needs and formulating a plan to accomplish a goal. The second step requires collaborative leadership, a concept that is both challenging and vital in synagogue life. Synagogues cannot be led by clergy or laypersons alone; how to create a working collaboration between both is at the core of congregational renewal. The underlying cause of synagogue politics is the diversity of opinions, tastes, styles, and needs of its members. This is certainly true when it comes to the kind of worship experiences people seek; prayer is often a matter of "different strokes for different folks." How can a congregation create a sense of community amid diversity? This is the third step in the process. Finally, in a fourth step that mirrors the first, Dr. Aron suggests that synagogues must honor the past while anticipating the future. It is often true that the "old-timers" and "regulars" who hold on to favorite practices, favorite melodies, favorite programs, and even favorite synagogue locations fail to recognize that change always happens. It is also true that new leadership can dismiss the past as irrelevant, forcing decisions that are more divisive than constructive. Dr. Aron warns us that healthy congregations are "tents" big enough to include and honor both the old and the new, to respect tradition while embracing change.

In this *tour de force,* Dr. Aron combines her prodigious knowledge of the current research in organizational development, congregational studies, and the sociology of the Jewish community with her substantial real-life experience in the field. No ivory tower academic, she has been in the trenches and knows the challenges of moving congregations into the future, primarily through her groundbreaking work in the Experiment in Congregational Education project. If I, along with my partner Dr. Lawrence Hoffman and our colleagues, have learned anything in our own work with congregations through Synagogue 2000—an institute to envision the synagogue of the future—it is that change is rarely easy. It takes time, patience, persistence, leadership, and vision. Yet, the potential payoff is enormous. At the conclusion of the book, Dr. Aron treats us to two inspiring case studies of congregations that have succeeded in becoming self-renewing, and, in the process, created the kind of spiritual community that reaches, teaches, and touches individual Jews, bringing them closer to God and to Judaism.

In the end, is this not what synagogues ought to be: self-renewing congregations of people, sacred communities that matter, that inspire, and that lead us to renew our own days? In this outstanding contribution to the field, Isa Aron has given synagogue leaders a vision and a path to become such a synagogue in the twenty-first century.

ACKNOWLEDGMENTS

In 1992, the Rhea Hirsch School of Education undertook a new project: the Experiment in Congregational Education (ECE). The initial goal of the project was to assist synagogues in becoming congregations of learners, in which more people were learning, at a higher level, in a variety of different ways. As the founding director of the ECE, I had the privilege of working with fourteen congregations directly and influencing many others indirectly. The theory behind this work and its practical manifestations, in both process and product, were the subject of my first book, *Becoming a Congregation of Learners: Learning as a Key to Revitalizing Congregational Life*.

As the project unfolded, my colleagues and I discovered that the goal of becoming a congregation of learners was, in itself, insufficient. Creating new educational opportunities is one thing; sustaining them is quite another. All of the ECE congregations created new programs, but in some the programs were isolated and relatively short-lived. In other congregations the initial educational innovations not only endured but served as catalysts for larger, more ambitious innovations and the development of a culture of learning. What accounted for the difference between superficial, transitory change and deeper, continual transformation? What conditions enabled new programs of learning to flourish? This book is my attempt to answer these questions by exploring four capacities of what we came to call the self-renewing congregation.

The process of discerning and defining these capacities was long and circuitous, and it would not have been possible without the assistance of many many colleagues. Accompanying me on the first leg of the journey were my fellow faculty members from the Rhea Hirsch School of Education, Professor Sara Lee, Dr. Michael Zeldin, and Dr. William Cutter. Their commitment to both action and analysis and their keen intelligence offered just the right mix of challenge and support. Sara, in particular, has been a close adviser to the ECE from its inception; many of the insights of this book originated with her.

The ECE has benefited from a stellar cast of consultants and staff members. Foremost among them has been Dr. Robert Weinberg, an organizational effectiveness consultant who was my closest adviser in the years that I served as director, and who succeeded me as the director of the project in 2001. Rob not only taught me many of the principles that found their way into this book but helped me outline several of the chapters and provided a much-needed close reading of both early and final drafts.

I owe an enormous debt to the two ECE researchers, Dr. Laura Samuels and Dr. Diane Schuster, with whom I coauthored several of the studies that are referred to in the book. Both of them spent untold hours with me trying to find patterns in the data and understand what it is that makes congregations "tick." Other ECE staff members who contributed, directly or indirectly, to my understanding of congregations as organizations include Marci Dickman, Susan Huntting, Dr. Cecile Jordan, Dr. Sam Joseph, Dr. Amy Katz, Edward Reynolds, Ms. Roslyn Roucher, Rabbi Randi Sheinberg, Dr. Susan Shevitz, Linda Thal, Dr. Jack Ukeles, Joy Wasserman, and Dr. John Watkins.

While reading, research, and the advice of consultants were invaluable, nothing could replace the concrete and direct experience of observing the progress of the fourteen congregations that participated in the ECE during its first ten years: Congregation Beth Am, Los Altos Hills, California;

Congregation Har Sinai, Baltimore; Congregation Shaare Emeth, St. Louis; Congregation Sinai, Milwaukee; Isaac M. Wise Temple, Cincinnati; Leo Baeck Temple, Los Angeles; Temple Beth Torah, Kansas City; Temple Emanu-El, Beverly Hills; Temple Emanu-El, San Diego; Temple Emanuel, Dallas; Temple Shalom, Newton, Massachusetts; Temple Sinai, Stamford, Connecticut; The Temple, Atlanta; and Westchester Reform Temple, Scarsdale. Their exemplary lay and professional leaders (too numerous to mention individually) taught me a great deal, not the least of which was how to take risks. I would also like to thank the foundations that supported the ECE during its first ten years: the Nathan Cummings Foundation, the Mandel Associated Foundations, the Covenant Foundation, and the Gimprich Family Foundation.

As I began writing the book I had the great fortune of having a research assistant for a summer. Miriam Heller Stern, who had just completed her first year of graduate school in education at Stanford, conducted all the interviews for the case studies that appear in chapters 3 through 6, and she wrote the first drafts of these case studies as well. She saw me through the initial uncertainties of how to organize the ideas that were floating around in my head, offering many important suggestions related to both structure and content.

The case studies in this book could not have been written without the insights, candor, and above all the generosity of lay and professional leaders, many of whom granted Miriam or myself two or three interviews, not to mention the follow-up e-mails. They include Veronica Abney, Susan Kippur, Sheryl Primakow, Ros Roucher, Dr. Yona Sabar, Dr. Sandy Silas, Lee Silber, Scott Stone, Richard Tell, Cyd Weissman, Cantor Judy Greenfeld, and Rabbis Jonathan Aaron, Alan Cohen, David Cohen, Laura Geller, Richard Jacobs, Rolando Matalon, Marc Margolius, Felicia Sol, Larry Sebert, David Stern, and Lewis Warshauer. Not all of them are quoted in this book, but all made key contributions to my understanding of what it takes to be a self-renewing congregation.

I was fortunate to be able to call on devoted friends and colleagues who read drafts of this manuscripts at various stages and did not stint on their critiques. I am indebted to Bill Aron, Rabbi Miriam Cotzin, Rabbi Karen Fox, Rabbi Laura Geller, Susan Huntting, Dr. David Kaufman, Professor Sara Lee, Dr. Riv-Ellen Prell, Dr. Susan Shevitz, Neal Schuster, and Dr. Robert Weinberg.

I feel especially fortunate to be published by Jewish Lights Publishing, whose professionalism and efficiency enabled me to focus on the writing without worrying about anything else. My editor, Elisheva Urbas, has been wonderfully supportive and encouraging, and publisher Stuart M. Matlins, managing editor Emily Wichland, and project editor Amanda Dupuis were always there to deal with my questions and concerns.

This book is dedicated to my husband of nearly thirty years, Bill Aron. Aside from his extraordinary generosity of spirit and unstinting support of my work, Bill has always served as my role model in reflection, proactivity, collaboration, and openness to change. My debt to him is incalculable.

1

The Self-Renewing Congregation

The synagogue is the institution American Jews love to hate. It is the Jewish organization they are most likely to join, and the one they are most likely to participate in regularly. It is also the most likely target of their ire and their humor. Nearly everyone has a favorite synagogue story—about a boring service, a callous member of the clergy, an outlandish bar mitzvah, a bitter controversy. An old joke tells of the Jewish Robinson Crusoe who builds two congregations on his deserted island: the one he attends, and the one he would never set foot in.

Beyond the jokes and critiques lies an undeniable truth: if there is one place that will preserve the Jewishness of the American Jew, that place is the synagogue. At any given time, forty percent of American Jews belong to a congregation; it is estimated that eighty percent have been members of a congregation at some point in their lives.[1] Whereas early attempts to address the "continuity crisis" focused on day schools and informal Jewish institutions, communal leaders and philanthropists eventually came to the realization that they could not bypass the synagogue. While day schools, summer camps, trips to Israel, and institutes for adult learning are all important vehicles for living a vibrant Jewish life, if one wants to reach the largest proportion of Jews, one must work with congregations.

The recent interest in synagogue "transformation" is a result of the acknowledgment, on one hand, of the enormous potential of synagogues, and the realization, on the other hand, that many have fallen short of their potential. Proponents of synagogue transformation have tried to identify exemplary congregations, analyze what makes them so effective, and teach other congregations how to operate in similar ways. It goes without saying that each "expert" has brought his or her own perspective to this task. Thus, there has been a healthy disagreement about which synagogues really *are* successful, which factors are key to their success, and how one might go about teaching these lessons to other congregations.

This book, and indeed the entire Synagogue 2000 Revitalizing Congregational Life Series, responds to the Jewish community's growing interest in, and accumulating knowledge about, synagogue transformation. The first volume in this series, *Becoming a Congregation of Learners,*[2] focused on learning as a vehicle for synagogue renewal; future volumes will deal with other aspects of congregational life, such as worship, healing, and social justice.

This volume is different from others in the series in that it focuses on the *ways synagogues operate,* rather than the *content of their operations.* A noteworthy congregation may be distinguished by its mode of worship, its innovative approach to study, its caring atmosphere, and so on. But over and above these content areas, a truly excellent congregation is one that does things in a thoughtful and deliberate manner, and that approaches all its activities with a reflective and experimental attitude. Excellence, I will argue, resides not only in program but also in process: the way in which a synagogue deals daily with both opportunities and challenges.

A Simple Mission but a Complicated Reality

The mission of the synagogue can be stated very simply: to help Jews connect with the Jewish Tradition and live by its precepts. But beneath this apparent simplicity lies a host of complex questions:

- Who interprets the Jewish Tradition? What happens when different members of a congregation have different interpretations? And who should have the authority to decide the synagogue's policies? For example, may men and women sit together at worship services? May women be called to the Torah? May women serve as rabbis and cantors? Should the liturgy be changed to include references to women in the tradition? Should the liturgy incorporate gender-inclusive language? The controversies over the role of gender in the synagogue are but a subset of the many conflicts faced by congregations as they try to reconcile the Tradition with contemporary norms and practices.

- What is the appropriate balance between helping Jews connect to the Tradition in the first place, and enhancing their Jewish practice once they become connected? How much energy should be spent on "outreach" as opposed to "in-reach?" Should worship services be oriented toward newcomers or regulars? What is the appropriate balance between single-session programs and long-term classes, and between programs for beginners and those for more advanced learners? Which activities should be oriented to targeted populations, and which should aim to bring the entire congregation together?

- Should congregations set standards for their members? For example, should children preparing to celebrate their bar or bat mitzvah be required to demonstrate their mastery of certain knowledge and skills? Should they be expected to attend services regularly or work for the betterment of the community? Should they be required to continue their studies after the celebration takes place? And what of adults? Other than paying dues, should they be required to engage in any core Jewish activities?

These are just a small sample of the issues with which synagogues must grapple regularly, whatever their size, location, or denominational affiliation. These questions are not easily answered, and one cannot expect that an answer that is satisfactory at one time will remain satisfactory in the future. While much has been written about the substantive issues themselves (such as the role of women in Judaism) and the various programmatic strategies they suggest (such as different ways of doing outreach), relatively little has been written about *how* these issues should be discussed and decided, and *how* the strategies should be chosen. In some congregations these issues are avoided altogether; at others they simmer just below the surface and can erupt at any point. Occasionally the issues become so divisive that they lead to the firing of a staff member, the resignation of a lay leader, or a split in the congregation itself.

Still other congregations have more productive ways of dealing with these issues, discussing them openly before they erupt, and soliciting diverse opinions so that everyone feels heard. These synagogues appear to be ahead of the curve. They spot trends early and take the time to analyze them carefully. A collective spirit of experimentation leads them to take risks, and these experiments are routinely monitored, evaluated, improved, and, when necessary, discarded. In short, these congregations have a kind of wisdom that enables them to spend their energy on essential, significant matters rather than unnecessary infighting.

What is wisdom, when applied to a congregation? And how is it acquired? As will be discussed below, the social sciences have much to teach us about organizational effectiveness, especially as applied to congregations. But the Jewish Tradition, too, has something to teach. As is appropriate, this book looks to Jewish texts to glean insight from them. These texts were written thousands of years ago in contexts vastly different from our own; they rarely speak directly to the issues faced by synagogues today. Yet, they contain some important, timeless truths about the human condition and about what is important in Jewish life. We begin, then, with what the Bible and some of its contemporary commentators can teach us about wisdom.

A *Midrash* on Attaining Wisdom

Think about the moment in which, according to the Torah, humanity first attained wisdom: the fateful moment in which Adam and Eve ate from the Tree of Knowledge.

We all learned the story as children: God created Adam and Eve, and placed them, along with the newly created plants and animals, in the Garden of Eden. In the Garden, all their needs were taken care of: "The Lord God caused to grow every tree that was pleasing to the sight and good for food" (Genesis 2:9). Adam and Eve were free to do as they wished, to eat of every growing plant, and to rule every living thing. Only one fruit was forbidden to them: the fruit of the Tree of Knowledge. Sure enough, in the very next chapter, at the serpent's suggestion, they violated the one commandment they were given. Eating of this forbidden fruit gave Adam and Eve a new awareness: "Then the eyes of both of them were opened and they perceived that they were naked" (3:7). It also led to their banishment from the Garden.

Centuries of commentary have been devoted to this pivotal act, which changed the course of human history as it is understood by both Jews and Christians. Why did Eve succumb to the serpent's goading? Why did Adam acquiesce to Eve's suggestion that he too should have a taste? What kind of new perception did Adam and Eve gain? And was this new insight worth the loss of their heretofore idyllic existence? Generally speaking, the story of Adam and Eve's "fall" is viewed as a great tragedy, the irrevocable loss of the perfect world that could have been theirs in perpetuity.

But a few commentators, including some classical Jewish mystics and some contemporary psychologists, look at this story differently. Summarizing this different line of interpretation, Noam Zion and Jo Milgrom write:

> [T]he so-called Original Sin was absolutely necessary, and even gave birth to the advancement of humanity, not its decline.... Despite the pain of growing up, humans earned greater

knowledge, greater self-understanding and greater responsibility due to eating the fruit from the Tree of Knowledge. There is no sense in returning to the innocence and childlikeness of the Garden of Eden. Far better is a world which cultivates an appreciation of the dangers as well as the possibilities inherent in a world full of people who know good and evil.[3]

Rabbi Lawrence Kushner takes this idea even further, seeing Adam's and Eve's act as a necessary stage in human development, a rite of passage deliberately devised by God:

> Adam and Eve are duped, not by the snake, but by God. They were lovingly tricked into committing the primal act of disobedience that alone could ensure their separation from God, their individuation, and their expulsion from (childhood's) garden.[4]

In this view God wanted, and perhaps even *needed,* Adam and Eve to violate the prohibition, for only through this transgression would they gain wisdom and autonomy. As Kushner points out, the day Adam and Eve left the Garden was the day they became fully human.

Perhaps, this *midrash* suggests, we are mistaken when we bemoan the human condition, wishing we didn't have to struggle to survive. Instead, we should appreciate our situation, knowing that when we struggle with adversity we are fulfilling our potential as thoughtful, knowing human beings.

While this perspective may seem pollyanish when applied to individuals facing catastrophes such as illness, war, and natural disasters that seem beyond their control, it makes a good deal of sense when applied to organizations. An organization that pretends it is living in an ideal world, or that longs for a "return" to such a world, is living in the false, preconscious innocence of the Garden of Eden. Like Adam and Eve, such an organization must eat from the Tree of Knowledge so that it may see things as they really are.

In the words of Michael Fullan:

It seems perverse to say that problems are our friends, but we cannot develop effective responses to complex situations unless we actively seek and confront the real problems which are in fact difficult to solve. Problems are our friends because it is only through immersing ourselves in problems that we can come up with creative solutions. Problems are the route to deeper change and deeper satisfaction. In this sense effective organizations "embrace problems" rather than avoid them.[5]

Imagine the typical "preconscious" synagogue. When it was first created, it may, in fact, have lived in a pristine state, much like Adam and Eve in the Garden. Its members may have formed a closely knit family, sharing common values and common assumptions about being Jewish. There may have been personality conflicts, and disagreements may have arisen from time to time. But the congregation's mission was clear, as were the lines of responsibility. The rabbi and the cantor led services, the lay leaders provided the financial support, and the membership attended faithfully.

It's not very likely that any congregation has ever lived such an idyllic Eden-like existence. But this illusion of stability and predictability is hard to shake. Some congregations long for a return to this mythical era; others operate on automatic pilot, as though, somehow, they are still living in the Garden. They proceed as though their mission is clear and unambiguous, never fully considering that "the way we've always done things" may need to change. Though they may tinker a bit around the edges, they rarely acknowledge that some essential and central issues need to be addressed. They are able, somehow, to overlook the fact that their membership has changed and that the environment has also changed. People live busier lives, farther apart from one another, and community is hard to find. Anti-Semitism (or the Holocaust, or the State of Israel) no longer serves as the unifying force that it once did. Intermarriage is more prevalent, and with it a host of new challenges. The timeless traditions of the synagogue seem further and further removed from the realities and aspirations of its members. Too many synagogues, unfortunately, have yet to confront these developments head on and to grapple with them.

If it took eating from the forbidden fruit and exile from the Garden of Eden for people to be fully human, what is the parallel act that will shake congregations from their complacency? How can synagogues become aware of their own "nakedness" and begin thinking about how to perfect themselves? No act of God will save our congregations. We must, on our own, acquire the wisdom that is the organizational equivalent of the knowledge and awareness attained by Adam and Eve. We must become self-renewing congregations.

What Is the Self-Renewing Congregation?

Social scientists have always been fascinated by the way in which the behaviors of an individual are affected by those of a larger group. While most early studies focused on peer pressure and mob psychology, a different line of inquiry began with the sociologist Kurt Lewin, who studied organizations and theorized about the factors that enable them to adapt and change. This interest intensified in the 1970s as the field of organizational development was born. Researchers watched intently as the fortunes of different institutions rose and fell, and attempted to discern the factors that contributed to their success and failure. Which corporations were able to adapt to changing economic conditions? Which schools learned to serve new, more diverse student populations and to embrace new approaches to teaching and learning? What enabled some institutions to embrace new technologies and to become technological innovators themselves? What led some to rethink their personnel policies and empower their workers?

As research into these questions began to accumulate, answers began to emerge. Some organizations, it seems, act more "intelligently" than others. They are open to new ideas, flexible in their outlook, thoughtful in their policies, and therefore better able to adapt to their changing environments. The wisdom of these organizations is different from, and not entirely dependent upon, the intelligence of the individuals within them. Smart, capable people working in isolation, or competing with one another, do not add up to a smart organization. The effectiveness of an organization is dependent on the synergy between its members.

Moreover, the "intelligence" of an organization is not a permanent characteristic. An organization that demonstrates its acumen, flexibility, and resilience in one era may, as many did, lose these capacities a few years later. Thus, rather than using an adjective to describe what such an organization *is*, it seems more appropriate to use an adverb, which would emphasize what it *does:* It scans and interprets its environment in search of potential issues and problems, explores a range of possible new directions, takes action, assesses the outcome of its actions, and, without missing a beat, begins the cycle anew. This organization not only articulates its vision but also monitors its progress toward that vision, and it is on the lookout for ways in which the vision is incomplete and in need of revision. In the words of Peter Senge, an organizational development consultant, this organization "is continually expanding its capacity to create its future."[6] Senge and others have used the term "learning organization" to characterize institutions that engage in this continuous cycle of action and reflection. Some who have applied the concept of the learning organization to congregations have used the term "learning congregation."[7] By contrast, I have chosen the term "self-renewing" to emphasize the reflexive and cyclical nature of this activity, the fact that much of the learning is internal, and that the learning is incomplete without concomitant action.

Four capacities[8] are the cornerstones to congregational self-renewal. These are collective capacities, over and above the individual abilities of congregants and staff. Each capacity enables the congregation to do the seemingly paradoxical—to hold fast to both ends of an apparent dilemma. They are:

- Thinking back and thinking ahead: being both reflective and proactive

- Enabling leaders to follow, and followers to lead: practicing collaborative leadership

- Seeing both the forest and the trees: creating community among diverse individuals

- Honoring the past while anticipating the future: balancing tradition and change

Each of these dual capacities is discussed in a separate chapter of the book (chapters 3 through 6). In each case I explain why both of these seemingly opposite capacities are critical for synagogues to cultivate. Drawing on organizational theory and research from the worlds of business, education, and government and on selected Jewish texts, I explore what each capacity entails. Drawing on sociological studies of religious organizations and on my own decade-long experience working with synagogues, I offer examples of the problems that arise when these capacities are absent and the benefits that accrue when they are present. Developing these capacities, and balancing one against the other, is no easy matter, and each chapter includes exercises designed to help a synagogue committee or task force understand and practice the capacity in question. It also includes text study guides that can serve as springboards for discussion. Finally, each chapter includes a real-life case study of a synagogue's efforts to develop the capacity in question.

Framing these four chapters are an introductory chapter and a concluding chapter. Chapter 2 reviews the recent history of American synagogues and explains why, at this juncture, it is critical that they develop the capacity to become self-renewing. At the end of the book, chapter 7 deals with two kinds of synergy—between the four capacities discussed in this book, and between the congregation as a whole and the individuals within it.

2

Inadvertent Change
vs. Conscious Self-Renewal

Why should synagogues aspire to become self-renewing? Why shouldn't a venerable institution that has served the Jewish people well for over 2,000 years keep on doing what it always has? Synagogues are not, after all, corporations, which are judged by the size of their profits. Nor are they like schools, which must meet governmental standards. Shouldn't congregations adhere to a timeless tradition? If so, why do they need to concern themselves with change?

These questions are misplaced because they assume that synagogues have not already undergone enormous changes. In fact, synagogues have changed continually over their 2,000-year history, adapting themselves to fit the social and political milieu in which Jews have found themselves. There is no doubt that synagogues will continue to change. The only question is: will these changes be timely or belated, careful or mindless? And while it would be inappropriate to judge a congregation by its earnings or the test scores of its members, congregations have much in common with other organizations. Operating in the same social context, synagogues are affected by many of the same demographic and cultural shifts that affect corporations and schools.

Becoming a self-renewing congregation requires that a synagogue re-examine, and perhaps reconfigure, itself in a way that is both faithful to the Jewish tradition and responsive to the changing situation of its congregants. This chapter begins with a very brief history of the synagogue as an institution, followed by a more extensive discussion of the evolution of American synagogues in the twentieth century. To meet the needs of future generations, I argue, the synagogue must continue to develop, but in a more purposeful and deliberate manner. To serve the Jews of the twenty-first century, synagogues must become self-renewing.

Changes in the Synagogue Over Time

Historians disagree as to whether the first synagogues were established in the period of the First Temple (built in approximately 1000 B.C.E.) or the Second Temple (rebuilt in 515 B.C.E.). They disagree, as well, as to whether the primary function of the earliest synagogues was prayer, Torah study, or both. All agree, however, that by the end of the Second Temple period, synagogues could be found throughout both Israel and the Diaspora. When the Second Temple was destroyed in 70 C.E., the synagogue became, by default, the focal point of Jewish life. Religious rituals that had been performed in the Temple were transferred to the synagogue, albeit in modified form. For example, *avodah* (the ritual sacrifice of animals and produce) evolved into *avodah shebalev*, the service of the heart, i.e., prayer.

Rabbinic leaders strove to impress on subsequent generations of Jews the idea that the synagogue was the rightful descendant of the Temple and heir to its legacy. One text put it in particularly poetic terms: "As the gazelle leaps from place to place and from fence to fence and from tree to tree, so God jumps and leaps from synagogue to synagogue to bless the children of Israel."[1] In a more didactic vein, a legend from the Talmud recounts an imaginary conversation between Abraham and God, in which Abraham seeks assurance that the Jewish people will never be destroyed. As long as they continue to bring sacrifices, God replies, Israel will be able to atone for their sins and prevent destruction. But what will happen, Abraham asks, after the Temple is destroyed and sacrifices can no longer be brought? God has an answer for this concern as well: Reciting the order of the sacrifices in the context of prayer will be seen as the equivalent of bringing sacrifices and will atone for people's sins.[2] In these teachings and others like them, the rabbis sought to establish the role of the synagogue, and of prayer, as central and essential.

Though the synagogue was primarily a place of worship and study, its functions expanded over time to meet the needs of the Jewish community. In many medieval communities, the synagogue doubled as an inn for travelers. And while separate institutions (such as schools and courts) arose in response to other communal needs, the synagogue often served as the place in which the community gathered, announcements were made, and rabbinic judgments rendered.

The Rate of Change Accelerates

When Jews immigrated to North America, their synagogues changed more dramatically and more quickly. Though the earliest American congregations were relatively modest, they served as the central Jewish address not only for worship and study[3] but also for companionship. The synagogue was the place to which Jews could turn in good times (such as weddings and circumcisions) and bad (such as poverty, illness, and death). "In colonial America," writes historian Abraham Karp, "synagogue and community were synonymous."[4] To quote historian Jacob Rader Marcus, "No colonial American Jewish community ever sheltered more than one permanent synagogue, and the local synagogue virtually exercised a monopolistic control over every Jew within its ambit."[5]

After the American Revolution, as Jews from different European countries continued to arrive in greater numbers, synagogues began to multiply and diversify. Nonetheless, three important patterns that had been set in the colonial era remained. First, synagogues continued to function as focal points for the Jewish community. Second, because the earliest synagogues were established well before the first rabbis arrived in North America, the practice of congregations hiring their clergy (rather than the clergy founding congregations) became an accepted convention. Third, in the absence of any centralized rabbinic authority, it was understood that any group, whatever its size and whatever its motivations, could start its own congregation.[6]

As American Jews became more established and assimilated, they began to model their synagogues after Protestant churches. "Following the Civil War, Jewish congregations across the country built new structures of monumental proportions and fantastic architectural style."[7] These "temples," as most were called, had a dual mission: perpetuating the Jewish tradition while adapting that tradition to fit with the exigencies of contemporary American life. Finding the right balance between adaptation and preservation has proved to be complicated and endlessly controversial. In the 1880s the controversies centered on the inclusion of English or German prayers and the introduction of mixed seating; today they are more likely to concern the style of music and the role played by diverse members, such as gays and lesbians or non-Jewish spouses. But whatever the specific issue, and whatever the denomination of the synagogue in question, the tension between adaptation and preservation remains a perennial dynamic.

The Rise of the Synagogue Center

In the late nineteenth century, a second tension in American Jewish life arose, which left an indelible mark on the American synagogue: the tension between Judaism as a religion and Judaism as an ethnicity. The concerns of the Eastern European Jews, whose mass immigration spanned four decades (1881–1921), tended to be more communal than religious. They were less interested in having a place to pray than in having a place to congregate, to commemorate lifecycle events, and to serve as a safety net in time of need. To attract and accommodate these Jews, a new kind of synagogue evolved, the "synagogue center." One prominent rabbi, writing in 1936, put it quite bluntly: "If the Synagogue as a *Beth Hatefila* (a house of worship) has lost its hold upon the masses, some institution would have to be created that could and would attract the people, so that the group consciousness of the Jew might be maintained. The name center seems to work this magic with thousands who would not be attracted to the place if we simply called it Synagogue or Temple."[8]

The synagogue center took as its guiding principle the tripartite function of a congregation—as a *bet tfilah,* a house of prayer; a *bet kneset,* a house of assembly; and a *bet midrash,* a house of study. Historian David Kaufman, whose study of the synagogue center is required reading for anyone wishing to truly understand synagogue life, notes that the synagogue center was a new kind of congregation, one that was "originally and quintessentially American."[9] In the synagogue center, "study" took the form of classes, primarily for children. "Assembly" was embodied in a series of social clubs and events, requiring a social hall and a catering facility. When the congregation could afford them, recreational facilities were added to the mix; hence the title of Kaufman's book, *Shul with a Pool.*

As it evolved over subsequent decades, the synagogue center became the perfect vehicle for and expression of the Judaism practiced by the generation of American Jews born between the two world wars. Most were born to Eastern European immigrant parents and raised in ethnically Jewish neighborhoods. Whether in response to discrimination or simply by preference, they tended to associate primarily with other Jews, even when they moved to more ethnically mixed suburbs. Herbert Gans, who studied Park Forest, a middle-class suburban housing project built in 1948, wrote that "from the very beginning it seemed to be important to Jewish Park Foresters to 'recognize' whether or not any of their neighbors were Jewish."[10] Very quickly, they formed a tightly knit social circle, created a Sunday school for their children, and began to think about establishing a synagogue. Their reasons for wanting a synagogue, however, had little to do with their interest in worship and much to do with their interest in impressing their non-Jewish neighbors.

> Most interesting in this demand for a congregation is the reason given by many supporters: "They'll have more respect for us, to show that we have arrived, that we're not merely a bunch of individuals." The "they" referred, of course, to the non-Jewish neighbors. This congregation movement was born not entirely of a religious impulse, but of one which attempted to demonstrate the solidarity and respectability of the Jewish community to the rest of Park Forest.[11]

Many suburban congregations were built out of a similar impulse, termed by Samuel Heilman (and others) the "Jewish edifice complex":

> That complex allowed both acculturation into America and a simultaneous self-conscious display of Jewish identity. The building of a synagogue could serve for the Jews who were moving into *terra incognita* as a kind of monument to their tribal identity. But it did not automatically exclude them from suburbia or from America. In America being a 'good Christian' and being a 'good citizen' were expected to mean by and large the same thing. As good Christians went to church, so good Americans were expected to also. If the Christians had their churches, the Jews could have their suburban temples, to prove that they had arrived and that they belonged in this new place.[12]

Judging by its popularity and longevity, the synagogue center should be considered a resounding success. "Whatever its congregational name, the American synagogue of today customarily perceives itself as a 'Jewish center.'"[13] In the 1950s and 1960s, the synagogue center did, in fact, evoke great pride and satisfaction. However, even during their heyday, synagogue centers did not appeal to the entire Jewish population. Only sixty percent of Jews were affiliated with a congregation at any one time.[14] Moreover, a much smaller number of Jews attended regularly. According to a 1958 poll, only eighteen percent of American Jews attended synagogue weekly.[15] To quote Samuel Heilman again:

> The suburban synagogue became a perfect reflection of the ambivalence of American Jews. It was built and joined as a sign of Jewish tribal consciousness and religious ethnic identity, but participation in its activities (and especially those that were particularly religious) was part-time at best, which served to signal that its members were busy doing other things and did not want to be completely identified with what went on inside or even to acknowledge that the synagogue played a large part in their lives.[16]

The Decline of the Synagogue Center

In retrospect, it should have been no surprise that the children who grew up in these suburban synagogues found much to criticize. Jewish baby boomers (to use the common sociological term for the generation born between 1941 and 1961) were more affluent and better educated by secular standards than any in Jewish history. As full participants in the American youth culture and Vietnam-era protests, they derided many of the institutions in which their parents participated, and their critiques of the synagogues in which they were raised were particularly harsh.[17] To quote Sidney Schwarz:

> [Baby boomers] pointed to the hypocrisy of their parents who dropped them off at Hebrew school and attended services only on the High Holidays. They mocked their own bar or bat mitzvah celebrations for being long on ostentation and short on religious significance. They pointed to their own lack of Hebraic and Judaic competency and used it as an indictment of their Jewish education.[18]

These critiques, first heard in the 1970s, have intensified in subsequent decades. In public speech and private conversation, in scholarly articles and the popular press, the synagogue center has been accused of being sterile and empty, catering to the masses rather than nurturing genuine community, and focusing on outward appearance rather than inward spiritual growth.

Many of these critiques reflect generational taste and are examples of the controversies related to adaptation versus preservation, alluded to above. For example, whereas one generation of Jews found the grand sanctuary with its high dome and raised dais spiritually uplifting, the next found it cold and impersonal, preferring a smaller space with circular seating. Neither space is inherently Jewish; the sensibilities and preferences of both generations were formed by the larger culture in which they came of age.

Music is another arena in which the conflict over generational preferences looms large. The founders of the synagogue center favored liturgical performances, with operatic cantors and large choirs. Baby boomers, on the other hand, tend to prefer folklike music and greater congregational participation. Each generation was influenced by the musical idiom and trends of its time.

Sidney Schwarz summarizes the conventional wisdom of the baby boomer generation when he offers the following prescriptions:

> The atmosphere must be casual and fun. Education must be maximally interactive and provide practical guidance for daily living. Worship needs to speak to the heart and not shy away from demonstrative expressions of joy and celebration. Ritual roles and organizational leadership must be as egalitarian as religious principles allow and must not be accorded on the basis of wealth alone. No effort should be spared in creating opportunities for small-group and one-on-one interactions to counteract the anonymity of large institutions.[19]

In his book *Finding a Spiritual Home*, Schwarz elaborates on the features of those congregations that are deemed most successful today, and he offers vivid descriptions and personal stories from four synagogues that meet his criteria. As a baby boomer myself, I find these descriptions immensely appealing. But it would be a mistake to ignore the lessons of history and to assume that the atmosphere that appeals to one generation will appeal to the next. Even as the synagogue centers of the mid-twentieth century seek to update themselves by emulating the preferred musical settings and adult programming of the late twentieth century, they are increasingly filled with a new generation of congregants. Termed by sociologists Generation X, these newer members are part of

> ...the 80 million Americans who were born between 1961 and 1981. This is the "buster" generation, the children of the so-called baby boomers. While they are a diverse lot, they also share many common cultural experiences related to advances in technology, the failed marriages of their parents, changes in the structure of the economy, and the liberation politics that transpired during their childhood and youth.[20]

There have been few, if any, studies of Jewish GenXers, as they are called, so it would be premature to make any generalizations about their religious outlook. However, the comments of Donald E. Miller and Arpi Misha Miller, writing about Christian members of this generation, are worth noting:

> One generalization that seems to be true...is that young adults are simply not attending traditional mainline churches in great numbers. This observation sometimes diminishes the fact that Xers are a deeply spiritual generation, seeking meaning and purpose while simultaneously avoiding what they perceive to be inauthentic attempts to mediate the sacred.... Their failure to commit to traditional religious and denominational struc-tures does not signal their lack of interest in questions of meaning and values. *Instead, it signals that new institutions are being birthed, and that current ones must be reinvented if they are to survive within this environment.*[21] (emphasis added)

Why Aspire to Become a Self-Renewing Congregation?

The observations of Miller and Miller point to the critical importance of becoming a self-renewing congregation. Given the way in which the needs and tastes of synagogue members (and potential members) have changed in the past century, it would be foolish to assume that they will remain fixed in the future. The need to balance adaptation to American society with the preservation of timeless Jewish values and practices will continue. Changing social and political realities will surely influence how Jews see themselves and how they see Judaism. New trends in music and the arts will alter people's aesthetic sensibilities, along with what they consider to be spiritually meaningful. The Internet may or may not transform how Jews interact with one another, but if the Internet doesn't, future technologies will.

Beyond the challenge of negotiating between adaptation and preservation, synagogues face another important challenge: to overcome what might be called a "service center" mentality. While the majority of Jews in the 1950s and 1960s were willing to pay dues to synagogues that they rarely attended, this mind-set has begun to erode. Younger congregants tend to view their synagogues as membership organizations, not unlike the automobile club. People join the automobile club because they anticipate the need for emergency road service or assistance in planning trips. They do not feel any emotional connection to the organization or any particular affinity with its other members. If the auto club represents or advocates a value they hold, such as highway safety, that may be an added bonus. But when it comes time to renew their membership, their calculation is likely to be purely instrumental: are they getting their money's worth? If the club's membership fee were to increase above the value of its services, most if not all would let their membership lapse.

While it would be an exaggeration to say that the American synagogue has become as unimportant and utility-driven as the auto club, there is a sense in which the analogy holds. Typically, congregants join a synagogue when their oldest child enrolls in either preschool or religious school; after the bar/bat mitzvah (or confirmation) of their youngest child, they think twice about whether they "really need" to retain their membership, and they may well drop out.[22] Congregations play into this "service center" mentality when they send out notices of membership renewal in the months before the High Holidays and require tickets for High Holiday worship.[23] Demographic studies indicate that an increasing number of Jews do not value what their synagogue has to offer sufficiently to make the financial commitment to join; this trend is likely to increase if the cost of synagogue membership and the rates of intermarriage keep rising. To fulfill their mission of perpetuating the Jewish tradition, American synagogues must overcome the service-center mentality.

They must look beyond the superficial needs of their potential members—for bar or bat mitzvah training or for High Holiday tickets—to their more enduring needs for community, spirituality, and psychological support. And they must learn how to meet these needs in ways that are in keeping with both the traditions and the sensibilities of their members. They must become self-renewing.

A New Perspective on Congregational Life

This chapter began with a question: is the concept of the self-renewing organization, first developed in the business world, appropriate for a congregation? The primary motivation for corporations to become self-reflective and deliberative is to help them stay ahead of the competition, to know what the next hot product will be *before,* not after, it is produced by its competitors. Does the synagogue need to develop this kind of advantage? Can't it simply stick to its traditional mission and its traditional formats?

My argument thus far has been that the synagogue has changed continually throughout its 2,500-year history. When Jews and Judaism evolved, their synagogues evolved with them. The main difference between the evolution of the first 2,400 years and that of the most recent one hundred is the rate of change. The synagogue of the twenty-first century must take as a given the need for continual transformation and revitalization at an ever-accelerating pace.

Now I would add a second argument for developing the capacity for self-renewal. Harsh though it may sound, synagogues must be competitive. In fact, the competition they face is keener than that faced by corporations. A manufacturer is in competition only with those who produce similar products; a congregation, by contrast, is in competition with all the demands on the time, attention, and commitment of its members. It competes with their work, their recreation, their civic activities, and a dizzying array of popular media. To prevail in face of such stiff competition requires that congregations be more responsive than ever to their potential members and more sensitive to their needs. The cases presented in this book exemplify the challenges faced by synagogues and the ways in which the most successful congregations marshal their intelligence, energy, and resources to meet these challenges.

A New Analogy for the Effective Congregation

In their landmark study *The Jew Within*, Steven Cohen and Arnold Eisen describe the fluid identities and commitments of American Jews in the following terms:

> The principal authority for contemporary American Jews, in the absence of compelling religious norms and communal loyalties, has become the sovereign self. Each person now performs the labor of fashioning his or her own self, pulling together elements from the various Jewish and non-Jewish repertoires available, rather than stepping into an "inescapable framework" of identity…given at birth. Decisions about ritual observance and involvement in Jewish institutions are made and made again, considered and reconsidered, year by year and even week by week. American Jews speak of their lives, and of their Jewish beliefs and commitments, as a journey of ongoing question-

ing and development. They avoid language of arrival. There are no final answers, no irrevocable commitments.[24]

What can Jewish institutions do, Cohen and Eisen ask, to increase the chance that the commitments these Jews make (however tentative and however individualistic) are Jewish ones? Their answer comes in the form of an analogy—synagogues must learn to operate like transit systems:

> Jewish institutions face a formidable task in this period of voluntarism and mobility. They must have a range of options available to every individual at every moment, so that when he or she is ready to seize hold of Jewishness or Judaism, the right option is there to be had. Jewish professionals more and more seem like the operators of a transit system. A bus must be ready and waiting at the bus-stop at the exact moment that the prospective Jewish rider appears. The fleet must be sufficiently large to be there whenever wanted, and it must be sufficiently diverse to take account of the diverse tastes and needs of its potential clientele.[25]

The synagogues of an earlier era could afford to operate like fixed and stable destinations, secure in their programs and confident that Jews would seek them out. The synagogues of tomorrow, though, will need greater fluidity and greater mobility. Like a transit system, they will need to travel to their riders, providing the appropriate vehicle at the appropriate stop at the appropriate time. A tall order indeed. But some synagogues have learned to function in just this way. Taking nothing for granted, they have learned to: reflect on the challenges they face and become proactive in meeting them; increase their expertise and their flexibility by practicing collaborative leadership; accommodate the diversity of their members while nurturing a holistic sense of community; and balance preservation and adaptation, tradition and change. In short, they have become self-renewing.

3

Thinking Back
and Thinking Ahead:
Being Reflective and Proactive

In June the professional staff and the co-chairs of the adult education committee gather to review a draft of the congregational learning brochure for the coming year. The following conversation takes place:

Synagogue Administrator: So what do you think? Looks great, no? And right on time, for once!

Assistant Rabbi: Do we have to keep offering Sunday morning Torah study? Attendance was dismal this year! Never more than four or five people, at best.

Senior Rabbi: One Sunday, when it was my turn to teach, only Sam and Sadie Shapiro showed up. It was so embarrassing, and so painful to get through the hour! I don't understand it. We used to get fifteen or more regulars. And the conversation was so lively. It used to be my favorite class.

Cantor: Don't you remember that we talked about this last summer? We were going to try to figure out what was wrong—is it the time slot? the topic? the format?

Senior Rabbi: Oh yeah. I was going to have a little conversation with the regulars. (Turning to the Educator) We were also going to do a little recruiting, weren't we? What happened to those ideas? (Turning to the chairs of the Adult Education Committee) And you were going to do a survey of potential learners, no?

First Co-Chair of the Adult Education Committee: We were?

Second Co-Chair of the Adult Education Committee: I think you were on vacation when it came up. Well, rabbi, I'm sorry, but it never got on our agenda. But could we talk about our committee's proposal for a series of debates about ethical issues? Everyone loves the idea, and we've even come up with a list of topics. Maybe we could substitute this for the Torah study?

Senior Rabbi: That's an interesting idea.

Synagogue Administrator: Well, if you want to get this into the brochure in time, I need topics and names of presenters within two weeks, at the latest.

Educator: It sounds like a good idea, but I wonder if that's the right time slot. And what message are we sending if we eliminate the Sunday morning Torah study? Does that imply that we don't value Torah study enough?

Senior Rabbi: Surely a debate on ethical issues would have to make reference to rabbinic texts and responsa. That counts as Torah also!

Second Co-Chair of the Adult Education Committee: I never thought about the connection between Jewish texts and the ethical debates our committee discussed. But it's an exciting idea. How can we make this happen?

First Co-Chair of the Adult Education Committee: Hey, wait a second. You can't put this new program on Sunday mornings. I can never come then, and neither can half of the committee!

Synagogue Administrator: Well, someone make a decision and get back to me by July 1.

Senior Rabbi: Unfortunately, I'm 10 minutes late for my 11 A.M. appointment, so we need to conclude this meeting.

Assistant Rabbi: We've raised and avoided some really important issues today, like: What are the adult learning needs of our congregants? What constitutes Torah study? What goals do we have for adult learning? When are we going to really talk about these things?

This dialogue points to one of the basic problems of synagogue life—how easy it is to run on automatic pilot until a crisis develops and it becomes necessary to grab hold of a quick fix. The Sunday morning Torah class has been perceived as problematic for at least a year. It is agreed that a full understanding of what is wrong requires additional information and a discussion of the overall goals of adult learning. But somehow a year has gone by without the data being collected and the issues discussed. With the brochure about to go to press, the group latches onto a new solution but has no time to explore the idea fully or consider any other alternatives.

Gilbert Rendle, of the Alban Institute, tells a similar story drawn from his experiences as a church consultant:

> I once sat with a governing board of thirty people in a congregation that was concerned its rate of growth was not keeping up with the rate of growth in the surrounding community. Ten minutes into the discussion one board member said that he had recently been reading a denominational newsletter and remembered a series of articles about doing ministry with single adults. The congregations highlighted in this article had grown significantly. "I move," he said, ending his speech, "that we begin a ministry to singles as a way of increasing our growth in membership." There was already a second offered to his motion before I had time to speak. But when I questioned the group, we discovered that none of the thirty people present was single.[1]

After asking a few more questions, Rendle discovered that not only were there very few singles in the congregation, but few singles lived in the rural area where this church was located. "Yet this congregation was poised and ready to 'do something' about their situation that would involve time, money, and people, with no possibility of addressing the real issues that made it hard for them to receive new members."[2]

These cases illustrate a pattern in congregational life that is all too common. When synagogues fail to be reflective, not fully attending to the issues that arise, they miss the opportunity to be proactive, intervening before the deadline looms or the problem becomes cataclysmic. Then, when it comes time to make a decision, they are unprepared to think carefully about the deeper issues or consider a range of options, and they fall back on easy answers. When it is discovered that the panacea is not working, the vicious circle of being reactive and unreflective begins anew.

This tendency to relegate complex problems to the back burner until they boil over may seem surprising, at first. As individuals, the key players in congregational life are, by and large, thoughtful and energetic. The professionals are conversant with many of the issues in contemporary Jewish life. Lay leaders are often accomplished in their field. Yet, somehow, the whole adds up to less than the sum of its parts.

One reason is that synagogue professionals are perennially overworked. There is always another phone call to be returned, another hospital visit that ought to be made, another meeting with the parents of a misbehaving student, a couple in need of additional counseling, a student who is struggling with her Torah reading, and so on. In the face of pressing day-to-day matters, long-range concerns inevitably fade into the background. The Jewish calendar itself may reinforce this tendency to live only in the present. The holidays come every year; no sooner does one end than it is time to plan for the next; who has time to reflect on whether the programs just mounted were appropriate or effective? Amidst the constant pressure, it is too tempting to repeat what one did last year, whatever doubts one may have had about its goals and methods.

For their part, members of lay boards and committees are volunteers who balance numerous other commitments with the time they give to the synagogue. When discussions of synagogue business get complicated, the result is more meetings to attend and more preparatory work to do. It is natural for them to favor discussions that are short and simple and to reach for the solutions that are right at hand.

To get beyond the malaise created when problems are ignored, and to prevent the mindless rush to a premature fix, a congregation must deliberately cultivate its ability to be both proactive and reflective. Before analyzing these capacities and offering suggestions as to how they can be developed, I want to consider a case, found in the Bible, in which being both proactive and reflective resulted in turning around a potentially deadly situation. This is the story of Avigayil, as it is recorded in chapter 25 in the First Book of Samuel.[3]

A Model of Proactive and Reflective Behavior

The story is set during the waning days of King Saul's rule. David, having been banished from Saul's palace, has attracted a group of six hundred or so followers with whom he roams the Judean hills. In deference to David's status as a hero, the local populace supplies his men with food. In turn, David's men offer the locals "kindnesses and protection."[4]

David sends a message requesting a "contribution" from Avigayil's husband, Naval, hinting broadly that this donation is in exchange for David's protection of Naval's sheep shearers. Naval, whose Hebrew name means "boor" or "fool," and whom the text describes as very wealthy but also as a "hard man and an evildoer" (verse 3), dismisses the messenger summarily. "Who is David?" he replies. "Who is the son of Jesse? There are many slaves nowadays who run away from their masters. Should I then take my bread and my water, and the meat that I slaughtered for my own shearers, and give them to men who come from I don't know where?" (verses 10 and 11). David's response to this insult is to tell four hundred of his men to gird their swords and prepare to attack Naval.

One of Naval's servants informs Avigayil, Naval's wife, of the message sent by David, and of her husband's response. (It is not clear whether the servant knows that David intends to attack their home—a point to which we will return.) Avigayil springs into action, "quickly [getting] together two hundred loaves of bread, two jars of wine, five dressed sheep, five *seahs* of parched corn, one hundred cakes of raisin, and two hundred cakes of pressed fig" (verse 18), which she sends ahead as a goodwill offering to David. Then she herself goes out to meet David, prostrating herself before him and delivering a long, eloquent speech, which begins "Please, my lord, pay no attention to that wretched fellow Naval" (verse 25). Avigayil makes it clear that had *she* been informed of David's request, it would not have been turned down. She herself knows that David has been chosen by God and that he will overcome all adversity to become the rightful king of Israel. She begs David to restrain himself from "shedding blood needlessly," which would be perceived as a sign of weakness on his part. And she concludes with a request: "And when the Lord has prospered my lord (namely David), remember your maid (namely Avigayil)" (verse 31). Upon hearing this, David praises Avigayil for her courage and her prudence, thanking her for "restraining me from seeking redress in blood by my own hands" (verse 33). "Go up to your home safely. See, I have heeded your plea and respected your wish" (verse 35).

Upon her return, Avigayil finds Naval drunk, so she says nothing until the next day. Naval takes the news badly: "his courage died within him, and he became like a stone" (verse 38). Ten days later, Naval dies; when David hears of Naval's death, he sends messengers to propose marriage to Avigayil. "Then Avigayil rose quickly and mounted an ass, and with five of her maids in attendance she followed David's messengers; and so she became his wife" (verse 42).

Avigayil and her servants demonstrate a remarkable ability to be collectively proactive and reflective. The servant is aware that Naval's response to David was inappropriate, and he speaks to Avigayil behind his master's back. As I indicated above, it is unclear from the text whether or not he knows of David's impending attack. It is also unclear what both Avigayil and the servants really think of David. Do they side with him because of some dissatisfaction with King Saul, or are they simply covering all their bases? Does Avigayil truly foresee the time when David will prevail over Saul, or is she simply out to flatter him? Whatever their motivations, it is clear that both Avigayil and the servants have considered their situation carefully and that they don't let either fear or inertia keep them from reaching out to David before David reaches them.

Like many biblical texts, the story of Avigayil's encounter with David leaves us guessing about many important details, including the decision making process both the servants and Avigayil went through. Were the servants aware of the foibles of their master, and did they routinely do "damage control" on his behalf? Did they debate whether to tell Avigayil what transpired with David, or were they accustomed to keeping her informed? Did they have any doubts about following her order, given the obvious danger it entailed? How did Avigayil come to the realization that David must be appeased? Had she been following his progress for a while? How did she get her information? How did she arrive at a judgment that was so different from Naval's? Did she have any compunctions at all about going behind his back?

The opacity of the text makes the proactive and reflective behavior of the characters seem effortless, fluid, and almost instinctive. In reality, however, group proactivity and reflection is likely to be self-conscious, deliberate, and even painstaking. The remainder of this chapter presents an analysis of the steps an organization goes through when it is proactive and reflective.

The Cycle of Proactivity and Reflection

Proactivity and reflection may seem at first like opposites. Being proactive carries with it connotations of jumping right in and *doing something*. Reflection, by contrast, requires that we pause and take stock. As individual decision makers we often feel the pull between thought and action. Our interest in mulling things over gets in the way of our desire to act decisively, and vice versa. This conflict becomes more acute in organizations, when the doers, who want to see results, lock horns with the conceptualizers, who love to consider all the angles.

But acting without sufficient forethought is like taking a shot in the dark. Conversely, reflection that does not culminate in action is merely an academic exercise or an intellectual parlor game. Reflection does not guarantee an intelligent, successful outcome, but it makes it possible for an organization to learn from its past. Being proactive affords one the opportunity to reflect while there is still time, and to act in a timely fashion before positions have become entrenched and opportunities lost.

Proactivity and reflection function best as a continuous cycle. Taking a proactive stance requires:

- routine scanning of the environment for potential challenges and opportunities.

As interesting problems or possibilities arise, reflection comes to the fore. This includes:

- stopping the action,
- shifting the focus so as to take a broader or deeper perspective,
- formulating a collective response.

Then it is time to be proactive again,

- overcoming inertia and taking action.

But there is no guarantee that the action will lead to the desired results, and every likelihood that new complications will arise. Thus, the cycle begins anew:

- scanning the environment to assess the effects of one's actions and to identify new challenges.

Thinking Back and Thinking Ahead: Being Reflective and Proactive 31

Routinely Scanning the Environment

It seems counterintuitive for an organization to be habitually proactive, continually on the lookout for new developments, positive or negative. Age-old maxims like "don't go looking for trouble" and "if it ain't broke, don't fix it" suggest that we should appreciate the status quo. Who wants to raise needless anxiety or hold additional meetings? Better to "leave well enough alone."

While this might have been useful advice for an earlier era, in which change happened very slowly, things move much more quickly today. Thus, it is essential that a congregation routinely take stock of its environment, which is composed of its current and future membership; its neighborhood; the surrounding congregations, both Jewish and non-Jewish; the local culture; and the larger social and political climate. What new trends can be discerned? Is the current membership aging? Are any new groups moving into the neighborhood? What political and social issues are of local or national concern? What new religious ideas and practices are "in the air?" These factors, and others like them, can have a profound impact on the synagogue. Becoming aware of these phenomena as they emerge enables a congregation to explore them fully and to consider a variety of possible responses.

Synagogue leaders are best able to scan their environment by keeping themselves informed—reading relevant publications, attending conferences, and networking with their peers at other congregations. But information alone is not enough. One needs to reflect on the data and assess their significance. This brings us to the next phase of the cycle: stopping the action.

Stopping the Action

The first step of reflection has been compared to observing Shabbat. The Torah commands us to both remember and observe the seventh day and keep it holy, because "in six days the Lord made heaven and earth, and on the seventh day He ceased from work and was refreshed" (Exodus 31:17). The Hebrew for "was refreshed," *va-yinafash,* derives from the root *nefesh,* which can be translated as "life force" or "essence." Without Shabbat, the work of creation was not completed;[5] Shabbat allowed God to return to God's essence. In marking that day, we humans can get in touch with what is essential and life-giving. Resting on Shabbat is not just a good thing to do, a nice reward for a job well done. It is an obligation we have—to ourselves, to our people, and to God. On Shabbat we are not only commanded not to work but also to engage in activities that will lead us to a spiritual rejuvenation. In the words of Rabbi Emanuel Rackman: "[T]he six days of toil are concerned with the means of life and the Sabbath with its ends. The six days of toil represent the temporal and transitory—the Sabbath represents the eternal and the enduring."[6]

One might ask why we need to be *commanded* to be refreshed or why this type of spiritual recharging needs to be scheduled in rather than taken as needed. Theological and halakhic considerations aside, the practical answer is that unless we build in regular opportunities for rest, and obligate ourselves to take advantage of them, it is too easy to pass by this opportunity, to be seduced by the need to complete one last task or do one additional chore.

We know how difficult it is for individuals to observe the mitzvah of Shabbat despite the teachings of the Torah, the injunctions of rabbis and teachers, and the sheer logic of having a day of rest. How much more so for congregations, which are not similarly commanded, to suspend their normal activities long enough to engage in thoughtful planning and deliberation. To do so requires setting aside time, and structuring that time so that the resultant discussion is indeed refreshing.

In addition to sufficient time, reflection requires a conducive atmosphere. The professional staff members of one congregation trained themselves to be more reflective by changing the venue of their staff meetings and setting a different type of agenda. Their meetings had been held in the office of the senior rabbi, with the agenda consisting of a series of reports. In the words of one staff member: "The atmosphere was competitive, as in the ways that the kids compete for dad's attention. It never felt particularly trusting, in terms of how we listened to one another. It wasn't an atmosphere where you could say 'this program is having trouble,' or 'I don't think I'm doing this as well as I can.'" A recognition of this problem enabled the staff members to make a few relatively simple changes. They moved the meeting to a more neutral space, and they restructured the agenda so that no more than one or two reports were given at a session. The senior rabbi modeled reflection by including questions and doubts in his own report. Over time, the staff members began to engage one another in conversation about important issues. Later, they were able to model this reflective behavior for the lay committees on which they served.[7]

An increasing number of congregations find that a board or staff retreat is an excellent venue for the kind of freewheeling thought and extended conversations that are difficult to sustain in the press of day-to-day concerns. In between these extended periods of reflection, another way of carving out time for thoughtful conversation is by including a text study component in all synagogue meetings.

TEXT STUDY AS AN OPPORTUNITY TO REFLECT

There are many compelling reasons why a congregation might decide to build regular text study into its meetings. In the Jewish tradition, study is more than just a good idea; it is a mitzvah, a commandment. It enriches people's lives and raises their level of Jewish literacy. It creates community and enables relative strangers to engage in meaningful conversation. More germane to the topic of this book, text study has an added, instrumental benefit: it can reconnect us with the core values of Judaism and help us think about what is really essential in our lives. *Becoming a Congregation of Learners* contains a story, told by Rabbi Richard Block, about a meeting of seventh-grade students, teachers, and parents, convened for the purpose of addressing a severe discipline problem:

Knowing that the atmosphere in the room would be charged, the rabbi and educators chose to begin the meeting with the discussion of a text from the Talmud. The text did not deal directly with the misbehavior of students, or the applicability of rules and punishments, but it raised issues regarding the kind of respect which all human beings have a right to expect. After twenty minutes of text study in *hevrutah,* one could feel the tension ebbing and a calm entering the room. The subsequent discussion of the problem at hand was quiet and reasoned. Participants were, Rabbi Block reports, much more open than they would have been had they not begun with the text study. Having gotten in touch with the most important issue, the respect of one human being for another, they were able to rise above petty recrimination and create a joint plan of action.[8]

Despite its many benefits, the introduction of text study into meetings may be met with resistance. Some congregants may feel intimidated by text study, especially in the presence of the rabbi; they may be hesitant to jump in and share their own opinions. The pressure to get on with the business at hand may lead participants (even those who study regularly in other venues) to see study as an unnecessary distraction or even as a waste of time. To serve as a springboard for reflection, text study needs to be carefully planned and skillfully facilitated.[9] Over time, even the most agenda-focused participants may come to see the text study portion of the meeting as a necessary reminder of the reasons that brought them to the synagogue in the first place.

The closer the theme of the text to the issue at hand, the more open people will be to engaging in study. Rabbi Gordon Tucker writes about a ritual committee's study of rabbinic and medieval texts relating to the giving of synagogue honors, which enabled it to craft a policy that was "true to the sources, consistent with synagogue needs and respecting of those who take pride in their heritage."[10]

Similarly, anthropologist Riv-Ellen Prell describes how the board of

Congregation Beth Jacob of St. Paul, Minnesota, regularly studies texts to inform its policy decisions. For example, in considering whether a private bar mitzvah luncheon could be held at the synagogue following a Shabbat service, they studied traditional sources on hospitality and community. Grounding the decision in Jewish texts had the added benefit of making it more palatable to the congregation at large.[11]

The Union of American Hebrew Congregations has created a packet of short texts that help to set the tone for a meeting and offer a Jewish perspective on some of the issues that synagogue boards and committees address routinely.[12]

On the next few pages are a handout with suggestions for how to prepare a short text study for a synagogue meeting, followed by two sample text study guides that have been used in the Experiment in Congregational Education. The first invites members of a board or committee to reflect on the qualities they need to have in order to perform their function. The second asks them to consider the extent to which their service to the synagogue committee is a mitzvah (commandment).

When text study becomes a regular part of synagogue life, it can help meeting participants get past their daily hassles and focus with greater clarity on the concerns of the congregation. In the words of one congregation president, "We put all the rest off to the side and become a group. Studying together puts us on common ground again."[13]

How to Use a Short Text as a Springboard for Reflection

Texts for group study can come from a variety of sources: from *parashat hashavuah,* the weekly Torah portion; from anywhere else in the Bible; from rabbinic literature, such as the *Midrash* (homiletical interpretations) or *Talmud* (the oral Torah); from the works of later commentators and thinkers; and from contemporary essays, fiction, and poetry as well. A variety of anthologies of rabbinic texts and other good source material can be found in any good library or Judaic bookstore.

Text study works best when it deals with an issue that is not black and white but invites different opinions and perspectives. Unless you have an extended period of time available for discussion, it is best to identify a single issue that the text raises. Try to frame this issue in the form of a series of short questions. This is not always so easy, so try out your questions on a friend to make sure they will focus participants on the issue you want to discuss. If you are using a biblical text and have found commentaries that offer several different answers, you may want to include those as well. Another approach, equally effective, is to contrast two texts that offer different perspectives on the issue.

It will be helpful to participants if you give them some background information, such as the source of the text, the biblical or historic context, or a brief biography of the author(s). This information can be inserted in a brief introduction or explained in greater detail in a written appendix or glossary.

Though you may want to read the text aloud in the beginning, do not assume that people will grasp it all at once; make sure a written version is available to everyone—in a book (when your text is from the Torah) or a specially prepared handout. Use a contemporary translation; it is difficult to follow a text with archaic or stilted language. If the original text is in Hebrew and some members of your group know Hebrew, include the Hebrew version. Either separately or in the same handout, write out the questions you would like the group to discuss.

If your group includes more than ten people, you may want to have participants work in *chevrutah* (with a partner, a traditional form of Jewish study). Rather than having each pair report back on its entire conversation, prepare a final, more global question, whose answer each pair can share with the entire group.

If you have planned your questions carefully, facilitating the study session will be easy. Give an introduction, which explains why you chose this text and what issue it raises for you. Then, stand back and let the participants answer the questions you have posed. Resist the temptation to respond to each comment; this is not a Socratic dialogue but a group conversation. If you have some comments you wish to make, save them for the conclusion.

Not everyone is comfortable speaking up in a group, and the thought of commenting on a Jewish text may seem intimidating to some people. So don't expect that everyone will participate, but do provide opportunities for them to speak. If everyone wants to talk at once, ask people to raise their hands. If one or two people monopolize the discussion, you may need to ask them to wait until those who haven't yet spoken have had a turn.

Facilitating text study may be intimidating at first, but with a little practice you will find it quite enjoyable.

The Qualities of a Good Synagogue Leader

Throughout Jewish history, the *mishkan,* the portable sanctuary that accompanied the Children of Israel in their travels through the desert, has been seen as the prototype of the synagogue. This text announces God's choice of Bezalel as the architect and designer of the *mishkan,* and it describes in just three words the qualities that made him God's choice. This text study invites us to examine these qualities and to see whether the same criteria apply to us as synagogue leaders.

> (1) And the Lord spoke unto Moses, saying: (2) See, I have called by name Bezalel, the son of Uri, the son of Hur, from the tribe of Judah. (3) And I have filled him with the spirit of God: with *chokhma,* with *t'vuna,* and with *da'at,* and in all manner of workmanship. (4) To devise skillful works, to work in gold and in silver and in bronze. (5) And in cutting of stones for setting and in carving wood, to work in all manner of workmanship. (6) And I, behold, I have appointed with him Aholiab the son of Ahisamach of the tribe of Dan. And in the hearts of all that are wise-hearted I have put wisdom that they may make all that I have commanded. (Exodus 31:1–6)

Commentators reading this passage focused on the qualities of Bezalel, enumerated in verse 3. They wondered why the Torah needed to use three different synonyms for wisdom: *chokhma, t'vuna,* and *da'at.* Their assumption was that there are no superfluous words in the Torah and that if the

Torah used three different terms, it meant to distinguish between three different types of wisdom. So what are these three different types?

Rashi, an eleventh-century commentator, offers the following answer:

- *Chokhma* is knowledge: what a person learns from others.

- *T'vuna* is understanding: the intelligent application of what has been learned.

- *Da'at* is inspiration.

- What, in your own words, is the difference between the three qualities? How might all three of these qualities be required of us in our role as members of this board or committee? How might we acquire all three types of wisdom?

- Commentators have pointed out that the Hebrew word *Bezalel* literally means "in the shadow of God." Why might the architect of the *mishkan* stand in the shadow of God? What would it mean for our committee to think and act as though we were "in God's shadow"?

TEXT STUDY 2

The *Kedushah* in Synagogue Leadership

This text explores the concept of *kedushah,* a key Jewish value, which, like many Hebrew terms, is difficult to define. It is most commonly translated as "holiness" or "sacredness," but this doesn't really help our understanding because these terms, too, are opaque. In biblical and rabbinic texts, *kedushah* was most commonly seen as residing in specific places (such as the Temple) or times (such as Shabbat) but also in people. This text study asks synagogue leaders to explore the degree to which their contribution to synagogue life entails *kedushah.*

> After the destruction of the Temple, the rabbis no longer emphasized the *kedusha* of places where God's presence was and the *kedusha* of things that were dedicated to God, but stressed the *kedusha* of human acts.... In simple terms, to be holy is to fulfill God's will and imitate God. The rabbis who wrote the formula *Baruch ata Adonai eloheinu melekh haolam asher kidshanu bemitzvotav vetzivanu*..."Blessed are You, *Adonai* our God, Ruler of the universe, who makes us holy with God's *mitzvot* and commands us..." understood that it is God who makes us holy by giving us the *mitzvot,* and that it is we who make ourselves holy by fulfilling the *mitzvot.* Both God and human beings participate in a divine-human partnership in fulfilling the commandment of Leviticus 11:44, "Because I *Adonai* am your God: you shall make yourselves holy *(vehitkadishtem)* and you shall be holy *(kedoshim)* for I am holy *(kadosh)."*
>
> Dan Judson and Peter S. Levi in
> *Theological Terms in the Talmud*[14]

As the text explains, the tradition sees us becoming *kadosh* when we fulfill ritual mitzvot, such as lighting Shabbat candles or hearing the sound of the shofar (ram's horn).

- If you were to focus on enhancing the *kedushah* that resides in you while fulfilling one of these mitzvot, would you do anything differently?

- To what extent is sitting on a synagogue committee or board also a mitzvah? To the extent that it is, should we as a committee be acting any differently?

Taking a Broader Perspective

Setting aside the time, creating a conducive atmosphere, and helping people get in touch with larger issues and concerns are only the first steps in reflection. A break in the action creates the potential for a new understanding and more intelligent decision making, but that potential is actualized only when we acquire new information or explore new ideas. Our thought patterns tend to run along familiar, well-worn paths unless we make a point of trying out different patterns. To become more reflective, we need to deliberately adopt perspectives that are unfamiliar.

In his book *Leadership Without Easy Answers,* Ronald Heifetz terms this practice "getting on the balcony."

> Consider the experience of dancing on a dance floor in contrast with standing on a balcony and watching other people dance. Engaged in a dance, it is nearly impossible to get a sense of the patterns made by everyone on the floor.... To discern the larger patterns on the dance floor—to see who is dancing with whom, in what groups, in what location, and who is sitting out which kind of dance—we have to stop moving and get to the balcony.[15]

How do we train ourselves to see things from the balcony? Heifetz proposes that we ask ourselves a series of questions designed to lift us beyond our immediate reactions and provoke us to think differently. These questions include the following:

1. What's causing the distress?

2. What internal contradictions does the distress represent?

3. What are the histories of these contradictions?

4. What perspectives and interests have I and others come to represent to various segments of the community that are now in conflict?

5. In what ways are we in the organization or working group mirroring the problem dynamics of the community?[16]

Another way we can broaden our perspective is to engage in what Lee Bolman and Terrence Deal call reframing. In their book *Reframing Organizations,* they discuss four "frames" through which organizational life may be viewed: structural, human resource, political, and symbolic.

- The structural frame directs one toward the roles and responsibilities people play. Is the division of labor appropriate and conducive to cooperation? Are the expectations and lines of authority clear?

- The human resource frame focuses on the needs of individuals and the extent to which the organization brings out the best in its members. Are the lines of communication open? Do people feel supported? Empowered? What can be done to be more inclusive and more responsive?

- The political frame deals with the distribution of resources and with the conflict created when different constituencies vie with one another for power and influence. What is the stake of each constituency? What alliances are formed, and how stable are they? To what extent is it possible to arrive at a compromise?

- The symbolic frame concerns itself with the way in which members of an organization can be motivated not by rational calculations (as stressed by the structural frame), not by attention to their needs (as stressed by the human resource frame), not by resources and the urge to control them (as stressed by the political frame), but by the values that are embodied in symbols and rituals. What early experiences have shaped the organization? What stories are told repeatedly, and what values do they represent? What new symbols, stories, or ceremonies might be used to reorient the organization's culture?[17]

Taken together, these four approaches present a more rounded and nuanced picture of organizational life than might be obtained from using the one or two that come most naturally. To develop the capacity for this more balanced four-frame understanding, one needs to be aware of the frame(s) one uses most commonly, and then cultivate an ability to use the others. For example, I tend to view situations from the structural frame. At meetings, I direct my attention to the tasks at hand, with only limited patience for tangents and side conversations. As a consequence, I may not register some of the symbolic, emotional, and political concerns of other participants. I can easily miss the subtle ways in which people use what may appear to be a simple discussion of tasks to express their feelings, jockey for power, or remind themselves of what is really important. With practice, I have learned that paying attention to these seeming distractions, and attempting to analyze them through each of the four frames, is often more productive than simply admonishing people to "stick to the agenda."

It is actually easier to develop the capacity to view things "from the balcony," whether through Heifetz's questions or through Bolman's and Deal's analysis, in a group. Various members of a committee or staff are likely to approach a situation differently. A discussion of these differences can lead people to an appreciation of divergent perspectives, assuming that the discussion is carefully facilitated and does not degenerate into a close-minded debate over which is the "right" view.

On the next pages are two exercises that were designed to help members of a group take on new perspectives. In addition, on page 60 is a case study, followed by an exercise in using Bolman's and Deal's four frames to analyze the case.

An "Appreciative Inquiry"

This exercise is adapted from a more elaborate process devised in *Congregations as Learning Communities* by minister and organizational consultant Dennis Campbell. It enables the leaders of a congregation to step back from their current problems and/or controversies and to appreciate the strengths of their congregation.[18] It is especially helpful in uncovering the stories and customs that congregants hold most dear, strengthening the group's ability to see the congregation through the cultural and symbolic frame. This, in turn, may help the leadership as it approaches a controversy or change. Depending on the time available, the first step can be done in groups of two, three, or four.

Time Required

Step 1: 10 minutes for each person in the subgroup, plus 15 minutes for overall discussion.

Step 2: 5 to 7 minutes for the report of each subgroup, plus 15 to 20 minutes for summary discussion.

Preparation

- Preassign members of the committee into subgroups of two to four, depending on the available time. Ideally, each subgroup should cover a range of constituencies, so the members are fairly new to one another.

- Make copies of Handout 2, which contains the interview questions for this exercise.

Facilitation

STEP 1:

Each subgroup should subtract 15 minutes from the time allotted to them, then divide the remaining time by the number of members. This will assure that each interview is of equal length. Participants take turns interviewing one another, using the questions in part 1 of Handout 2. They then discuss the questions in part 2.

STEP 2:

The larger group reconvenes, and each subgroup presents its answers to the questions in part 2. The concluding discussion might pose any of the following questions:

- What did you hear that surprised you?
- Is there anything you will do differently, now that you have heard from others in the group about what matters to them?
- How can our committee or board make use of the information we have gleaned from this exercise?

Interview Questions for an "Appreciative Inquiry"

Part 1

In Part 1 of this exercise, you will take turns interviewing the members of your group. To find out how long you have for each interview, subtract 15 minutes from the time available to your small group, then divide the remaining time by the number of people in your group. Use the following questions to structure your interview:

1. How long have you been a member of this congregation?

2. Think back on a time when you felt most fulfilled or most excited about your involvement in the synagogue; describe the situation and what made it so rewarding.

3. What do you value most about the synagogue?

4. What is the most important thing the synagogue has contributed to your life?

5. What, in your opinion, is the key ingredient of our congregation?

6. Make three wishes for the future of our synagogue.

Part 2

After everyone has been interviewed, think about the common themes that have emerged from all of the interviews:

1. What does the congregation do for its members?

2. What do people seem to value most?

3. Are there any other things that haven't been mentioned yet, but should be?

4. If you had a magic wand, what would your group wish for the congregation?

Note on adapting these questions: If your group is a specialized committee (such as the education or social action committee), you might want to focus more specifically on that aspect of congregational life.

A Limiting Assumptions Exercise[19]

This exercise, adapted from a similar one in *Becoming a Congregation of Learners: Learning as a Key to Revitalizing Congregational Life,* provides an opportunity for members of a committee or board to gain a different perspective on what they are doing. Groups that have used it have found that it gives them new insight into aspects of synagogue life they have taken for granted.

Preparation

Prepare two flip charts with markers; ask two members of the group to take turns writing (since the answers will be coming quickly).

Time Required

Part 1: 45 minutes

Part 2: 20 to 30 minutes

Part 3: 2 minutes for each subgroup's presentation, plus 20 minutes for discussion

Facilitation

PART 1

Participants sit in a semicircle (with two or three rows, if necessary). The facilitator asks people to brainstorm the assumptions that congregants (or they) bring with them to the congregation. Some of these statements may be true, and some false; these will be discussed in part 2. Part 1 is a brainstorming exercise, so there are no wrong answers. The recorders take turns writing down people's statements. If participants get stuck, the facilitator can prompt them by asking some more specific questions, such as "What assumptions do we have about worship? about learning? about social action?"

PART 2

Divide participants into groups of three or four. Each group gets one or two flip chart pages with the assumptions on them.

- Begin by noting the assumptions you believe to be true.

- Then choose two or three assumptions you would like to challenge because you believe them to be erroneous; rewrite each assumption so that it becomes one your group can affirm. For example, one assumption brainstormed in part 1 might be "Committee members aren't expected to do any work between meetings." This assumption could be rewritten to clarify what committee members *are* expected to do.

- In the last few minutes, each group prepares to present one or two of their rewritten assumptions to the larger group.

PART 3

Each subgroup presents its rewritten assumptions. Then the following questions are posed:

- What have we learned about our congregation by examining our limiting assumptions?

- If we were to replace the limiting assumptions with the rewritten version, how might our congregation be different?

- What might our board/committee do to help replace some of the limiting assumptions in people's minds?

Formulating a Collective Response

In individual reflection, the shift from analyzing a situation to forming a response may be imperceptible, because the wording of an issue often contains within it an implied solution. In group reflection, the implicit must be made explicit, because what is obvious to one person may be anything but obvious to the next. Thus, the final step in organizational reflection is articulating and obtaining consensus on a response.

The critical role of language in creating consensus is illustrated by Riv-Ellen Prell's account of Beth Jacob's struggle with the issue of decorum. The synagogue had experienced rapid growth in its membership, and in the number of children attending services. The congregation values the participation of its members and had always had an air of informality about it, but behavior deemed acceptable when the congregation was small seemed less tolerable as it grew larger. Congregants described the problem in various ways. Some focused on inappropriate dress, such as wearing jeans and tennis shoes on the *bimah* (dais); others were bothered by the misbehavior of children and their apparent lack of respect; still others complained about the level of chit-chat during services.

Controversies related to decorum are not uncommon in synagogue life. What is remarkable about Beth Jacob's case is the way in which Rabbi Morris Allen framed the issue—as the "inevitable cleavage between synagogue as a community and synagogue as a sacred place."[20] He believed that the problem of decorum was a by-product of Beth Jacob's success in encouraging active participation. This made people more comfortable with worship and made the sanctuary a less forbidding place. Given the range of lifestyles and parenting styles among congregants, it was understandable that the behavior of some would seem offensive to others. Resisting attempts to promulgate a dress code or to simply chastise the offending congregants, Rabbi Allen saw in this issue an opportunity to "reassert synagogue values and principles." After much discussion, the ritual committee

> acknowledged that it was virtually impossible to fix decorum
> as a matter in and of itself, let alone to imagine consequences

for those who would not consent to it. They settled instead on a language that would place decorum within their own vision of Judaism and community.[21]

The committee ultimately decided to produce a one-page statement entitled "Decorum at *Shul*," which translated the issue into one concerning "community and the presence of God in our midst." Included in the statement, which was reproduced in the synagogue bulletin, were guidelines that covered a range of behavior in the sanctuary. In addition, weekly reminders about appropriate behavior were issued from the *bimah,* and the supervision of children was tightened. Still, they acknowledged to themselves that the issue would never be fully resolved.

This expansive and nonjudgmental way of dealing with a potentially divisive issue not only defused the situation but served an educational purpose. The key to the committee's success was the way in which Rabbi Allen outlined the problem, which created a common ground and reminded people of their shared values and principles. With that as a baseline, it was relatively easy to arrive at a thoughtful response.

While there must be many similar cases, in which insightful and persuasive congregational leaders (whether lay or professional) formulate a problem in a way that creates grounds for a consensus, many other cases remain conflicted, with different parties clinging to their own formulations of "what is really going on." Often productive discussion is hampered by the lack of a common understanding of the problem at hand. The following exercise is designed to assist people in articulating a problem in a way that is acceptable to all parties and, further, to explore a range of alternative solutions.[22]

Exploring a Complex Issue
and Finding an Appropriate Response

Complicated issues are made even more complex when different people define the issue differently and then latch onto particular ways of addressing the issue without considering other alternatives. This exercise was devised to address both of these problems. In part 1, the group works to articulate a common definition of the issue. In part 2, it works to generate a wide range of solutions or responses, and then consider which of these solutions are most appropriate.

Preparation

No special preparation is needed, other than supplying a flip chart with lots of paper and making copies of Handout 3, which contains questions to guide the group through this exercise.

Time Required

This is difficult to predict precisely. Depending on the nature of the problem and the diversity in the group, it could last between 1 and 3 hours. If time is limited, you might allot 1 to 1½ hours to part 1, then ask a subcommittee to do part 2 on their own, reporting their conclusions at a future date.

Facilitation

Lead the group through the questions in Handout 3.

Exploring a Complex Issue

Understanding the Issue

- How do you understand this issue? What are some reasons why this issue has emerged at this particular time?

- Think about how this issue has arisen in your congregation, and take a few moments and write out (on your own) a statement of the issue, as you understand it. (Write the different statements on a flip chart, so that everyone can compare them.)

- (If the definitions are very different) What are some key elements that contribute to this issue?

- Together, work on a common statement of the issue.

Formulating Responses

- What are some alternative solutions/responses? (Generate as many as possible.)

- What values and assumptions lie behind each of these alternatives?

- What are the pros and cons of each alternative?

- What are some consequences (both intended and unintended) that might result from each alternative?

● Although the same range of solutions is theoretically open to every congregation, certain solutions will be more or less appropriate for some congregations. Which alternatives seem most promising *for your congregation,* and why?

● What are some first steps in pursuing the alternatives you deem most promising?

Some Overall Concerns about Reflection

Having analyzed the steps involved in reflection, I want to address two questions that often arise. First, in a self-renewing congregation, who is actually doing the reflecting? Many synagogues are too large to have everyone involved in decision making. So who should be involved in these kinds of conversations? Second, how much reflection is enough? How many issues can be discussed following the careful steps outlined above? Is there such a thing as being too reflective?

Choosing a Group to Develop a Reflective Capacity

The town meeting is an American tradition that is alive and well in some small towns, and in some small congregations as well. While some town meetings are more deliberative then others, the idea of an entire congregation's members talking to one another is appealing. However, once the membership of a congregation grows beyond 150, this kind of simple democracy is no longer feasible.[23] In a typical congregation, several different groups are convened regularly: the professional staff, the governing board, standing committees (devoted to such matters as ritual or membership), and ad hoc committees convened for particular purposes (such as a search for a new staff member or the building of a new facility). All these groups would benefit from being more reflective, but where is the best place to start? Which group will have the most potential to succeed?

Some questions to consider are these: Which group already has, among its members, some highly reflective individuals? To which group could additional members be added most easily? Which group deals with issues that merit reflection but are not too divisive or too overwhelming? In which group would increased reflection have the greatest impact? Additionally, how much weight should be given to each of these factors? For example, more reflection on the part of the board of directors might have the biggest impact, but its current members may not be so reflective, and enlarging the group may prove complicated and divisive. A standing committee, on the other hand, can easily be expanded, but the issues it deals with may not be of concern to other synagogue leaders. The answers to all of these questions will vary from one synagogue to another.

A different approach is to create an entirely new group, whose expressed purpose is to be reflective. It might be called a long-range planning committee or a futures task force. Organizational theorist Edgar Schein advocates the use of such a group, which he terms a "temporary parallel learning system," because he believes that only a new entity—one not saddled with ongoing tasks—can offer its members the psychological space they need to think differently. "[S]ome part of the organization must become marginal and expose itself to new ways of thinking, so that it can be objective about the strengths and weaknesses of the existing culture."[24] Schein suggests that this new entity comprise a mix of insiders and outsiders; by extension, I would suggest that there be a combination of old-timers and newcomers, lay people and professionals, people who are active in different parts of the synagogue and some who are inactive.[25]

There is, however, a danger in cultivating a group that is marginal by design—it may easily become marginalized. The literature on education reform is replete with examples of task forces and exploratory teams that are perceived as elitist and resented for having been shown some favoritism.[26] One synagogue that participated in a synagogue change project found that members of its task force, who attended a national retreat together, "were incredibly moved by the experience, but unable to explain to others, who were not there, what precisely moved them." In the words of the rabbi:

> When people reported back to the community it was totally incomprehensible. It was not an experience that could be easily translated, because it was so emotional. Anyone who was skeptical at the outset was even more skeptical when people were unable to articulate what they had experienced, and what their new goals were. All too quickly, people stopped wanting to hear any more about it.

The advantages and disadvantages of working with a standing committee versus a task force must be weighed carefully. At the very least, those who begin with a task force should be careful to include on it many members of the standing committees.[27] Conversely, those who begin with a standing committee should select one that includes a core of people inclined toward reflection, and relatively few people whose urge to see results makes them impatient with extended conversation.

Yet a third possibility is worth considering: restructuring the synagogue's governance so that one or more committees or subcommittees are given explicit responsibility for reflection. For example, in several synagogues that participated in the Experiment in Congregational Education (ECE), the ECE task force evolved into a "designated reflector." At Temple Sinai of Stamford, Connecticut, the new role of the ECE task force was explained in the following way:

> The ECE's role...is to act as the agent for facilitating transformational change in the synagogue. In a corporate environment, we would be the equivalent of a strategic planning arm. We do not have "line" responsibility; we do not actually implement anything as ECE (of course, many members involved in ECE help implement many activities at the Temple). We are, however, perhaps the only group with the luxury of not having an immediate operational responsibility, so that we can think about the bigger picture and make recommendations to the Executive Committee. Also, our task forces and working groups have had the ability to engage in a level of study regarding particular issues which has been unusual for Temple Sinai. We hope to continue this emphasis on the study of issues relating to Temple Sinai's ability to live up to its mission statement and strategic values.... We feel fortunate to have an Executive Committee that is willing to place its trust in us to analyze these issues and make recommendations to them.[28]

Recently, the ECE task force completed a year-long study of the synagogue's governance, which included an analysis of the minutes of the board, interviews with key leaders in the congregation, consultation with movement leaders and other congregations, and extensive deliberation on solving perceived governance problems. Their recommendations included a reduction of the size of the board and a consolidation of the committees "to align with strategic values, clarify roles and responsibilities, and reduce jurisdictional uncertainty and overlap."

The following case study describes how Congregation Sinai of Milwaukee restructured its board in a different way, which also allowed for extended reflection on important issues. This process of restructuring was not without its conflict, but in the end the goal of increased reflection was achieved to everyone's satisfaction.

CASE STUDY
Introducing Reflection to Board Meetings at Congregation Sinai, Milwaukee

Congregation Sinai is the smallest (445 member units) of three Reform synagogues in the Milwaukee suburbs. Change happens slowly in this congregation, whose members' initial reaction to suggested changes is likely to be "but we've *always* done it that way."

The congregation's choice of Sheryl Primakow as president was, in itself, a departure from the norm. Though Sheryl had been a member of the board for eight years, she had not served as an officer before assuming the presidency. Instead, her primary leadership position at the congregation had been as the co-chair of a task force designed to transform the synagogue into a congregation of learners.

Sheryl came into her new position critical of the way the board had functioned in the past. In her view, the twenty-five–member board tended to micromanage too many things—from the time of services to the color of the walls. They were so concerned with details that they rarely had time to reflect on the larger issues facing the congregation. Meetings were dominated by reports from standing committees, which tended to be boring. Few of these committees were very active, some consisting of only the board member who chaired them. After extensive discussion with Rabbi David Cohen, Sheryl determined that one of her goals would be to make the board both more efficient and more reflective; she also hoped to involve a wider group of volunteers in substantive decision making.

Sheryl approached her first board meeting as president with these goals in mind. On the agenda for that meeting was a report from a committee on governance, which had been convened by the outgoing president. The report called for a system of ad hoc committees to deal with some of the more practical issues that typically came before the board. As the governance committee saw it, their proposal had several benefits: it would free the board to discuss long-term policy matters; it would create meaningful work for a wider group of volunteers; and, by encouraging the ad hoc committees to take their time, discuss each issue carefully, and do the necessary research, it would begin to create a culture of reflection in the congregation.

The board meeting, held in June 2001, was a disaster. In the words of Rabbi Cohen, "The agenda dealt with a series of issues relating to change. We began with a heated discussion about delegating some of the board's critical decision making power to the education committee. From there we went to the governance committee's report on restructuring the board. Many board members felt threatened. Accustomed to their oversight role, they viewed the committee's recommendation as (to quote one member) a 'power grab.'"

A fierce debate erupted between those who had crafted the proposal, who were cast as "insiders," and the others, who felt excluded. The proposal's proponents felt wounded; its opponents felt threatened and angered. As is his custom, Rabbi Cohen was quiet during most of the meeting, though his participation in the governance committee indicated his tacit approval of their proposal. By the end of the meeting, however, Rabbi Cohen could no longer restrain himself. "I felt compelled to state publicly that in my fourteen years as a rabbi, it was the first time I felt like I was witnessing a *machloket lo l'shem shamayim* [an argument that was *not* for the sake of heaven]. People began focusing on each other, as opposed to the issue at hand. Some people started trembling, and even crying." Sheryl came away from the meeting shaken. "Their response really threw me. I didn't know whether to cry, or interrupt them and try to explain it better, or just walk away."

In debriefing the meeting, Sheryl, Rabbi Cohen and the immediate past president came to the realization that they had asked the board to assimilate too much, too soon. As Rabbi Cohen put it, "Though we had created a deliberative process in the congregation's programmatic life, we had not done so in its administrative life. We needed to begin infusing the board with the same reflective ethos that we had evolved for other parts of the congregation." After that conversation, Sheryl recalls, "I was able to put it in perspective. I recognized the board's passion, and found it to be very healthy. I knew we had to clarify the points of confusion, and proceed much more slowly."

Since the board was not scheduled to meet in July, Sheryl and the executive committee had two months between meetings to take stock and to think about how to improve the atmosphere at future meetings. Rather than take up the governance discussion again in August, they decided to put it off until a day-long retreat could be scheduled in October. In the meantime, Sheryl began sending out more frequent and more detailed e-mails to the board members in an effort to keep them better informed.

At the August meeting, Sheryl asked the board to divide into small groups to discuss one item, but she did not call attention to the fact that this was a departure from how things had been done before. To address the insider/outsider problem that had surfaced at the June meeting, she and the other members of the executive committee tried to be listeners rather than monopolizing the conversation, as they sometimes had in the past.

Because of several extenuating circumstances, the board retreat had to be postponed. But over the next few months, it became clear that a retreat dedicated to issues of governance would probably not be needed, since many changes were already under way. Though talking about changes in the governance structure was threatening to some board members, implementing these changes without much discussion was much simpler. The *divrei torah,* or text study discussions, at board meetings were now focused on the topics of leadership or team building. Sheryl was circulating the minutes from executive committee meetings to the rest of the board, to alleviate the feeling of "us versus them" and to build the trust necessary for productive dialogue. The board members were having more extended "good and welfare" discussions at the end of each meeting, thus ending on a positive note. They were gradually shifting how they operated as a group. The changes seemed to be evolving from the inside rather than imposed from the outside, and they seemed to be working.

That fall, the congregation faced a new challenge: whether or not to cap its membership, in light of the fact that the sanctuary had been filled to capacity on the High Holidays. This was an emotional issue, since the congregation has long been committed to being small and to having all its members at the same worship service. In previous years, the board might have limited the discussion and made its decision at a single meeting. Now, however, they framed the issue more broadly: What is positive about growth? What is negative about growth? What are our limiting assumptions? They posted the responses for everyone to see. Sheryl suggested that they wait until the next meeting before voting, giving people time to reflect further. Without the pressure of having to reach a decision on the spot, everyone had a chance to share opinions and feelings.

By the next meeting, there was enough distance from the first discussion that Sheryl was able to suggest forming an ad hoc committee to research and reflect on the issue and to bring written recommendations back to the board. A few months earlier, the board would have been much more reluctant to delegate this responsibility, and the suggestion would have sparked a contentious debate. Now, however, people felt differently. Since the various viewpoints had been posted and recorded, everyone felt heard. Those who had previously perceived themselves to be outsiders now felt more involved and better able to trust an ad hoc committee. The board defined the committee's charge and moved on to the next item on the agenda.

Appointing ad hoc committees with short-term assignments gives the board an opportunity to broaden its perspective, see problems in context, and plan more deliberately for the future. In addition, as Sheryl notes, "ad hoc groups create more opportunities for volunteers to engage in meaningful work, instead of just buying the cups for a program." People are more willing to volunteer their time for a substantive task with a defined end; if the experience of researching and planning together proves satisfying to the first groups, this may encourage others to become involved.

In August, when Sheryl was asked what would help the board become more reflective, her response had been a board retreat. She thought the group of twenty-five would need a full day and an outside facilitator to discuss the proposed governance changes. Only four months later, she believed that talking about governance was no longer necessary, since things were already changing at a pace that was comfortable for everyone. The board was gradually moving toward a structure and a process that enabled it to be both reflective and proactive.

Viewing a Case through Bolman's and Deal's Four Frames

Bolman's and Deal's four frames, discussed on pages 44–45, are helpful tools for discussing a case like the one of Temple Sinai. This exercise takes a group through such a process. The exercise includes three steps:

Step 1: Review the four frames, using Handout 4; each person identifies the frame s/he uses most comfortably.

Step 2: Divide into four groups (one for each frame) to analyze the case, using the questions in Handout 5 for guidance. Each group devotes most of its time to that frame but considers the other frames as well.

Step 3: The groups present their analyses and consider the insights they have gained about their own congregation from the four-frame analysis.

Preparation

Make copies of the case and of Handouts 4 and 5 for each participant.

Time Required

Step 1: 10 to 15 minutes
Step 2: 15 to 20 minutes
Step 3: 15 to 20 minutes

Facilitation

Step 1: Distribute copies of Handout 4, which summarizes the four frames. Ask people to review them and to think about which frame seems to embody the usual way they think about institutions. Divide people into four groups accordingly. The groups need not be of equal size, but each should have at least three or four members, so you may need to ask some participants to switch groups. Give each group copies of the case and of Handout 5.

Step 2: Small groups read the case aloud and discuss the questions in Handout 5. They need not discuss all the questions, but they should be prepared to report back their answers to questions 3 and 4.

Step 3: The large group reconvenes to hear reports from the small groups. General discussion of the case follows. If there is time, consider other situations in your congregation that might be illuminated by a four-frame analysis.

Optional: Give participants Handout 6, which gives the author's analysis of the case.

A Summary of Bolman's and Deal's Four Frames

- The *structural frame* directs one toward the roles and responsibilities people play.

  Questions asked by this frame:

  - Is the division of labor appropriate and conducive to cooperation?

  - Are expectations and lines of authority clear?

- The *human resource frame* focuses on the needs of individuals and the extent to which the organization brings out the best in its members.

  Questions asked by this frame:

  - Are the lines of communication open?

  - Do people feel supported? Empowered?

  - What can be done to be more inclusive and more responsive to people's needs and feelings?

- The *political frame* deals with the distribution of resources and the conflict created when different constituencies vie with one another for power and influence.

  Questions asked by this frame:

  - What is the stake of each constituency?

- What alliances are formed, and how stable are they?

- To what extent is it possible to arrive at a compromise?

- **The *symbolic frame* concerns itself with the way in which members of an organization can be motivated by the values that are embodied in symbols and rituals.**
  Questions asked by this frame:

  - What early experiences have shaped the organization?

  - What stories are told repeatedly, and what values do they represent?

  - To what extent do the actions of people in this situation exemplify these values?

  - What new symbols, stories, or ceremonies might be used to reorient the organization's culture?

Which frame seems most familiar and/or comfortable to you? Which do you usually use when thinking about an organization?

Based on Reframing Organizations, *by Lee Bolman and Terrence Deal (San Francisco: Jossey-Bass, 1991).*

Analyzing a Case Using One of Bolman's and Deal's Four Frames

This handout can be used as a guide for applying Bolman's and Deal's four frames to all the cases in this book or to any case study of congregational life. After reviewing the frames (see Handout 4), divide into four groups, and assign each group a different frame to apply to the case. (For instructions on bringing the groups together, see the instructions in Exercise 4.)

Read the case aloud.

1. What aspects of the situation does your frame direct you to look into?

2. What new insights does this frame give you? What aspects of the case does it explain?

3. What advice might this frame offer the various characters in this case?

4. What aspects of the case does this frame fail to explain?

5. Based on what you know about the other three frames, what insights might they add?

6. Think of a situation that has arisen in your congregation that is, in some way, similar to the incident described in this case. What new insight into that situation have you gained from this discussion, using the four frames?

A Four-Frame Analysis of the Case "Introducing Reflection to Board Meetings at Congregation Sinai, Milwaukee"

- The *structural frame* invites us to look more closely at the ways in which the governance of a synagogue works. Before restructuring, the board used the same process to discuss issues that were large and those that were small, issues that came up through the committee structure and those that didn't. Consequently, its deliberations on large issues were overly hurried and not sufficiently deliberative. Under the new plan, this would have changed. But there was no precedent for ad hoc committees, and some board members worried that the new division of labor might not be appropriate and that the board might become a rubber stamp. The governance committee needed to persuade the board that the process they suggested allocated more time for weightier issues, but also that the board would retain its authority in decision making. The president's initial strategy for dealing with the board's resistance—to hold a board retreat to clarify its role—fits with this frame, as well.

- Looking at this case through the *human resource frame* directs our attention to the feelings of the board members, particularly those not on the governance committee. They were unprepared for the change and felt excluded from the process. The president should have taken more care to prepare people for this change. She might have circulated a written draft of the report and solicited people's feedback in advance; alternatively, she might have presented the proposal as a discussion draft rather than a formal proposal. Either way, she should have realized that the proposal would encounter some resistance. After the debacle, the president began to operate out of this frame. She reached out to the board members who felt excluded, and she tried to listen to them more carefully. She set aside more time for "good and welfare." As the board members felt more invested and consulted they became more open to the president's subsequent process suggestions.

- Although the proposed restructuring was explained in logical terms as a bid to increase efficiency, the *political frame* calls attention to the shifts in power that it suggested. Some on the board perceived the proposal as a power grab—a feeling that was exacerbated by the first item on the agenda, which could also be interpreted as taking power away from the board. The antidote to this kind of political resistance is to share power and to show a willingness to compromise and negotiate, both of which the president did. She backed away from the proposed change and set it aside; she made a concerted attempt to share as much information as possible between meetings. As the members of the board felt more empowered they were more amenable to sharing power with other committees.

- Finally, the *cultural and symbolic frame* points to the emotional impact of the proposed change, which created a sense of loss and made it difficult for some to see its logical benefits. The fact that the new president had not come up through the ranks in traditional fashion might have exacerbated the situation, signaling to old-time board members that the congregation's time-honored traditions were being upset. When this new president's first act was to suggest a change in procedure, this sense of dislocation intensified. The cultural and symbolic frame reminds us of the importance of rituals to mark transition and loss and to celebrate symbols of the new reality as well. By bringing texts about leadership and teamwork for the board to study, the president signaled that her new approach was anchored in the Jewish tradition. In retrospect, she might have selected an old-timer on the board to present the governance committee's proposal; she might also have done more to recognize the contributions of the board under the "old" system.

Is There Such a Thing As Too Much Reflection?

The three steps of reflection—stopping the action, trying on new perspectives, and formulating a response—are time consuming and cumbersome, especially when a group is unaccustomed to this kind of deliberation. When the habits of unthinking or impulsive decision making are ingrained, practicing reflection will take a good deal of time and should be reserved for a few issues that merit this kind of attention. An appropriate subject for an experience of reflection is one in which the problem is bothersome but not contentious, and neither too obvious nor too complex. The experience of collectively discussing and resolving a difficult issue can be rewarding when facilitated well. If, in addition, the outcome proves to be successful, the group will be eager to try it again. These types of discussions become easier with practice. Eventually, reflection will be incorporated into the synagogue's culture. Then the process of decision making will seem as smooth and easy as it appeared to be in the story of Avigayil.

Even in the most reflective congregations, however, some decisions will need to be made quickly, and some long-held practices and assumptions will remain unquestioned. If we had to think deeply about everything we did, it might take us an entire day to get up, get dressed, and eat breakfast. The art of reflection includes the ability to discern which issues are worthy of extended conversation and which are not. Excessive and prolonged deliberation has the potential to be paralyzing, and many congregational boards and committees have fallen into this trap. This is why it is important to balance being reflective with being proactive, taking action in a timely fashion.

Cycling Back to Proactivity: Overcoming Inertia and Taking Action

In the story of Avigayil we see just how important it is to be proactive. As soon as the servant brought Avigayil the news of Naval's miscalculation and David's response, she sprang into action. As the text says, "Avigayil quickly got together two hundred loaves of bread..." (I Samuel 25:18) and "When Avigayil saw David, she quickly dismounted..." (verse 23). Had Avigayil delayed, the story might have had a different ending.

As the mistress of the house, who clearly had the trust and loyalty of her servants, Avigayil had a decided advantage. By contrast, when decision making is in the hands of a group, it is easy for inertia to set in while each participant waits for the other to act first. This is particularly true for synagogues, where the lines of authority are ambiguous. The board may select the top professional(s), but the professional staff has a good deal of input into the composition of both the board and the committees. Thus, the lines of responsibility are often unclear, especially when one considers the varying degrees of power and influence wielded by different professional and lay leaders.

At times, a synagogue group created for the purpose of reflection can get so caught up in talk that it finds itself unable to act. One synagogue, for example, created an umbrella group dedicated to reflect on the congregation's educational programming. It soon found that participation in the group's admittedly fascinating discussions seemed to siphon off the time and energy people might have devoted to action. In the words of one participant:

> We allowed people to talk for so long, now no one wants to volunteer to *do* anything. We channeled all of our willing people into [the group], and we are afraid to ask them to do any more. It was even difficult to find people to serve on the board.

The synagogue ended up cutting back on the number of meetings of this group, but restructuring, so that its recommendations could flow more easily to the committees that would implement them. Eventually, they were able to right the balance between reflection and action.

An unfortunate example of inertia in a synagogue board appears in journalist Paul Wilkes' book *And They Shall Be My People,* which chronicles a year in the life of a congregational rabbi. The synagogue began the year with a large deficit, which increased as the year went on. The problem was discussed repeatedly by the board and an ad hoc fundraising committee, and various strategies were considered. Some of them were attempted, but with little success; the only solution seemed to be to cut the budget.

> After some torturous board meetings, during which blame was amply apportioned but no real plan was developed, the board, in essence, turned to the rabbi, saying they would put off slashing the budget for several months if *he* could come up with a financial plan. One especially vocal member was even grumbling that the financial predicament was the rabbi's fault after all; he had not organized the parlor meetings that were supposed to instill a new spirit of generosity among the congregants. The rabbi had difficulty controlling himself when the responsibility for the financial welfare of Beth Israel was tossed back into his lap—especially as he looked around the room at the men and women present who were talking about saving a thousand dollars here and there. Many of them were moderately wealthy, many were successful business people who were as familiar with cash flow and spread-sheets as he was with the Torah and *Midrash*. He wondered why this, too, was his job. He was never supposed to organize the parlor meetings; it had simply been one of the many ideas he had advanced.[29]

Failing to be proactive when the budget shortfall was first identified, again when the idea of parlor meetings was raised, and even later during the three months' grace period left the board no chance of dealing with the financial situation in a deliberate manner. By the end of the year, there was no time to be reflective, and the only option left was to cut salaries and eliminate a staff position.

By contrast, an example of coordinated reflection and action can be found in the second synagogue studied by Riv-Ellen Prell: Beth El of Minneapolis.[30] The rabbi and professional staff had been thinking about how to raise the level of Shabbat observance. In consultation with the board and various committees, they envisioned a series of educational programs throughout the year that would focus on bringing Shabbat into people's lives. The "Celebrate Shabbat" initiative was kicked off by a powerful Yom Kippur sermon that focused on the joy of Shabbat, and suggested that Shabbat could become a celebration to be savored, rather than an obligation to be endured. What struck me in reading this ethnography was not the eloquence of the sermon; sermons, no matter how moving, rarely lead to long-term changes in behavior. Most impressive about "Celebrate Shabbat" was the coordinated barrage of programming and promotion that began in the days after Yom Kippur, and continued throughout the year. The reflection of the congregation's leaders led them to prepare, in advance, a coordinated action plan, which effectively conveyed a consistent and compelling message—a message that did indeed lead congregants to increase their Shabbat observance.[31]

The need to balance reflection with action poses a formidable challenge for any organization, particularly one that requires large numbers of volunteers. There is no magic formula for goading a committee into action, but I have found one exercise to be especially helpful in overcoming inertia. This exercise, adapted from a more elaborate one devised by Edgar Schein, serves as a tool for analyzing organizational culture. In particular, participants come face to face with the ways in which the organization's stated values are undercut by the unstated, but no less real, messages it sends out. It may take a while for participants to begin peeling back the layers and exposing some of the contradictions. But confronting discrepancies between what the congregation preaches and what it practices (and these discrepancies exist in every congregation) can serve as a wake-up call, spurring congregational leaders to action.

An Exercise That Can Move People from Reflection to Action

In every organization, there is a gap between the values that are stated publicly and the values that underlie its customs and practices. The purpose of this exercise is to help synagogue leaders confront this discrepancy and reflect on what might be done to align their stated values with their practices. The exercise asks participants to imagine, first, a promotional film on the congregation, and, second, a documentary film, and then to compare the two. This activity is enjoyable and cathartic but can become very sobering at the end. It can be used to reflect on the values of the entire congregation or of a particular area, such as education or worship.

Preparation

Collect multiple copies of recent public relations materials, as well as the congregation's mission and/or vision statements, if these exist. Make copies of Handout 7, which contains instructions for the small groups.

Time Required

1 to 1½ hours (see below for breakdown)

Facilitation

Part 1: (5 minutes) Explain the overall purpose of the exercise, then divide into subgroups of three to five participants. The exercise will work best if there are three or four subgroups.

Part 2: (15 minutes) Subgroups work separately, following the instructions in Handout 7.

Part 3: Subgroups report back (5 minutes for each group), plus 15 minutes for discussion:

- What do these film clips convey about the way we do things in this congregation?
- What would they teach an outside observer about the values that are important to our congregation? (List these on a flip chart.)

Part 4: (20 minutes) Subgroups follow second half of handout.

Part 5: Subgroup presentations (5 minutes for each group), followed by overall discussion, 20 to 30 minutes:

- What do these film clips convey about the way we do things in this congregation and about the values that underlie them? (List these on a flip chart.)
- What are the main differences between the scenes you imagined in the public relations film and those you imagined in the documentary film?
- What would the documentary film teach an outside observer about the values of our congregation?
- What are the differences between these values and the ones we listed earlier?
- What might our board/committee do to address these discrepancies?

Moving from Reflection to Action

First Subgroup Session

Look over the publicity materials you have been given. Imagine you are creating a promotional video for your congregation. What scenes might you include? What might the narrator say? Be as descriptive as possible. (It's OK to use humor.)

Second Subgroup Session

Now imagine you are creating a documentary film that aims to tell the truth about your congregation. What scenes might you include? Again, be as descriptive as you can, and feel free to use humor.

Reflection and proactivity are complementary capacities that work best when practiced together in reciprocal fashion. Being proactive enables a congregation's leaders to look ahead and to discern the issues that require attention. Reflection enables them to understand the issues, their causes, and a range of possible solutions. Then it is time to be proactive again, selecting a solution and putting it into practice. In the course of doing so, new issues will undoubtedly arise. And so the cycle begins anew.

4

Collaborative Leadership: When Leaders Learn to Follow and Followers Learn to Lead

An increase in the level of reflection in a synagogue committee can have a powerful ripple effect. Over time, members of the group gain an appreciation for one another's talents and perspectives and (ideally) a tolerance for one another's limitations and blind spots. They find that they can rely on one another to bring in new ideas, ask difficult questions, keep the discussion from getting bogged down, and so on. A subtle shift in the balance of power occurs as the group develops a collective sense of responsibility. The process of collaboration has begun.

Collaboration and reflection go hand in hand; each can serve as a catalyst for the other. In addition, collaboration gives synagogue leaders both the impetus and the courage to be proactive. But collaborative leadership doesn't come easily. Some people equate hierarchy with respect; they question whether more collegial relationships are appropriate to the sanctity of congregational life. Others like the idea of collaboration in theory but find it difficult to put the theory into practice.

This chapter begins with a discussion of the limitations of top-down leadership and why corporations, schools, and government agencies have begun to explore ways of becoming less hierarchical and more collaborative. It looks at the particular challenges to collaborative leadership in synagogues from the perspective of the leader, from the perspective of the followers, and from the perspective of the collaborative group as a whole. And it describes what some synagogue leaders have done to meet these challenges.

Hierarchical Leadership

Traditionally, Judaism has been seen as a system of principles and laws, known as *halakhah* (literally, the way). The *halakhah,* which prescribes all of a Jew's actions, derives from the Torah, was elaborated in the Talmud, and is spelled out in detail in rabbinic codes, which date back to the Middle Ages and continue to be augmented today. Though the basic *halakhot* (laws) are taught to all observant Jews early in life, the finer points of the *halakhah* and the application of *halakhot* to new situations are left to rabbinic authorities to elucidate. Thus, hierarchical leadership is essential to the operation of traditional Jewish communities, in which the rabbi is referred to as the *mara d'atra* (literally, the master of the place). To this day, Jews who see themselves bound by the *halakhah* tend to accept the rabbi as their ultimate authority.[1]

But hierarchical leadership is also found in liberal synagogues that do not adhere so strictly to the *halakhah.* Whether by deliberate choice or by unthinking convention, American synagogues have tended to model themselves after corporations, with the rabbi serving as a kind of CEO. Typically, the rabbi and other senior staff members are hired by and are accountable to an inner circle of congregants, who serve on the board of directors and on the key standing committees.

Not surprisingly, this same form of concentrated authority can be found in many churches. George Parsons and Spead Leas offer the following example:

One congregation started in the early sixties, led by a dynamic and effective pastor. People respected and admired him greatly. He loved his role as the expert on how to "do church." No decisions were made without first coming to him for approval. No one would think of doing something at the church without his involvement and blessing. Committees were always small, usually the same people serving year after year.... If people did not like the style of the pastor or the activities of the church, they were not without choices: they could acquiesce or leave.[2]

In such a congregation, the authors point out, "keeping control seems appropriate...because the leaders believe themselves to be the experts; others with less experience and training will not be as well informed and will not make appropriate decisions."[3]

Though many other aspects of congregational life have come under criticism in recent years, the hierarchical nature of synagogue leadership has gone largely unchallenged. Many efforts to change synagogues assume that the traditional hierarchy is entirely appropriate. Assuming that the rabbi should be the key player in synagogue revitalization, these efforts focus almost exclusively on the rabbi as a sole change agent. In fact, Sidney Schwarz, whose critique of the synagogue center was discussed in chapter 2, goes so far as to argue that the problem of the synagogue center is that the rabbi *is not given sufficient power.* His book *Finding a Spiritual Home* presents portraits of four exemplary congregations, each led by a charismatic rabbi.

[I]n each case...the rabbi played a much more central role in shaping not only the worship service but also the organizational culture.... When the rabbi is permitted to pursue a particular vision as the spiritual leader of a community, it can powerfully motivate and inspire synagogue members.... People drawn to such a community become not only loyal followers of the rabbi and his or her vision but advocates and missionaries for that vision as well.[4]

The synagogues portrayed in Schwarz's book are indeed warm spiritual communities that inspire congregants to participate fully in Jewish life. But though the rabbis in these congregations have a great deal of personal charisma and influence, they also work collaboratively with their congregants in a variety of ways. In Beth El of Sudbury Valley, Massachusetts, for example, congregants led the effort to create a congregational siddur. In Schwarz's own congregation, Adath Shalom of Bethesda, Maryland, congregants participated actively in the drafting of the synagogue's mission statement. And B'nai Jeshurun in Manhattan, another synagogue profiled by Schwarz, has been trying to move away from a leadership centered on the charisma of the rabbi, as will be explained in the case on pages 101–104.

Beyond the question of the kind of leadership that is practiced in a few highly successful congregations lies a larger, more important issue: Is hierarchical leadership good for synagogue life? Edwin Friedman, a rabbi and a psychotherapist, and one of the first to apply systems theory to congregational life, thinks not. Though a powerful, charismatic rabbi can attract devoted followers and serve as a unifying force, charismatic leadership is a double-edged sword. "The emphasis on the personality of the leader tends to personalize issues,...with the result that emotions and issues become harder to separate from one another."[5]

David Teutsch, former president of the Reconstructionist Rabbinical College, echoes Friedman's concerns. The source of contemporary rabbinic authority, he argues, goes beyond either the traditional halakhic model or the more contemporary corporate model. Much of its power derives from the role played by rabbis at critical moments in the lives of congregants, as officiants in lifecycle ceremonies, and as counselors in time of distress. But the deep personal ties that inspire awe, respect, and even love can also lead to antagonism, especially toward rabbis "who maximize the more dramatic, awe-inspiring aspect of their role as a priest."[6]

> When rabbis internalize the priestly role, they sometimes
> understand themselves as *klei kodesh,* holy vessels. This not

only legitimates their uniqueness and power in the community; it implies that they are always above reproach. That claim creates resentments around issues of power and blame, as well as a belief that rabbis do not understand what "real life" is about because they do not participate in it.[7]

This type of antipathy can seep into contract talks and other budget negotiations, making them unduly contentious.

Ronald Heifetz, whose concept of the "view from the balcony" was discussed in chapter 2, makes a similar point about charismatic and hierarchical leadership in any organization:

> The lone-warrior model of leadership is heroic suicide. Each of us has blind spots that require the vision of others. Each of us has passions that need to be contained by others. Anyone can lose the capacity to get on the balcony, particularly when the pressures mount. Every person who leads needs help in distinguishing self from role and identifying the underlying issues that generate attack.[8]

The concentration of an organization's leadership in one individual, or in a small cohort of lay leaders, is problematic in other ways as well. Sensing that they are likely to be overshadowed and/or overruled by an inner clique, other congregants may be loath to volunteer their time. Potentially strong staff members may decline positions or leave after a few years. No one wants to feel that his or her contributions to an organization are not appreciated.

A dynamic leader or group can generate a great deal of enthusiasm for a proposed change, but when responsibility for the change rests on the shoulders of a single leader, or even a small group, that enthusiasm is contingent on the leaders' presence and can easily evaporate in their absence. For example, in one synagogue, an educator with a great deal of personal charisma introduced a host of family education programs that generated a great deal of interest and excitement. But when the educator moved to a different city, the excitement wore off, and participation in the programs dwindled, because the congregation as a whole had never solidified its commitment to family education. Research on changes in corporations corroborates this point. If the CEO is "the only visible champion" for an initiative, the initiative fails when the CEO's attention turns, as eventually it must, to other matters.[9]

The Benefits of Collaborative Leadership

Thus, religious organizations are not the only ones finding themselves increasingly dissatisfied with hierarchical leadership. In the past twenty-five years, calls for a different model of leadership have come from the worlds of business, government, and education. Advocates for this new type of leadership have given it various names: "facilitative,"[10] "constructivist,"[11] and "adaptive."[12] I have chosen the term "collaborative" as best expressing the concept that this type of leadership is rooted in a partnership—among members of the professional staff, and between lay and professional leaders in general.

Underlying these newer conceptions of leadership are several common themes, which should sound familiar to readers of this book:

1. Organizations and societies are never "finished"; rather, they are continually beset by problems and challenges.

2. These problems can be managed and even resolved temporarily but are never completely solved; the management of organizational and societal problems requires a continual balancing act, a series of trade-offs.

3. The leader's role is not to solve problems but to help people to articulate and define problems and to weigh the pros and cons of a range of possible solutions.

4. Leadership, under these circumstances, requires facilitative skill in bringing together diverse constituencies and both empowering and supporting them as they work together to articulate their problems, explore the universe of possible solutions, and reflect on their actions.

From this perspective, leadership is not a characteristic inherent in certain types of people or built into certain types of roles, but a set of attitudes and behaviors. In the words of Ronald Heifetz:

> Rather than define leadership either as a position of authority in a social structure or as a personal set of characteristics, we may find it a great deal more useful to define leadership as an *activity*. This allows for leadership from multiple positions in a social structure.... It also allows for the use of a variety of abilities depending on the demands of the culture and situation. Personal abilities are resources for leadership applied differently in different contexts.... By unhinging leadership from personality traits, we permit observations of the many different ways in which people exercise plenty of leadership every day without "being leaders."[13]

From the concept of leadership as an activity in which many can and should partake, it is only a small step to the concept of leadership as residing in a group rather than an individual. This conception of leadership has been put forth by William Drath and Charles Palus of the Center for Creative Leadership:

> [Leadership is] the process of connecting people to one another and to some social activity, work, enterprise; ... [it is] that which creates commitments in communities of practice.[14]
>
> The shift in viewpoint here involves moving from seeing the individual as the seat of leadership toward a view that the source of leadership lies in meaning-making in which all members of the community participate to some degree or another.[15]
>
> The purpose of the process of leadership in this view is therefore not to create motivation; rather it is to offer legitimate channels for members to act in ways that will increase their feelings of significance and their actual importance to the community. The question for an individual in a position of authority is no longer how to get people to do what is needed but how to participate in a process of structuring the activity and practice of the community so that people

marginal to its practice are afforded the means to move toward the center of that practice. In other words, how can the contribution of each person in the community of practice be made increasingly important and increasingly appreciated for its importance?[16]

In religious institutions, the case for collaborative leadership is even more compelling, for the mission of these institutions is not to sell a product or even to deliver a service but to create spiritual communities that nurture and challenge their members. If, as I argued in chapter 2, one of the problems facing synagogues is that they have become like fee-for-service organizations, the only way to turn them back into communities is by giving congregants a vital stake in the full range of their activities. As Rabbi David Stern, of Temple Emanu-El in Dallas, writes: "The idea of broadening and universalizing a sense of investment is vital."

> [T]he person at the top may be the least accessible person in the institution. If the vision is vested in the person who is hardest to get to, how are other people going to hear what the vision is? People who enter our congregation's communities enter through the outlying boundary. It's precisely the person at the outlying boundary who needs to know the vision. It's the congregant they see in the hall who is not an officer. It may be that the person who is there that day to pick up the sisterhood cookbook is the first person who articulates the vision for that person visiting.[17]

Rabbi Felicia Sol, of Congregation B'nai Jeshurun in Manhattan, makes a related point. For a congregation to function as a community, "people need to have meaningful encounters on a regular, if not daily, basis." In most congregations it is impossible for the rabbi to be the only fulcrum of these meaningful encounters. It is essential that a large number of congregants create community through their everyday encounters with one another.[18] The case on pages 101–104 explains the structure B'nai Jeshurun has created to make this happen.

Learning from Ezra the Scribe

What does collaborative leadership entail? How can synagogues give their members the sense of belonging and responsibility that would encourage them to step up to leadership? In subsequent sections, I analyze the challenge faced by each of the parties in the collaboration and offer examples of how different synagogues have met these challenges. But I want to begin with what might seem to be an unlikely primer for this new type of leadership—the Bible. For the most part, biblical leadership is hierarchical. Though he had a brother to help him communicate and a council of judges who served under him, Moses clearly stood apart in his leadership as being the only one to communicate with God "face to face." After Moses, the Israelites were led by a series of judges, prophets, and kings, who, though less powerful than Moses, could hardly be called collaborative.

But in one of the last books in the Bible, the books of Ezra-Nehemiah, we find an impressive example of collaborative leadership as displayed by Ezra the scribe. Ezra's story begins in Babylonia, where the Jews had been living in exile since 586 B.C.E., when the army of Nebuchadnezzar destroyed the First Temple. Babylonia itself was conquered, first by the Assyrians, and then by the Persians, and in 538, King Cyrus of Persia allowed the Jews to return to Jerusalem and to rebuild the Temple. Over the next decade or two, the building of the Temple proceeded in fits and starts; scholars believe it was completed around 520. The situation of the Jewish settlers in the land of Israel remained precarious; Jews lived in poverty and were subject to threats by the surrounding people.

About a century later (scholars cannot be sure of the exact date), Ezra, "a scribe expert in the Teaching of Moses which the Lord God of Israel had given" (Ezra 7:6), received permission to lead a delegation from Babylonia to Jerusalem. In addition to being a scribe, Ezra was a priest; the text traces his lineage, generation by generation, back to Aaron, the brother of Moses. As the text explains, "Ezra had dedicated himself to study the Teaching of the Lord so as to observe it, and to teach laws and rules to Israel" (7:10).

The text emphasizes just how special Ezra was by stating that his request was granted "in its entirety, thanks to the benevolence of the Lord toward him" (7:6).

Given Ezra's pedigree and reputation, "one anticipates a grand figure to step onto the stage and perform marvelous deeds." Instead, writes biblical scholar Tamara Eskenazi, "the book presents a rather unassuming person...who does not readily use the enormous powers that have been bestowed upon him, but lets others take the initiative and make decisions."[19]

> Ezra's chosen method involves persuasion, example and appeal, rather than coercion.... At the core of Ezra's activities is the transfer of power and knowledge from himself to the community as a whole. He does so by example, delegation of power, joint decision-making, reading of the Torah, and finally departing, leaving the community and the Torah in each other's care.[20]

Ezra's approach to leadership stands in stark contrast to that of Nehemiah, a cup-bearer to King Artaxerxes, who received permission to return to Jerusalem at roughly the same time[21] and becomes the governor of Israel. When Nehemiah learned that the Israelite inhabitants of the land had intermarried with their non-Jewish neighbors, he "censured them, cursed them, flogged them, tore out their hair" (Nehemiah 13:25) and forbade them to continue this practice. Ezra, by contrast, went into mourning, fasting and prostrating himself before God. This attracted a crowd of onlookers, who began weeping. It was not Ezra but a member of the community who acknowledged the people's transgression and proposed that they all take an oath to expel their non-Israelite wives. Later, at the people's request, Ezra convened a tribunal to examine each case and to ensure that proper amends were made.

Similarly, though Ezra's stated mission was to teach Torah to the people, he waited to be asked before reading the Torah aloud in public (Nehemiah 8:1). He shared the podium with Nehemiah and the Levites, who were given the role of explaining the text to the people. The account of this public reading of the Torah begins in the singular ("he read," verse 3), but then shifts to the plural ("they read," verse 8) to include the Levites. Through this reading the people discovered, on their own, the commandments to celebrate the festival of Sukkot (verse 14).

> Ezra apparently does not tell them but enables them to find God's commandments in Moses' Torah. He acts as a midwife between the community and the Torah and does not keep himself between the two any longer than is necessary. As soon as his task is complete, and the community can find for itself God's commandments in the Torah, Ezra fades away.... Ezra has accomplished his task: Israel is able to approach the Torah, to know it, and carry it out.[22]

Looking closely at Ezra's actions (with Eskenazi as our guide), we can learn a great deal about collaborative leadership. It involves a good deal of listening to the people's requests, concerns, and suggestions. It means waiting for people to discover certain truths on their own, on their own timeline. Collaborative leadership doesn't require that the titular leader mask his or her own opinions or feelings; Ezra is quite open in his distress about the mixed marriages. But there is a difference between expressing one's concerns (as Ezra does) and taking unilateral action (as Nehemiah does). Ezra models utmost self-restraint, letting the people accept responsibility for both the problem and its solution.

The sections that follow offer a closer look at these ingredients of collaborative leadership, based on scholarly work in the fields of business and education, on research on church and synagogue life, and on my own experiences in working with congregations. The first section considers collaborative leadership from the perspective of the leader—the rabbi, the professional, or the committee chair. The second deals with what is required of those who were previously simply "followers." The third focuses on the joint challenges faced by collaborative teams.

The Challenge for Leaders

Collaborative leadership poses a formidable challenge to anyone who has become accustomed to leading in a more hierarchical fashion. Rather than simply assessing a situation and taking action, the leader must become much more of a follower, practicing self-restraint, listening carefully, framing issues, and acting as a facilitator rather than a didactic teacher.

Practicing Tsimtsum

Consider Nehemiah's response to the intermarried Israelites. Because he believed that they had transgressed and that this transgression must be stopped immediately, he censured, cursed, and flogged them and issued an order prohibiting mixed marriage. Nehemiah was not a self-centered autocrat, and his primary goal was not to assert his own authority or to "show people who's the boss"; he simply saw a problem and went about solving it in a manner that seemed to him to be direct and effective. Had we not been offered an account of Ezra's very different approach to the same situation, it might not occur to us that Nehemiah had other alternatives at his disposal.

Similarly, the actions of a seemingly autocratic professional or lay synagogue leader may stem not from arrogance but from a failure to understand that there are other ways of handling things. Thus, the first task of the leader who wishes to become collaborative is similar to the first step of one who wishes to become more reflective: it is simply to refrain from acting, to leave room for others to come forward.

In an article that became an instant classic when it was written nearly thirty years ago, Eugene Borowitz compares the restraint that Jewish leaders ought to practice to *tsimtsum,* the kabalistic concept of God's contraction in the act of creation. Summarizing the thinking of the sixteenth-century mystic Isaac Luria, Borowitz writes:

> [Luria] boldly suggests that creation begins with the act of contraction, *tzimtzum.* God does not initiate the existence of other

things by extending himself. There would be no place to be, no area of non-being or partial being in which they might exist. Hence to create, He must first withdraw into Himself. God must, so to speak, make Himself less than He is so that other things can come into being.[23]

Leaders of Jewish institutions, Borowitz writes, have much to learn from this model of leadership, in which "the leader withholds presence and power so that followers may have some place in which to be." Borowitz likens the leader's act of *tsimtsum* to that of a parent

> ...who has the power to insist upon a given decision and a good deal of experience upon which to base his judgment.... [T]he urge to compel is almost irresistible. Yet if it is a matter the parent feels the child can handle—better, if making this decision and taking responsibility for it will help the child grow as a person—then the mature parent withdraws and makes it possible for the child to choose and thus come more fully into his own.[24]

Anyone who has ever been in a similar situation with a child, a student, or even a friend knows how difficult it is to practice *tsimtsum,* but also how, ultimately, this act of self-restraint allows the other person to develop more fully.

Listening

David Stern writes: "Shared leadership is a leadership of listening." He reminds us that early in his reign King Solomon had a dream in which he asked God for a *lev shomeah,* a listening heart (I Kings 3:9). "Already [in this early work] our tradition makes the link between listening and wisdom, between listening and understanding, and between listening and leadership."[25]

Collaborative leaders listen because they know they don't have all the answers, and they know that their "followers" may well have a different perspective or a new approach. With this in mind, some new rabbis or congregational presidents, upon assuming their position, convene a series of parlor meetings, encouraging congregants to share their views on the congregation. Likewise, congregations considering expanding or relocating their facilities now routinely hold focus groups to find out how both staff and congregants use the current facility, and the kind of space they might like to have in the future.

It's important to distinguish, however, between listening that is genuine and listening that is a public relations gimmick. In recent years, many politicians have embarked on "listening tours" before announcing their candidacies. This kind of "listening," which seems designed to reinforce what the potential candidate wants to hear, gives true listening a bad name. To truly listen means to suspend prior judgment and remain open to new ideas. This poses a challenge to both lay and professional synagogue leaders, because they are likely to have spent years thinking about certain issues and to have developed a great deal of expertise in these areas. It is not easy to sit quietly through a discussion of a topic that one has studied in depth and about which one has formed a considered opinion.

While collaborative leadership involves listening, it does *not* involve acquiescence. It would be impossible to agree with everyone (especially when there is a debate within the synagogue) and equally impossible to implement every suggestion, no matter how creative and persuasive it is. The art of listening sincerely without making undue promises takes practice. It may be reassuring to know that congregants are often satisfied with being heard. In a recent article on the controversies surrounding changes in worship, one church member was quoted as saying, "We are always able to talk with the pastor. We may not always get what we want, but we always know we have been heard by her."[26] This remark was meant as a compliment, not a critique. In a similar vein, Felicia Sol reports that for many congregants at B'nai Jeshurun, it is often sufficient to know that a process has been followed and that some lay people have been involved in making a decision. "Even when there are complaints, the leadership can point to a particular part of the process and say 'here is where that is being addressed.' Then people feel heard."

Framing the Discussion

The previous sections have alluded to the expertise many synagogue leaders, both lay and professional, bring to their positions. The cantor, for example, knows a great deal about synagogue music; how wasteful it would be if others could not learn what he or she has to offer. The chair of the membership committee, to take another example, may have years of experience observing the fluctuations in membership; informed decision making would take into account his or her observations and conjectures.

Though leaders who are more powerful and entrenched must practice *tsimtsum* so that newer leaders can find their voice, there is definitely a place for the wisdom and expertise of the veteran in framing discussions and making information available. Rather than simply advocating a particular approach, the role of the expert should be to guide people through complicated issues. This involves providing an overview of the key concepts and issues, and making resources available for those who want to pursue them more fully. For example, at a meeting of the education committee of the religious school at Temple Emanuel of Beverly Hills, several parents began complaining about how bored their children were and how little Hebrew they had learned. Realizing that members of the committee did not know very much about either Hebrew or language instruction, the educator, Cheri Ellowitz, resisted the urge to launch into a long defense of her program. Instead, she devoted a series of meetings over the next few months to the evaluation of the Hebrew program. She distributed articles and invited a guest speaker to inform the committee of the factors that had led her to make certain curricular choices. Together, they discussed different approaches to Hebrew instruction and the pros and cons of each. With this framework as a background, the committee was able to understand the choices that had been made and to suggest specific changes.

Acting As a Facilitator

This role of the leader follows closely upon the previous one. In a hierarchical system, the leader's responsibilities are enormous: identifying the problem, finding the solution, lobbying with the appropriate parties, dealing with the opposition, and overseeing implementation. In collaborative leadership, the leader's role is to make sure that his or her partners work together to identify the problem, investigate an array of possible solutions, weigh the alternatives carefully, and lay out a manageable plan for implementation. The role of the titular leader, then, is to ensure that this process proceeds at the right pace—neither too quickly nor too ponderously. To accomplish this, the leader will need a great deal of facilitative skill, structuring a process that will enable the group to work together effectively.

An entire volume could be written (and several have been) on how to facilitate meetings effectively.[27] In addition, many people have gained facilitation skills through their work or volunteer activities, and they can be asked to help out. The following are some of the questions I ask myself when I facilitate meetings:

1. *How shall I set the agenda?* With whom do I need to consult? Should I ask for additional agenda items in advance? At the meeting itself?

2. *How will I give participants appropriate opportunities to voice their opinions?* Meetings that consist of endless discussion quickly become boring and tedious. Nonetheless, participants need to share their opinions, especially since talking things out helps to clarify people's thinking. Is there a brainstorming technique I can use? Would it be appropriate to break people into dyads or triads for a 5- to 7-minute discussion? Could people be asked to write down their ideas on Post-it notes that are displayed on the wall, so everyone will have an opportunity to see them?

3. *How can I encourage good listening? How will I make sure that everyone's opinion is heard with respect?* Can people be given statements to read in advance? Should I take notes on a board or a

flip chart to focus people's attention? What kind of gentle, humorous comment can I offer to defuse the negativity of those who sit scowling, whispering, or passing notes while others are speaking?

4. *How can I focus the discussion and keep people from rehashing the same positions?* At what point can I summarize the debate and announce that the floor is open only for ideas that haven't yet come up? How can I curtail the discussion nicely but firmly when people violate this rule?

5. *How should we reach our decision?* Should the decision be made by vote or by consensus? Should people have an opportunity to vote for more than one option by using a multivoting technique, such as giving everyone five stickers to distribute to the options of their choice?

The Challenge for "Followers"

Collaborative leadership poses an equally formidable challenge to the followers, particularly in a synagogue context, and particularly in relationship to members of the clergy. It takes time for the average congregant to overcome feelings of intimidation and to make a commitment to long-term engagement.

Overcoming Intimidation

As difficult as it is for members of the clergy to practice *tsimtsum,* it is equally difficult for congregants to see them as partners. Rabbis and cantors play important symbolic roles at critical times—when congregants are in the hospital, when they come in for counseling, and when they celebrate lifecycle events. It is not so easy to get past the vulnerability or gratitude that one felt at those moments and engage with a member of the clergy as a partner. Thus, at the first meeting of a new congregational task force, the coordinator placed packets with participants' names around the table; instinctively, she put the rabbi's packet at the head of the table. Both the task force chair (who expected to be at the head of the table) and another member of the team (who objected to having *anyone* at the head) made comments about the seating arrangement, to which the coordinator replied, "but he *is* the rabbi."

True collaboration requires open debate, which may leave participants feeling uneasy. At another congregation, a heated (though amicable) debate broke out between the rabbi and a member of a committee. Later in the day, it occurred to this congregant that she had never challenged any of "her rabbis" before. Though an experienced and highly regarded professional on the outside, in her capacity as a synagogue leader she had always instinctively deferred to the rabbi.

David Stern tells the story of a meeting in which he and the educator engaged in some "intellectual sparring."

> I could see that the lay leaders sort of blanched. Another staff member came up to us afterward and said, "You know, that was kind of terrifying." I asked what they meant, and they said, "Well here you are the senior rabbi and it was very clear that you don't know the answers to these questions."[28]

As this anecdote indicates, congregants may not be the only ones to feel intimidated in a collaborative situation. The educator at yet another congregation spoke quite frankly about feeling out of her league as a member of a group of high-powered lay leaders:

> In my own professional life, I know that I am an expert on working with children. [When I work with adults] it's always as a teacher and as an expert on their children. Now I am working with a group of people that has nothing to do with children. These people are extremely successful in their fields— they are different from anyone I've ever worked with or known before. I see myself better on a kibbutz than in this environment. I was quiet the first few months because I was the little girl.... Working through this made me feel much stronger as a professional.[29]

The discomfort experienced by members as a team gropes its way toward collaborative leadership is compounded by the fact that new role definitions rarely remain fixed but continue to evolve. One congregant compared her frustration in clarifying her role as a collaborative leader to that of a parent trying to figure out a child's developmental stage; by the time the parent has identified the stage, the child has already progressed to the next one. In collaborative leadership, as in parenting, relationships change continually.

Bringing in One's Expertise

It is common for accountants and lawyers to bring their expertise to a synagogue board. But after their initial hesitancies are overcome, other lay leaders (and perhaps some professionals as well) will, it is hoped, discover that they have expertise that can benefit the congregation in some way. I have already mentioned the facilitation skills that people in a variety of professions, including social work, teaching, and marketing, have acquired. Once people who have skill in facilitation realize that a meeting in a synagogue is not radically different from any other meeting, and once the rabbi or committee chair indicates a desire for some help, this is a natural avenue for "stepping up" to leadership.

At some point, those who were English majors or who have led Great Books discussion groups will discover that they have some good ideas about how to lead Torah study—after all, the Bible is one of the "great books." Musicians, both amateur and professional, have much to contribute to worship services and holiday celebrations. Educators and academics can be helpful in thinking through educational issues as well as in planning programs. And what synagogue could not benefit from the assistance of public relations specialists and graphic designers, not to mention other artists?

Unfortunately, some volunteer congregants turn out to be unhelpful or difficult, which is why it is important to recruit a broad pool of congregants and to set the expectation of collaboration from the outset. If each congregant volunteer is assigned to a staff supervisor or lay mentor, it will be easier to keep track of how the volunteer is doing and to give the volunteer timely feedback. If, after repeated feedback, the volunteer fails, for whatever reason, to fulfill the congregation's expectations, he or she can be reassigned to a more suitable task.

The following case describes the system devised by Congregation B'nai Jeshurun to increase the level of both support and accountability among congregants who perform the mitzvah of *bikur cholim* (visiting the sick).

CASE STUDY

Making *Bikur Cholim* (Visiting the Sick) a Shared Responsibility at Congregation B'nai Jeshurun

Congregation B'nai Jeshurun, on Manhattan's Upper West Side, is known for its lively and spiritual Shabbat services, social activism, and dynamic rabbinic leadership. Founded in 1825, BJ (as it is commonly known) had once been a flagship congregation of the Conservative movement. But its membership had declined over the years, and it was nearly moribund in 1984, when Rabbi Marshall Meyer came on board. Clearly, Rabbi Meyer's approach filled a previously unmet need, because by 1990 the congregation had grown to 1,000 member units. Even after Rabbi Meyer's untimely death in 1993, the congregation continued to thrive under the leadership of Rabbi Rolando Matalon; by 1995, when Rabbi Marcelo Bronstein joined the staff, there were over 1,600 households. Today the membership stands at 1,800 households, and the staff includes three rabbis, a *hazan* (cantor), and 25 full-time professionals.

This rapid growth was gratifying to the congregation's leaders but also a source of consternation. They knew that they had to move from a "Mom and Pop Shop" mode of operation, wherein things "just happened organically," to one that was more structured. New professional staff had been added to perform tasks that had been handled by volunteers when the synagogue was small. But even with additional staff members, the standing committees did not have the resources or personnel to reach out to the periphery of the congregation. For example, in the "spiritual pledge" that congregants are asked to fill out and bring to Yom Kippur services, many had pledged to participate in the mitzvah of *bikur cholim* (visiting the sick), but few of these potential volunteers had ever been called, and many of them felt frustrated that their offer to help had gone unacknowledged.

Clearly, a new structure for volunteers was needed. But bureaucracy and hierarchy were anathema to the spirit of this congregation. In the words of Rabbi Felicia Sol, "BJ is the kind of community where everyone wants to be well informed and intensely involved." The challenge was to create a structure that would cultivate new lay leaders and enable a larger number of congregants to feel connected to the daily life of the congregation, not just the wonderful Friday night services.

To meet this challenge, the congregation engaged in a strategic planning process. The result was an umbrella structure with seven steering committees. Each steering committee is staffed by a board member and a staff member or rabbi. To quote Rabbi Sol: "Clarity was very important. This new structure of defined roles, relationships, and responsibilities helped to create a culture of shared leadership that congregants felt they could trust."

One of the steering committees was "Creating Kehilla," which had under it committees related to *bikur cholim* (visiting the sick), *hevra kadisha* (supporting the bereaved), singles, gays and lesbians, interfaith families, *hakhnasat orchim* (welcoming strangers), book groups, and *havurot* (fellowship groups).

After a year-long discussion about how to restructure *bikur cholim,* Susan Kippur, a longtime member of the congregation, was asked to co-chair the committee. Susan knew from personal experience that the system was not working as well as it could; she had been one of the many who had volunteered but never been called upon. Drawing on her experience as an organizational development consultant, Susan led her co-chair, the social work consultant who staffed the committee, and Rabbi Sol, the rabbinic liaison, through a visioning process. They met several times over the course of a month to ask themselves: "What would the *bikur cholim* committee like to be known for? What is the major work that should be done? How should it be structured? How could we create direction for the committee?"

They concluded that five different subcommittees were needed to cover five different tasks:

- visiting the sick
- maintaining the *misheberakh* (prayer for healing) list
- education and communication (so that the entire congregation would be taught the value of *bikur cholim*)
- helping to bring frail elderly members to the synagogue and other places
- organizing special events (such as visits to a nearby nursing home)

The different tasks allowed for varying levels of involvement—from making phone calls to organizing to actual visitation. Leadership teams for each of these tasks were assembled, and those who had volunteered to help were called and asked which team they would like to join. For the task of visiting the sick, three teams were created. The rabbi and social work consultant receive the requests for visitors; they notify the co-chairs to select and mobilize a team that will provide support. The co-chairs convey the assignments and provide managerial guidance where needed, team leaders oversee the visitation for the duration of the illness, the rabbi serves as the spiritual leader to the teams, and the social work consultant provides professional support.

The shifting of responsibility from a single staff member and a small committee to this more elaborate team structure was a complicated process. It was not easy to find appropriate team leaders. Some congregants are wonderful, caring volunteers but are not yet skilled at administration; others, who have managerial responsibilities at work, are not eager to take on additional ones at the congregation. In addition, the team leaders are now responsible for training their team members in the intricacies and subtleties of dealing effectively with people who are made vulnerable by illness. "In a corporation or academic environment, there are often selection and development programs in place to build the requisite skills," Susan Kippur reflects. "But in a spiritual community, you frequently need to build these capabilities from scratch, capitalizing on people's raw talents and good intentions." Over time, co-chairs, team leaders, and staff members have become more adept at handling these challenges.

For Susan Kippur, *bikur cholim* was just part of her journey. For many years, her career and her family came first. Then she decided she wanted to use her business skills in a new setting "where the values are intimately linked to my values, unlike at a bank or corporation." Since becoming the co-chair of *bikur cholim,* she has also taken advantage of adult learning opportunities and has joined the board. Learning the different rules of leadership in a volunteer context has been eye-opening but also spiritually fulfilling.

Bikur cholim is just one example of how a collaborative leadership model has expanded the "inner circle" to include more people in the daily spiritual life of the congregation. As Rabbi Sol notes, "Suddenly people are bringing challahs to people who can't get out before Shabbat. One person who underwent surgery volunteered after she recovered, because being visited was such a nice experience." Feeling "connected" is becoming less dependent on knowing the rabbis and more linked to knowing one another.

Making a Commitment for the Long(er) Term

Many synagogues limit the potential for collaborative leadership by setting very short terms (of only one or two years) for their lay leaders. This "revolving door" policy may have been instituted to attract new leadership ("don't worry, you only have to commit for a year or two") or to prevent the leadership from becoming too insular, but it makes it difficult for truly collaborative leadership to take root. As will be discussed below, it takes time for partners who share leadership responsibilities to develop a common language, adjust to one another's strengths and limitations, and learn to work together productively. This suggests that the "laboratory" or "incubator" for collaboration be a task force or committee that can require a longer term commitment (of two years, at least) for its members. Having forged a partnership under these circumstances, members of the committee might then go on to serve positions in the governance structure that carry more limited terms. The case in chapter 3 (pages 61–65) provides an example of how this was done at Congregation Sinai in Milwaukee.

The Joint Challenge

By far, the biggest challenges to collaborative leadership lie in the work that all participants must undertake together:

- evolving a vision that is truly shared
- clarifying roles in decision making
- rethinking the division of labor

Evolving a Shared Vision

It is often said that shared vision is a prerequisite for successful collaboration, but that way of stating it puts the cart before the horse. A truly shared vision is an amalgam of the separate visions of the various members of the group; it is not something that can be borrowed, negotiated, or cobbled together. Shared vision is the by-product of a genuine meeting of the minds. This requires trust, honesty, and tact. And it takes considerable time to develop.

A great deal has been written about the appropriate timing and format for vision statements.[30] Should an articulated vision precede action or be derived from it? Are short, pithy statements inspirational or platitudinous? My experience in the Experiment in Congregational Education has led me to conclude that the process of visioning is more important than the product. People who have not participated in articulating or discussing the vision will not have internalized it sufficiently for it to guide their actions. Thus, some congregations have chosen to set aside their vision statements, however compelling, as they brought on a new cadre of lay leaders. They decided to begin "from scratch," repeating with the new group many of the visioning exercises they have used in the past. In some cases, the second, third, or fourth drafts of the vision statement were very similar to the first draft. In others, subsequent vision statements made some substantive changes, giving the leadership new direction and insight.

Becoming a Congregation of Learners contains a chapter on the process of visioning, including nine exercises that have been used with a variety of congregational groups. Many of these exercises can be adapted to focus on topics other than learning, for use in a variety of synagogue committees and with the board as well. The exercises that follow are modified versions of the exercises in that book; each is accompanied by suggestions for adapting the exercise in different contexts.

Reflecting on Our Best Synagogue Experiences

In this exercise, participants reflect on some of their best synagogue experiences. They analyze these experiences and arrive at some general principles about the factors that contribute to them. Handout 1 suggests one way in which this assignment might be framed.

Preparation

An instruction sheet for participants will be required. See Handout 1 for a possible model.

Grouping of Participants

Small groups with five participants each.

Time Required

30 to 40 minutes for the small groups, and 3 to 5 minutes for each group to report back.

Facilitation

Each group can work on its own, following the instruction sheet.

Record Keeping

The list of principles can be used as a point of departure for Exercise 2, the Synagogue Bulletin of the Future.

Reflections on Our Own Best Synagogue Experiences

In Small Groups

Think for a moment of a very positive synagogue experience you have had. It might have taken place in this synagogue or in some other congregation, when you were a child, a teenager, or an adult.

- **What factors or conditions made this a particularly positive experience for you?** (Possible factors might include the nature of the activity, the setting and ambiance, the role of the professionals, the role of the other congregants, or any factors that made you particularly open to having a good experience.)

- Take turns sharing both the experience and the factors that made it so successful. As people talk, have someone list the factors or conditions. Notice how many of these are mentioned more than once.

- After everyone has had a turn, spend some time analyzing and prioritizing the list. Which items can be combined? Which seem to be most important?

- Pick your group's top five priorities.

- Turn each of these five into a sentence that explains what the factor is and why it is important. Write them on newsprint to be shared with the other groups.

The Synagogue Bulletin of the Future

The Synagogue Bulletin of the Future is simply a device for people to imagine the kind of planned programs and unplanned activities that might happen if a synagogue were to live by the principles enumerated in Exercise 1. This exercise could be used immediately after Exercise 1 or at a subsequent meeting. It could also be used independently, with the principles of a good synagogue experience deduced at the end.

Alternative 1

Small groups of three to four for 30 minutes, plus 2 to 3 minutes for each group to share at the end.

Alternative 2

- Small groups of three or four for 30 minutes
- Groups share (3 to 4 minutes each)
- A different set of small groups of five for another 30 minutes
- 2 to 3 minutes for each group to report back

Facilitation

ALTERNATIVE 1

Participants should be given the list of principles of a good synagogue experience, as generated in Exercise 1. Working with a few of these principles, they should imagine what the synagogue's bulletin might look like in 3 to 5 years, when these principles are built into every aspect of the synagogue's life. One group might be assigned to write the calendar of events; a second, the lead article; a third, the rabbi's column, etc.

ALTERNATIVE 2

Alternately, participants are not given a list of principles but are simply asked to imagine an issue of the bulletin written at some future date, when the synagogue has arrived at "an improved state." Each group is asked to write a different monthly feature. After they share their products, they are broken into different groups, with each group looking at one part of the bulletin. What can they deduce from this article, column, or calendar about some of the principles followed by their "new and improved" synagogue?

In addition to visioning exercises, text study can serve as an excellent springboard for discussing a congregation's vision and the complementary roles of different leaders in perpetuating that vision. The following text study can lead to a stimulating discussion of shared leadership in service of a common vision.

How to Keep Judaism Alive:
A Talmudic Debate

It seems that even in the days of the Talmud, there was concern about keeping Jewish traditions alive, as can be seen from this text, taken from tractate *Bava Metzia* 85b:

> When Rabbi Hanina and Rabbi Hiyya used to quarrel, Rabbi Hanina would say:
>
> Do you dare to quarrel with me? Even if, God forbid, the entire Torah were to be forgotten, I would be able to restore it by myself, relying on my powers of argumentation.
>
> Rabbi Hiyya would respond:
>
> Do you dare to argue with me? Consider what I have done to ensure that the Torah will not be forgotten:
>
> What do I do? I go out and plant flax, and after the flax is processed I proceed to weave nets from it. When the nets are ready, I go out and catch a deer and give the meat to needy orphans. From the skins of those deer I prepare scrolls, upon which I write the Five Books of the Torah.
>
> Then I go to a town where there are no other teachers and teach the Torah to five children, one book to each child. Then I teach the six orders of the Mishnah to six children, one order to each child. And I say to each of the children: "Now I have to leave to teach elsewhere; until I return, teach one another Torah and teach one another Mishnah."
>
> Thus my efforts ensure that the Torah is not forgotten in Israel.

Both Rabbi Hiyya and Rabbi Hanina have the same goal in mind—ensuring that the Torah will not be forgotten. But they have very different ideas about how to achieve this goal.

- How would you describe their different methods?

- Both these accounts read more like outlandish tall tales than accurate descriptions or realistic plans. Why do you think the rabbis exaggerated in this way? What points were they trying to make?

- Which rabbi's method do you think would be more effective and why?

- Why do you think the Talmud includes both of their statements?

- What lessons can we in our synagogue learn from each of these approaches to preserving the Jewish tradition? What can lay leaders learn from this text? What can professional leaders learn?

Finally, vignettes that paint vivid portraits of a range of synagogue experiences can spark people's imaginations and challenge their preconceptions of synagogue life. A discussion of people's reactions to these vignettes can also help a group evolve a shared vision. A selection of vignettes that might serve this purpose can be found in chapter 2 of *Becoming a Congregation of Learners* and also in Sidney Schwarz's book *Finding a Spiritual Home.*[31]

Clarifying Roles in the Process of Decision Making

Collaborative decision making can mean different things in different contexts and is best thought of as a continuum of possibilities. At one end are situations in which a group of lay and professional leaders deliberate together and arrive at consensus. At the other end are cases in which an individual or small group retains the prerogative to make the decision but seeks input from others. In between the two end points lies a range of possibilities for involving different people in the discussion of the issues involved and for giving people a voice in making the decision. Different situations may call for different approaches.

At the collaborative end of the continuum lies the concept of a worship care committee, described by Lawrence Hoffman in his book *The Art of Public Prayer.* As the subtitle of the book *(Not for Clergy Only)* suggests, Hoffman believes that improving synagogue worship requires that a group of lay and professionals work together "to ask hard questions in the certain knowledge that no one will be scapegoated and everyone will be safe, no matter what the problems turn out to be."[32] Following Hoffman's advice, Temple Emanuel of Beverly Hills formed a worship care committee for its Shabbat morning *minyan.* In the year since its inception, the committee has considered the seating arrangement, the length of the service, the introduction of certain liturgical innovations, and the requirements for celebrating a bar or bat mitzvah in the *minyan.* It spawned a subcommittee to review and revise the loose-leaf *siddur* it has been using. Co-chaired by two lay leaders, the committee periodically holds open meetings

after services to solicit feedback and encourage new ideas from all participants. The rabbis and cantor, who attend all meetings, believe that open-
ing up decision making in this way has given congregants a greater stake
in the *minyan*. Evidence of this lies in the increased number of Torah readers and text teachers, and the initiative taken by members to expand the
minyan to holidays in addition to Shabbat. (The development of collaborative leadership at this *minyan* will be discussed in greater detail in the
case in chapter 7, pages 223–230.)

At the opposite end of the continuum are congregations that have
chosen to leave decisions about worship in the hands of the clergy; collaboration, in this case, involves soliciting continual feedback. For example, in Congregation B'nai Jeshurun in New York, the clergy are deeply
committed to experimentation and believe that a ritual committee would
curtail their flexibility. They continually look for ways to keep the worship
experience fresh and to maintain a sense of intimacy in what has become
a very large congregation. As they experiment they ask the congregants to
"bear with them" but also to share their reactions through letters, e-mails,
and faxes. They have instituted a week-night conversation with the rabbi,
which meets several times a year in an effort to encourage dialogue on a
range of liturgical, educational, and halakhic issues.

Similarly, in Temple Emanu-El of Dallas, which was founded by
Classical Reform Jews and retains many members who identify with
Classical Reform ideology, the rabbis decided that the time had come for
them to wear *kippot* (skullcaps) and *tallitot* (prayer shawls) on the *bimah*
(dais). Though the decision was made by the rabbis, the manner in which
the change was introduced was highly collaborative. Knowing that this
issue could serve as a lightening rod for many who felt disenfranchised by
the Reform Movement's increased use of traditional ritual and symbols,
key lay leaders worked with the senior rabbi to devise a process for introducing this change. They began by teaching about ritual garb to a variety
of groups, such as adult education classes, the ritual committee, and the
board. With the board, in particular, "the discussion lasted a very long time

and was intense and emotionally charged."[33] This reaction gave the lay leaders second thoughts—not about the decision itself, which they saw as the purview of the rabbis, but about the time line for its implementation. They decided to create additional opportunities for teaching and discussion and to introduce *kippot* and *tallitot* more gradually, over the course of a summer.

Rethinking the Division of Labor

Moving toward collaborative leadership requires, by definition, a blurring of roles and a renegotiation of responsibilities that were previously taken for granted. This is similar to the situation faced by many married couples. Before the days of women's liberation, the tasks of husbands and wives were dictated by convention: men went to work; women stayed home and took care of the children. Today, with more women working outside the home and men more actively involved in parenting, a whole new set of questions arises: Who stays home to take care of a sick child? Who does the shopping, cooking, and cleaning? Anyone who has lived in a dual-income household knows how much discussion, debate, trial, and error are required before these roles and responsibilities are clarified. There is no correct answer that applies across the board. Every couple must find its own solution to this problem and be prepared to make continual adjustments as the need arises.

The situation of collaborative leaders in a congregation creates similar ambiguities that require a similar process of negotiation. When congregants take on roles that were traditionally left to professionals—teaching classes, for example, or making decisions regarding rituals—a certain discomfort and uncertainty is to be expected, especially at first. It is not uncommon, at least at the beginning, for things to fall through the (newly formed) cracks. For example, a committee chair who moves toward a more collaborative style of leadership may appropriately expect members of the committee to take on additional tasks.

This represents a big change for congregants who have previously seen their role as simply showing up for meetings. Once committee members begin to take on new responsibilities, the chair faces a new challenge—how to oversee and coordinate the work. "Responsibility charting" is an excellent technique for clarifying responsibilities when a new and more complicated situation arises or when a committee would like to tackle a familiar situation in a different way. Handout 2 explains how to use this technique.[34]

Responsibility Charting

Responsibility charting is a technique that was devised to help working teams coordinate their various tasks and work together well. Begin by creating a chart with as many rows as you have tasks (leave room for the extra tasks you will discover along the way). List each task on a separate row. Create a separate column for each person who will be involved in these tasks. They can be involved in four different ways, as indicated by four letters:

- *R* stands for the person (or people) *responsible.*

- *A* stands for the person (or people) who must *approve.*

- *C* stands for the person (or people) who must *be consulted.*

- *I* stands for the person (or people) who must *be kept informed.*

On the following page is an example of a responsibility chart for the preparation of bar and bat mitzvah students at one congregation.

As the chart is being filled in (and when it is complete), ask yourselves the following questions:

1. What type of coordination is built into this structure?

2. What additional coordination might be needed?

3. What are the advantages/disadvantages of this arrangement? What are the "weak links" in the chain, and how might we reinforce them?

Steps in Preparation for Bar/Bat Mitzvah	Rabbi	Cantor	Educator	Teacher	Bar/Bat Mitzvah Tutor
Learning Hebrew	C		A	R	I
Study of prayers (meaning and fluent decoding)—special class during 7th grade	C	C	A	R	I
Meeting with family 8 months before the bar/bat mitzvah	R				
Creation and updating of bar/bat mitzvah handbook given to family	A	A	R		
Coordination and correspondence regarding all meetings with tutor and rabbi		R			
Individual tutoring 1x/week about the content of Torah portion and fluency of decoding and chanting	I		A	I	R
5-session workshop for families re: service	R	R	R		
3 meetings with bar/bat mitzvah candidate re: *d'var torah*	R				
First rehearsal with family (review service, *haftora*, and *d'var torah*)		R			
Second rehearsal with family (review service, Torah service, and *d'var torah*)	R				

Every collaborative group needs to develop procedures for keeping its members informed. Though minutes are especially critical in a collaborative situation (where key members may, from time to time, be unable to attend meetings), they represent only the bare minimum of what is required to maintain good communication. People rarely read minutes very carefully; consequently, they rarely retain what they read. If possible, one member of a collaborative group should serve as a coordinator, communicating with members by phone and e-mail. Alternatively, the group might develop a buddy system so that people who are absent are kept informed in between meetings.

A wonderful example of the power of carefully orchestrated collaboration comes from Riv-Ellen Prell's ethnography of Congregation Beth El of Minneapolis. When the senior rabbi resigned, the congregation was unable, after a six-month search, to find a replacement. The lay leadership, which had always been strong, stepped into the breach. The synagogue's president worked with the assistant rabbi to prioritize every task, restructure the staff to take on some new responsibilities, and recruit congregants to take on others. "The board leadership learned by hard work how many tasks its clergy undertook on a daily basis."[35] Though the congregation felt bereft at the loss of their rabbi, they did not let this loss hold them back but launched the impressive "Celebrate Shabbat" initiative discussed in chapter 3.[36]

The Downside of Collaboration

This discussion of the need for careful coordination hints at some of the problems that accompany collaborative leadership. Collaboration requires time and attention to group process, both within the collaborative group and between the group and the rest of the congregation.

Collaboration Is Time Consuming

Obviously, collaboration requires considerably more time than a more hierarchical system; no congregation has the luxury of making every aspect of congregational life collaborative. Just as many decisions must continue to be made without extended reflection, many situations can and should be managed by a single individual or a small committee. Collaboration should be reserved for areas in which it would be important to have a greater investment on the part of congregants, decisions that are more carefully considered, and areas in which significant change is contemplated.

It would be logical to assume that the time required for collaboration might deter volunteers from becoming involved, and this must certainly be true for some potential leaders. My own experience, on the other hand, corroborated by recent research on synagogue life, indicates that many lay volunteers are attracted by the idea of collaborating with one another and with the synagogue professionals. They relish the opportunity to engage in high-level discussions about important matters. In the words of one member of a collaborative team, "I like to come here; it's affirming. You get good ideas, things get beaten around, and you're making changes that work."[37] Another member of the same team added,

> This is my workout for the brain. It is like a physical workout— you may drag yourself to get there, but you feel so good when you are done. It is so hard to carve out the time, and we are so overcommitted, and our kids are so overcommitted, but when I get here it is so much fun. When I walk out of here I just want three to four more hours without any interruptions to keep my mind on it.[38]

The Need to Establish Appropriate Norms

The early stages of collaboration are likely to be filled with both excitement and apprehension as people who are only partially aware of one another's skills and working styles begin to work together. Though many will find the process invigorating, disagreements will inevitably arise. This is such a common occurrence in the life of groups that Tuckman and Jensen, in their work on the stages of group development, characterize the second stage as "storming."[39] While some degree of "storming" is probably inevitable, its ferocity may be tamed by careful attention to group process at every stage.

Early on, before any serious problems arise, members of the group should devote some time to getting to know one another and discussing how they will work together. Exercise 3 on pages 122–123 is adapted from the writings of Linda Lambert and enables members of a group to share some of their expectations and to create an initial set of ground rules.[40]

Another tool that collaborative groups have found useful is a simple one—dedicating a small amount of time at the end of each meeting to filling out a written evaluation. From this feedback, the group can make adjustments to its agendas and modes of operation. The evaluation form found on pages 124–125 is adapted from one developed at Westchester Reform Temple.

Creating Ground Rules for a Working Group

This exercise asks members of a newly formed committee, task force, or professional team to analyze some of the best experiences they have had in a working group and to extrapolate from those experiences some guidelines for how their group will operate.

Step 1:

FREEWRITE (7 to 10 minutes)

Each participant is given a pencil and a sheet of paper and is asked to recall an experience in a working group (in any context, paid or volunteer) that was particularly effective in accomplishing its goals and particularly rewarding for its members. Participants write notes to themselves about this experience and about what made the experience so special.

Step 2:

SHARING THE STORIES (10 to 15 minutes)

If the group contains six or more participants, divide into subgroups of three or four. Participants share their experiences and, if time permits, begin to analyze the elements that made these group experiences so positive.

Step 3:

APPLYING THE PRINCIPLES TO OUR OWN SITUATION

(15 to 20 minutes)

Reconvene as a larger group. Ask these questions:

- What group norms or expectations made these experiences so powerful? (Keep a list of these on a board or large newsprint.)

- Which of these norms might we want to establish for our synagogue committee?

- How can we establish these norms?

Keep a record of these norms and expectations, to be sent out with the minutes and kept on hand as a guideline for deliberations.

An Evaluation Form
to Assess a Meeting's Effectiveness

Meeting Evaluation Form

● How would you rate each part of our meeting?

	Very Useful	Somewhat Useful	Not Useful
Part 1 *(fill in content)*	1	2	3
Part 2 *(fill in content)*	1	2	3
Part 3 *(fill in content)*	1	2	3

● What might we do to make our meetings more useful?

● One of the most important things I learned today is…

● Name (optional):

Attending to Group Process

All the collaborative synagogue teams I have observed or studied have found that internal communication among members of the team has consumed not only more time but also more energy. In the words of one synagogue professional:

> It isn't just time—it's freshness, it's crispness. You've got to be listening carefully, you've got to be attuned to what's going on, you've got to be reading the messages behind the message and all those things of human dynamics and group dynamics that are fun and fascinating. The problem is, they all come when you're not always so fresh and when you've got a thousand other things going on and your energy level may be lower, or your patience level may be lower, or you are just preoccupied.[41]

At some point, nearly all groups find themselves in situations in which the need for careful and/or honest communication was overlooked or neglected, which resulted in mistakes being made, deadlines missed, tasks neglected, and/or feelings hurt. Chris Argyris, an organizational theorist, argues that a major source of group tension is the natural tendency to jump from a slim piece of evidence to an often incorrect conclusion. From a brief remark, or even a person's tone of voice, we leap to conclusions about who that person is and what that person believes. Anita Farber-Robinson offers the following anecdote, which illustrates this point:

> Larry and Martin served on a committee together. They were trying to redesign something that wasn't working well. Martin had an idea. Larry, a large and muscular man, hunched over with his chin on his hand and his elbows on the table. He furrowed his brow and appeared to grimace. Martin did not know Larry well, but feeling intimidated, he dropped the idea he had advanced and withdrew a little.... Eventually one of the other ideas that had been presented was adopted and put into operation. A few months later Larry was sitting with Martin over

coffee. "Martin," Larry asked, "there is something I've been meaning to ask you. You had that great idea last spring when we were working on the new design, and almost as soon as you presented it, you withdrew it. I was really disappointed that you did that. I thought it was the best idea that had come forward." Martin was stunned. "I stopped advocating for it when I could tell that it was making you angry."... Larry now was the one who was stunned. "I never was angry.... And I thought for sure you had withdrawn the idea from discussion."[42]

In retrospect, Martin realized that he had made an incorrect inference about Larry's reactions to his idea. Had he probed more deeply and asked Larry what he was thinking, rather than simply assuming that the furrowed brow meant disapproval, he might have realized that Larry was concentrating on what he thought was an intriguing idea.

This kind of "leap to inference" is very common. We rarely have time to "stop the action" to discern what lies behind one person's nod of the head or another's sarcasm. Learning to interpret people's subtle nonverbal messages correctly takes time and is always uncertain. When we know a person well, our inferences are likely to be correct. But when people in a group are just beginning to work together, unchecked inferences can lead to lost opportunities (as in the anecdote above) at best, and serious conflicts at worst. Lay leaders, in particular, may find it difficult to get past their unchecked and often erroneous assumptions about the motivations of members of the clergy. Mindful of this possibility, members of a collaborative group should take care to, in Farber-Robinson's terms, "travel down the ladder of inference" and test out their interpretations.

Over time, the members of a collaborative team will get to know one another's strengths and weaknesses quite well. The teaching skills of one, the facilitative skills of another, and the hard work of a third will have come out, along with one member's tendency to wait until the last minute, another's overly critical comments, and yet a third's failure to return phone calls. The more honest and open group members can be in giving one another feedback, the stronger the collaboration will be. Often the person receiving the feedback is fully aware of the problem and will be relieved to have it out in the open. An open discussion will allow the group to reassign certain tasks, bring on a new member to fill the gaps, or, in some cases, help a member to become aware of not fulfilling his or her responsibilities. While "firing" a volunteer is extremely uncomfortable, reassigning that person will often solve the problem. Some collaborative teams have found it worthwhile to hire a process consultant to help them define and redefine their roles, communicate their concerns more openly, reflect on their strengths and weaknesses as a team, and handle any crises that arise.

Obviously, a good deal more could be said about creating and maintaining the conditions necessary for productive relationships within a group. Fortunately, many good books can be found on this topic.[43]

The Danger of Becoming Too Insular

In Jensen and Tuckman's schema, a group goes through four stages: forming, storming, norming, and performing.[44] As members of a group get past storming to performing, they develop their own shorthand and their own jokes and rituals. But, as Parsons and Leas point out, the collegiality of one group can actually serve as a barrier to the involvement of those outside the circle.[45] When a collaborative group becomes too insular, it creates another kind of hierarchy—between the collaborative "insiders" and everyone else. The special access that members of the group have to the top lay and/or professional leaders, and the closeness that can develop within such a group, can become a source of resentment to those who do not share that privilege. More than one collaborative group in the Experiment in Congregational Education had the experience of unwittingly undermining their ultimate objective of creating a congregation of learners by antagonizing members of the board or standing committees. It took a good deal of effort to turn these situations around, and the proverbial ounce of prevention should be on everyone's mind.

Parsons and Leas suggest that "the first step toward moving away from excessive collegiality would be—not to have people work alone, but—to explore ways to establish several centers of collegiality rather than one or a few."[46] In other words, a synagogue can diminish the insularity of a single collaborative group by forming additional collaborative groups. The more collaborative groups there are, the less they are likely to be seen as privileged and exclusive. Members of early collaborative groups can be given responsibility for helping later groups create their own norms of collaboration, which not only breaks up the clique but also takes some of the pressure off the professionals.

The Ultimate Rewards of Collaboration: A Focus on Primary Jewish Acts

A famous dictum in *Pirkei Avot* (Ethics of the Fathers) says that the world stands on three things: on *torah* (learning), on *avodah* (worship) and *gemilut chasadim* (righteous deeds). To live a full Jewish life, a Jew must engage in each of these primary activities. In too many synagogues, however, these pillars of Jewish life are upheld by only a small segment of the congregation. Learning is relegated to the religious school or to the adult education program, which rarely draws more than ten percent of the congregation. Worship services are held weekly (and in some congregations daily), but only a small core of regulars actually attend regularly. Good deeds are seen as the province of the social action and "caring community" committees.

Truthfully, few synagogues are structured in a way that would enable every member to participate in these core Jewish activities, because most are so dependent on professional leadership. Hiring staff members to lead multiple opportunities for learning, worship, and good deeds for all congregants would require a budget larger than that of even the largest and most wealthy synagogue. Increased participation requires that congregants teach one another, take a more active role in leading worship, and reach out to one another and to the community at large.

This, ultimately, can be the most important benefit of collaboration. When more people are invested in thinking about how to make the synagogue a better place and in assuring that these ideas become a reality, these people are drawn closer to the core of Jewish life. Just as decisions can no longer be left to the rabbi or the top tier of lay leaders, so primary Jewish acts cannot be left to them either. It is no accident that in the same year the lay leadership at Congregation Beth El stepped in to take over some of the responsibilities of their former rabbi, the "Celebrate Shabbat" initiative proved to be so successful. Ultimately, leadership and participation go hand in hand.

5

Seeing Both the Forest and the Trees: Creating Community amid Diversity

The earliest American synagogues served as the locus of Jewish community for the first waves of Jewish immigrants. Because Jews were often excluded from certain neighborhoods and social clubs, but also because of their own ethnic loyalties, they continued to fraternize primarily with other Jews well into the 1950s. Much of this fraternization took place in congregational settings.

Today we no longer need to find social outlets that are exclusively Jewish because we have become fully integrated into American society. We may enter any profession, live in any neighborhood, and join (nearly) any social club. We have become so desirable as marriage partners that our intermarriage rate is over fifty percent. But full participation in American life has come at a price—the loss of our Jewish connections and, in many cases, other social connections as well. As Jews became more affluent, and moved out of their immigrant neighborhoods, the value of community was overshadowed by the value of individual achievement. Having become fully Americanized, we, like so many other Americans, are victims of our own preoccupation with autonomy and privacy. Americans at every socioeconomic level feel increasingly isolated but unclear about what to do in response. On one hand, we are searching for spiritual and emotional connections; on the other, we are loath to make the compromises it takes to live in a true community. In the words of sociologist Robert Wuthnow:

> Individualism . . . once meant being responsible for ourselves *and* our neighbors. But [contemporary Americans] have replaced this traditional concept with a more radical individualism that looks out for number one at the expense of everyone else. . . . Most people, however, seem to believe at some level that this self-centered individualism is no way to live. . . . They value their individual freedom, but go through life feeling lonely. They desire intimacy and wonder how to find it.[1]

This ambivalence is reflected in social philosopher Barry Schwartz's first-person account of the founding of a new synagogue:

> [T]here was a very deep longing in people to belong to something, something that was larger than any individual, and would accept, nurture and protect those who had made commitments to it. There was a very deep longing in people to make this congregation, this community, their "haven in a heartless world."[2]

Yet, even as they searched for an overarching sense of belonging, Schwartz's fellow congregants hesitated, wondering what compromises they might be called upon to make:

> [H]ow much [could] individuals be expected to submerge their individual autonomy in the service of building a community? What, in other words, was a person giving up, and what was she getting, if she decided to become one of us?[3]

Given our ambivalence, it is not surprising that American Jews find it difficult to articulate just what they are looking for in a community. This chapter begins by considering several definitions of community in search of one that will suit contemporary American synagogues, whose members differ in a variety of ways. It goes on to consider some ways a synagogue can create a sense of community despite (or perhaps because of) this diversity.

Defining Community

"Community" is a term with multiple meanings. It can refer to a large, amorphous collection of people (such as the "American Jewish community") or a small, carefully defined entity (such as "a classroom community") and to many types of groupings in between. In an effort to be more specific (and to indicate their own preferences), people often preface the word "community" with adjectives like "genuine" or "face-to-face." What they mean by this, usually, is that "real" communities should be small. So, for example, John Westerhoff, a Protestant minister and theologian, argues that churches should not exceed 300 families.[4] Rabbi Lawrence Kushner mentions a similar figure, arguing that

> Real community is not merely a loose association of dues-paying members. It is composed of people who know and care, or who at least want to know and want to care for one another, who might prefer not to be seen together in public but who are nonetheless stuck with one another. And that means you need at least a fighting chance of knowing everyone's names.[5]

If size alone were a determinant of community, the majority of synagogues and churches in America would function as genuine communities. But neither Kushner nor Westerhoff, nor any other commentator on congregational life, sees size as a sufficient criterion. Research done by sociologist Penny Edgell Becker helps explain why. Becker studied the twenty-one churches and two synagogues of Oak Park, Illinois, dividing them into four categories based on the type of community they aspired to be. The other three categories will be described in greater detail later in this chapter; here

I want to focus on one particular category, the "Family" congregation. "Family" congregations see one of their core functions as facilitating close, family-like relationships among their members. Congregants have "a feeling of belonging, a knowledge of important events in each other's lives, and a sense of caring and support in times of crisis."[6]

All six of the "Family" congregations in Becker's study were small and were quite ambivalent about growing larger. Congregational leaders were well aware that expanding their membership would increase their tight budgets and give them additional person-power. But they worried that new members might not "fit in" or might advocate for changes in worship or religious education. Moreover, these congregations shared a common limitation—they had great difficulty dealing with differences of opinion. They tended to avoid controversial issues, whether within the congregation (such as changing the Sunday school curriculum) or in the larger community (such as propositions on the state ballot). When conflicts did arise, they tended to be seen in personal terms—as problems of personality. "The tendency to label those who disagree as troublemakers can lead to an atmosphere of mistrust and resentment that simmers under the surface of the family-like closeness of these congregations."[7] Clearly, small size alone does not assure that a congregation will have a sense of community; if it did, these "Family" congregations would be more open to newcomers and better able to air their differences.

A second adjective that is sometimes used synonymously with "genuine," as a modifier for community, is "all-encompassing." An all-encompassing community is one that touches every aspect of its members' lives. There is an underlying assumption that everyone is there for the same reasons and feels comfortable with the community's norms and expectations. In Schwartz's words:

> If you are faced with an all-encompassing religious community, you have but one question to answer: do you join up or not? Once you decide to join up, you simply understand and accept the fact that this decision will affect everything you do.[8]

Anthropologist Riv-Ellen Prell uses the term "communities of choice"[9] to describe congregations that aspire to be all-encompassing. Communities of choice take it as a given that their members share an explicit, coherent religious ideology. Though not all members may abide by the congregation's norms in practice, it is assumed that they ascribe to them in theory. As long as congregants are able to articulate their synagogue's ideology to potential members, and as long as these new members join because they agree in principle with this ideology, the essential unity of the congregation will be preserved.

But when a significant number of new members join for nonideological reasons—because their family or friends belong, because the synagogue is close to their home, or because they have heard that it is, for whatever reason, "a good place to be"—the closely woven fabric of the community of choice begins to fray. Congregants are no longer bound together by a set of basic premises about what being Jewish is, or what the congregation's essential activities should be. Thus, all-encompassing communities tend to be very traditional, very new, or very small. It is nearly impossible to rewind the clock and turn large and/or heterogeneous synagogues back into communities of choice.

I believe that neither size nor like-mindedness is a determining factor in creating community within a synagogue. Based on Becker's research and my own experience, I would argue that a genuine community is one that acknowledges and even welcomes the diversity among its members, but is able to imbue them with a sense of shared purpose. A synagogue functions as a community when it is embracing, but not confining; purposeful, but not single-minded; unified, but not because differences among congregants are submerged.

Congregations that are neither very traditional, very new, nor very small have members who differ along several dimensions—their reasons for joining, their religious ideology, demographic factors such as socioeconomic level or lifecycle stage, their taste, and their level of participation. The next sections deal briefly with each of these differences.

Diversity in Congregations

Reasons for Affiliating with a Synagogue

As discussed in chapter 2, relatively few of the Jews who founded a synagogue in the newly built suburb of Park Forest in the late 1940s did so from either a sense of religious obligation or a desire to deepen their spiritual connections. Rather, they sought to impress their non-Jewish neighbors and to establish the Jewish equivalent of a Christian Sunday school for their children.[10] Subsequent generations have had different motivations. Some join out of a sense of obligation to their families, or because it seems like "the right thing to do"; others join because they are on a spiritual journey or because they want to reclaim their heritage. However, based on the time of year (late summer or early fall) and stage in the lifecycle (having school-aged children) when people tend to join, it seems clear that primary motivators for many congregants are to observe the High Holidays, to enroll children in nursery or religious school, and to celebrate lifecycle events, particularly bar/bat mitzvah. While none of these reasons for joining are bad, they do pose problems. When adult members are more interested in what the synagogue represents than in the activities it offers, and when they are more concerned with the programs it offers for their children than for themselves, synagogue membership becomes a means to an end rather than an end in itself. The synagogue becomes the umbrella organization for a series of discrete activities. In short, it becomes a "service center" rather than a community.

Religious Differences

Judaism can be viewed in different ways: as a religion, a nationality, or an ethnicity. Mordecai Kaplan attempted to bridge these different perspectives by defining it as "an evolving religious civilization;"[11] the compound wording highlights the fact that there is no one way to be Jewish. In the first half of the twentieth century, for example, secular Judaism flourished, and people saw, variously, the Yiddish language, the Hebrew language, Zionism, being an intellectual, participating in the labor movement, or supporting civil rights as the essence of their Judaism.

There were also many Jews who did not explicitly identify themselves as secular but were not quite religious either, as can be seen in this old Harry Golden joke:

> Everyone knows my father was never a *shul*-goer—all of a sudden, in his old age, he starts going to *shul* every Shabbat.
>
> So I asked him, "Pop, what are you doing, going to *shul* every week?"
>
> Pop asked me, "You know my friend Goldberg?"
>
> "Sure," I said, "Goldberg is a real religious guy, a regular *shul*-goer."
>
> "Right," said Pop. "Goldberg goes to *shul* to talk to God, and I go to *shul* to talk to Goldberg."[12]

Like Golden's father, contemporary Jews are much less interested in ideological matters. Summarizing the findings of their research on marginally affiliated Jews, Steven Cohen and Arnold Eisen write: "Ideological disputes over which a great deal of ink has been spilled in the annals of modern Jewish thought blur in the eclectic and fluid commitments that are now the rule."[13]

> A generation or two ago, Jews such as those we interviewed might well have found other, "secular" outlets for Jewish participation, that did not require synagogue attendance. Or, when they did go to services, they might have seen that act as merely a social performance, something Jews do to express and maintain Jewish community.... Now, freed of the need to declare "party allegiance" to one or the other of the accepted credos of modern Jewish adherence, religious and secular, our subjects seem more content to experience what is there to be experienced, and to take the meaning as it comes.[14]

Demographic Diversity

Any synagogue that has been in existence for more than a decade can probably count among its members people of various ages and stages in the lifecycle. Inevitably, these different populations look to the synagogue for different things. Some, like single adults and parents of young children, are looking for opportunities to meet others like themselves. Others may be looking for a more intergenerational experience. To complicate things further, different people at different stages in the lifecycle may have similar interests but incompatible schedules.

Some congregations have significant numbers of immigrants from diverse countries. In Los Angeles, for example, it is not uncommon to find first-generation and second-generation Persian, Israeli, South African, and Russian immigrants in the same congregation along with those whose parents, grandparents, and even great-grandparents, were born in the United States. These groups have different customs and different ways of behaving in synagogue.

Most divisive of all are differences in income. Congregants in lower income brackets, for whom paying dues is already a financial stretch, are put in a difficult position when the congregation asks for additional contributions. They may feel intimidated by the lavish style of fundraising events and lifecycle celebrations. For their part, congregants of greater means may feel that they are shouldering too much of the financial burden.

Differences in Taste and Style

Closely related to demographic differences are differences of taste and style, particularly in liturgical music. Rabbi Jeffrey Summit describes the controversy that surrounded the introduction of a new Friday night service at Temple Israel in Boston. Scheduled at an earlier time slot, this service was more informal and participatory than the "regular" service. It was held in the atrium rather than the sanctuary, with congregants facing one another, in close proximity to the clergy; a guitar, rather than an organ, was used. Older members of the congregation "hated" the service, which they considered to be "too Jewish."

> [T]here is quite a bit of traditional chant to the service, which the older members associated with Conservative and Orthodox prayer. Many older members found this service to be "too involving, too participatory, absolutely without decorum."... [T]he changes in style were no laughing matter for the older generation. They wanted a service primarily in English, so that it would be intelligible and understandable. Very much Americans, they were embarrassed by what they perceived as the disorderliness of traditional Jewish prayer.[15]

Disagreement over styles of worship is a common phenomenon, not only in synagogues but in churches as well. As his research into Jewish liturgical music progressed, Summit found that his Christian colleagues were concerned with many of same issues.

> Both Catholic and Protestant worshippers wanted to affirm the unity of their church by the simple act of singing together, yet congregants brought very different ideas of what they should sing, how it should be orchestrated, and who should sing it. In the words of an Episcopal priest, "People don't like to change or be challenged that much. These days, discussions about music and liturgy always seem to be contentious.[16]

James Wind, director of the Alban Institute, terms these controversies the "worship wars."

> [M]any who want to [pray] find it difficult to deal with others who want to do the same thing, but in a different way. In many churches and synagogues, lines are being drawn between groups colliding over differing worship traditions, styles and preferences. Musicians line up against clergy, newcomers against old-timers, reformers against traditionalists, formalists against informalists, one ethnic group against another.[17]

Though the most common stylistic disagreements seem to center on liturgical music, controversies related to taste and style arise in other areas of synagogue life as well. For example, while most congregants would acknowledge the necessity for fundraising, there can be considerable disagreement about the form that fundraising can take. Similarly, while everyone would agree that Torah study is an important part of the Shabbat service, some prefer sermons given by the rabbi, whereas others prefer participatory text study and discussion.

Differences in Levels of Involvement and Commitment

Every congregation has members who are active and members who are inactive; those who participate regularly in study, worship, and/or social action, and those who attend only a few times a year; those who can be counted on to volunteer, and those who do little more than pay their dues. To some extent, these differences overlap with and reinforce other differences. For example, those with a more traditional religious perspective are more likely to attend worship services regularly, and those who are better off financially are more likely to serve on the synagogue's board. This creates a vicious circle, in which the congregation's leadership is drawn from a limited portion of its membership and, in turn, orients its programming and its services to this narrow constituency.

Insiders and outsiders tend to be ambivalent about one another. Congregants in what sociologist Samuel Heilman calls the "active core" are frustrated by the low attendance at services or the lack of participation in other activities, but they can easily empathize with those on the periphery. They themselves may have been less active in an earlier period, and can easily imagine becoming less active in the future. In the words of a congregant in Central Synagogue, one of the Conservative congregations Heilman studied, "You flow in and flow out."[18] Underneath it all, Heilman argues, insiders realize that they are, in a sense, being subsidized by those who pay comparable dues but do not participate as fully. They enjoy the intimacy and the smaller scale afforded by the "no-shows."

> Paradoxically, even as the inner circle seeks, at least in princi-
> ple, to draw others into the core and its activities, they are also
> likely to react to the presence of too many outsiders in the syn-
> agogue with ambivalence at best, and disdain at worst. Yes,
> they like a big turnout for services, but they also (at Kehillat
> Achim) support the smaller alternative services and or (at
> Central Synagogue) desire a small retreat-style setting or an
> intensive learners' service that will also "make greater
> demands" on the participants. In a sense, some wish to sepa-
> rate themselves from those who are less engaged and involved,
> to present themselves as a more dedicated class of Conserva-
> tive Jew.[19]

Those on the periphery have their own set of ambivalences. Their low level of participation is mostly a matter of choice; they lead busy lives and have other interests and commitments. At the same time, many yearn for a deeper spiritual life or for a sense of belonging, but they feel uncomfortable and even unwelcome at the synagogue. "The synagogue is sometimes a closed club to those overwhelmed by how much they do not know about Judaism and the mechanics of synagogue ritual."[20]

Creating Community amid Diversity

What can congregations do to bridge the gaps between their various constituencies? Can the disparate subgroups transcend their differences, and come to see themselves as part of the same community? Among the strategies synagogues have devised are the practice of *keruv* (literally, "drawing near"), the creation of *havurot* and *minyanim,* discussions and study sessions aimed at creating a shared sense of purpose, and careful attention to the way in which tensions are explored.

Reaching Out to the "Marginally Affiliated"

In *Succeeding at Jewish Education,* an ethnographic study of a Reform synagogue, Joseph Reimer describes Temple Akiva's concerted effort to "reach out" and "embrace" constituencies who were perceived by themselves, and by others, to be marginal.

> The rabbis were aware that there are many Jews who perceive themselves to be marginal to the Jewish community because they are not living a traditional lifestyle; they may be single, widowed, or divorced, married to a non-Jew, or gay or lesbian. These marginal Jews imagine synagogues to be the province of the straight-and-narrow Jews, and in the case of Temple Akiva, the well-heeled, well-educated Jews. That perception itself becomes self-sealing; as fewer and fewer Jews see themselves as fitting the definition of the Jewish mainstream, the circle of synagogue members in fact grows smaller.[21]

The synagogue staff launched a series of efforts aimed at reaching out to these "marginal" Jews, members and nonmembers alike. In so doing, they had an opportunity to reiterate their definition of community as a place that could embrace, and draw strength from, diversity.

Because relatively few synagogue members attend services or study sessions regularly, it is quite possible for many to see themselves as marginal. To counteract this sense of alienation, some congregations go out of their way to reach out to both newcomers and long-time members. One of the categories of congregation identified by sociologist Becker was the "community" congregation, which attempts to create "an intimacy [which], while genuine, is also highly planned. Congregations of this type see 'plugging in' to one of the congregation's many organized activities [as] a key to making friendships and being part of the community." Each time she visited one of these congregations, Becker reports, "people were quick to greet me...and to ask especially what kinds of activities I enjoyed, so that they could put me in touch with the right contact person."[22]

The Hebrew term for this type of active welcoming and engagement is *keruv,* which, as mentioned earlier, literally means bringing people closer—in this case, to the tradition and to one another. *Keruv* can take different forms. Some synagogues, for example, sponsor a series of get-togethers for new members. These sessions might include community-building mixers, interactive text study, and first-person testimonials from congregants involved in a variety of congregational activities. Similarly, many synagogues have found that the year or two before a child's bar or bat mitzvah is a time when parents are particularly open to exploring their Jewish commitments and becoming engaged in Jewish activities. Capitalizing on this teachable moment, these congregations have scheduled a series of family education sessions, whose goal goes beyond bar or bat mitzvah preparation to community building and enabling parents to find a spiritual connection. It is easy to imagine how this concept might be applied to other lifecycle events, including birth, marriage, and bereavement.

The following personal account from Victor Gold, a law professor in Los Angeles, exemplifies how one point of contact—a counseling session with his rabbi, Rabbi Laura Geller of Temple Emanuel in Beverly Hills—opened doors to other ways of becoming involved in the synagogue:

> My Mom died in early 1999. Some months later I visited Rabbi Geller to discuss my continuing grief and need to find meaning in Mom's death. Rabbi Geller convinced me that this loss could be transformed into a positive turning point in my life. She gave direction to my search for meaning by urging me to become an active Jewish learner and volunteer in projects both within and outside Emanuel. Because my Mom's death was the catalyst, my contributions as a volunteer and my growth as a Jew provide the meaning for which I was searching. It's like creating a memorial with one's acts rather than in stone or with dollars.[23]

Victor's experience was so meaningful to him that he helped start a project at Temple Emanuel, "Torah of Our Lives," that seeks to connect mourners to one another and to the congregation as a whole. Inviting his fellow congregants to participate in this project, Victor wrote:

> Judaism recognizes a close connection between mourning and community. Mourners are sustained by the *shiva minyan,* visits from friends, and gifts of food. In fact, many Jewish congregations started as burial societies to provide service and support to those who mourn. Community is essential to mourners because it demonstrates that, even in the face of death, we are not alone.[24]

To create community amid diversity, a congregation must begin to view every point of contact as an opportunity for *keruv.* Any occasion in which people might show up for one purpose (parents' orientation at religious school, for example, a baby naming, or mitzvah day) becomes an occasion to build community and to demonstrate the richness of the congregation's offerings. This is not easy to accomplish because it requires the planners of these activities to take a holistic perspective. The educator is already overburdened without taking on the additional assignment of creating a learning experience for a baby naming, and the planners of mitzvah day may be overwhelmed by the thought of adding worship and/or study to an already full and complicated day.

Synagogues typically deal with large and intricate tasks by dividing them up, with the expectation that these tasks can be done in isolation from one another and require only loose coordination. Taking a more holistic, less fragmented approach requires considerably more planning and more staff time. This liability must be weighed against the potential benefit—the greater involvement of congregants, who may be motivated to lead fuller Jewish lives as a result. This will, in turn, strengthen the community, ultimately creating a larger pool of potential leaders and planners.

Creating Subcommunities within the Congregation

Synagogues have always had subcommunities, such as sisterhoods and men's clubs, within them. Typically, however, these groups served a primarily social function and were not oriented toward any of the three core Jewish activities: *torah* (study), *avodah* (prayer), and *gemilut hasadim* (good deeds). By contrast, activities that build community should be more than simply social occasions; they should, argues sociologist Robert Wuthnow, be catalysts for significant emotional and intellectual engagement:

> We may know some of our neighbors well enough to wave as they whiz by on their way to work in the morning. We may stop to chat once in a while or take them pumpkin bread at Christmas as a neighborly gesture. We may even consider them our friends. It is more doubtful that we have ever discussed our most cherished values with these neighbors.... The same may be true of the people we know at church. Sitting together in the pews on Sunday morning, we may feel that there is much in common among us. But do we know that? Skeptics, at least, ask: Have we ever opened up to these people by admitting our fears, discussing our deepest anxieties, or sharing our most basic dreams and aspirations?[25]

In an attempt to deepen the interactions among their members, churches in the late 1960s began to sponsor small groups devoted to fellowship, Bible study, and/or prayer. Rabbi Harold Schulweis is credited with bringing this concept to synagogues when he introduced *havurot* (fellowship groups) at Valley Beth Shalom in Encino, California, in 1970. The idea of synagogue *havurot* spread rapidly, particularly in the western United States.[26] A 1981 study conducted by Gerald Bubis and Harry Wasserman found that leaders of congregations with *havurot* credited them with fostering not only warmth and friendship but also a sense of engagement with Jewish life.

More recently, *minyanim*—smaller, more participatory worship services—have been seen as another way of creating community, particularly in congregations that are large and diverse. Rabbi Stephen Pearce of Congregation Emanu-El of San Francisco is credited with having coined the term "synaplex" to designate a synagogue that offers multiple worship services to accommodate a range of congregants and to create more intimate prayer communities.[27] One such alternative prayer service, the New Emanuel Minyan, is discussed in the case presented in chapter 7.

Do *havurot* and *minyanim* enhance or inhibit the overall sense of community in a congregation? Does congregants' close connection to their subcommunity strengthen or loosen their ties to the congregation as a whole? Bubis and Wasserman found that membership in a *havurah* tended to increase both people's loyalty to and their level of participation in the synagogue. But this greater investment in Jewish life in general, and the congregation in particular, sometimes made people more critical, as one rabbi noted:

> Through *havurot* people have become more critical of temple programs. They are more critical of the religious school. They have rising expectations, and more sophisticated ways of making judgments. *Havurah* has not taken away from the centrality of the synagogue. It has reinforced it. There is now a greater consciousness of Jewish values and, with some people, a desire to make their lives more Jewish.[28]

Today few would question the value of *havurot* in helping to build community. But the value of alternative services is still up for debate. The following case recounts an attempt by Temple Emanu-El of Dallas to reverse this trend in order to create a more unified community.

CASE STUDY
Balancing Community and Diversity
at Temple Emanu-El, Dallas

Temple Emanu-El is a large (2,800-member unit) Reform congregation founded in 1872 by German Jewish immigrants. Though its roots in Classical Reform remain an important part of its identity, there are many (both relative newcomers and third- and fourth-generation members) who have more traditional leanings.

To accommodate its large and diverse membership, the congregation has, for over a decade, offered a variety of options for Shabbat prayer. The "main" Friday night service, held in the large and formal sanctuary, maintains its Classical Reform format, with music performed by the Temple's renowned choir under the leadership of its musical director (the congregation had never had a cantor). For those who prefer more informal and participatory prayer, other services have been created: a less formal service in the chapel, and "Sabbath Prayer, Sabbath Peace," a service with a guitar and some alternative liturgy, that meets twice a month. Once a month there is also a Tot Shabbat service on Friday evening, so that on any given Friday night, between two and four services are held. There are also several services on Shabbat morning to accommodate both b'nai mitzvah and regular attendees.

Each of these worship services has its own constituency, and there is relatively little overlap among them and hence no overarching sense of community-wide prayer. This has concerned Rabbi David Stern, the senior rabbi, who has begun to question the "more is better" approach, which in his opinion has contributed to the "balkanization" of worship.

The rabbi and numerous congregants discussed ways in which the entire congregation could become more united in worship. Many concluded that if the "main" Friday night service were more participatory and included newer music, it could serve as the focal point for creating community at Temple Emanu-El. To use terminology introduced by Cantor Benjie-Ellen Schiller, the music in the sanctuary was unparalleled in its sense of "majesty" and "meditation" but lacking in a sense of "meeting."

An opportunity for change presented itself when the congregation's longtime music director announced his intention to retire. At this point, the ongoing discussion of the role of music in worship intensified. For a long time, many at Temple Emanu-El had argued that the way to make the sanctuary service more appealing to the congregation as a whole was to hire a cantor, who would introduce new music and more congregational singing. Others resisted this suggestion, especially those who adhered to Classical Reform ideology. These congregants were already perturbed by the temple's recent move toward more traditional observance, which included a greater use of Hebrew and the clergy's decision to wear *tallitot* (prayer shawls) and *kippot* (skullcaps) on the *bimah* (dais). Many congregants saw worship as an internal, aesthetic experience, which did not require congregational singing and might, in fact, be disrupted by it. Even those who did not identify with Classical Reform might be opposed to hiring a cantor, out of loyalty to the choir (whose central position in the service, they perceived, would be overshadowed by a cantor) and out of a general reluctance to change a time-honored worship tradition.

Because this large cultural change was likely to encounter resistance in some sectors of the congregation, the synagogue's leadership decided to convene two separate committees—a music search committee and a transition committee. This paralleled the committee structure that had been used when Rabbi Stern had been brought on as the senior rabbi. Creating the same structure for the search for a musical director would, they hoped, send a strong symbolic message about the importance of this position. In putting together these committees, they sought representatives from the full spectrum of worship orientations. In addition, they looked for individuals who would be honest about their own opinions but open to opposing views. They wanted a group that would represent the diversity of the congregation but also reach a decision that was in the best interest of the congregation as a whole.

The music search committee first worked to define a new vision for the music program and then articulated a list of expectations for the person who would realize that vision. Near the top of the list were both new and old goals: enhancing participation and maintaining the role of the choir. Then the committee met with well over a hundred congregants from dozens of different committees (such as the worship committee, the religious school committee, the older adults committee, and so on) as well as with the professional staff, to solicit their views about the future role of music at the synagogue (both within worship and within the congregation in general). On the basis of this input, the committee concluded that the person who could best achieve these goals would be a cantor.

Parallel to the meetings of the committee, a concerted effort was made to inform the entire congregation and to solicit people's feedback:

- Two distinguished visiting cantors were brought in for two different Shabbatot to demonstrate what a cantor might contribute to the service. At the *oneg shabbat* that followed each service, congregants were asked for their reactions.

- Members of the search committee wore buttons that said "Ask me about the music program."

- The rabbis stressed repeatedly that their doors were open for discussion of this topic.

About six months into the process, the committee presented its recommendations to the board, and the board authorized the committee to begin a search for a cantor. A letter went out to the congregation announcing the decision. Two town hall meetings were also convened to solicit additional feedback. Since attendance at these meetings was low, the committee assumed that people were relatively comfortable with the decision.

They were mistaken. Suddenly, a process that had been smooth, thoughtful, and delicately handled encountered a significant challenge.

In response to the announcement, a congregant who had not attended any of the town hall meetings, and had not approached any of the rabbis or lay leaders, sent a letter to the entire congregation, asking people to join him in trying to overturn the board's decision. He encouraged people to attend the upcoming annual meeting to voice their protest. About 750 people showed up to the annual meeting—a sharp increase from the more typical 150.

There was frustration on all sides. Those who opposed the decision felt that their voices hadn't been heard. Others were angered by the dissenters, who had ignored the ample opportunity to speak before the decision was made and only came forward afterwards. "We felt frustrated, because we had worked so hard at making this an open process," Rabbi Stern notes. "But once we got over it, we realized that despite our attempts to hear people, many didn't feel we had listened." In an effort to be as accommodating as possible, the president announced that a special congregational meeting would be held in three weeks to address the issue, and that the search for a new cantor would be suspended in the interim.

The meeting packed the social hall, with over eight hundred people. The president, the outgoing music director, and the senior rabbi each shared their thoughts on the process and outcome of the committee's work. Their speeches celebrated the diversity of the congregation, and the need to respect the past, but also to move forward to meet new challenges. Then microphones were made available to anyone who wanted to speak, and congregants of all ages came forward: fourth-generation members and new members; b'nai mitzvah kids and parents. People spoke passionately, those in favor of hiring a cantor far outnumbering those who were opposed. The meeting lasted until the last person wishing to speak had an opportunity to do so. The rabbi and president concluded with an apology for allowing people to feel that they hadn't been heard. They stressed their commitment to continue listening and the value they placed on diversity, even as the congregation moved forward with a clear sense of purpose. A burst of applause followed. People felt that the congregation was coping in a healthy way with the challenge of change.

Even those who were against hiring a cantor came away feeling that the meeting had been productive.

In light of the support expressed at the meeting, the board decided to resume the search for a new cantor and to continue to invite visiting cantors to open the congregation up to new possibilities. The congregant who had sparked the initial protest continued in his attempt to derail the search. He circulated a petition calling for a special congregational meeting to revise the bylaws, so that the board's authority to approve a search for a cantor would be suspended. The congregational meeting was held, and the board's authority was endorsed by an overwhelming majority.

While a number of individuals still have misgivings about the congregation's new direction in worship, the search for a cantor continues. The congregation too continues to move forward, more aware than ever of its diversity, and of both the blessings and challenges of change.

Creating a Shared Sense of Purpose

Programs alone will not create a sense of community. *Keruv* is essential, and subgroups such as *havurot* and *minyanim* create important opportunities for congregants to interact with one another in substantive ways. But moving congregants beyond a "service-center" orientation requires repeated reminders that the overall purpose of synagogue life is not merely to educate their children or to celebrate lifecycle events but to enable *all congregants* to live more Jewishly. Given everything that has been said about the ambivalence of Jews toward their Judaism, and their varied reasons for joining congregations, it should not surprise us that this purpose has become obscured. Synagogues cannot assume that a shared sense of purpose exists or that it will develop naturally; rather, they must actively work to establish and promote it.

In each church or synagogue she studied, sociologist Becker inquired into the common threads that united the congregation. Based on her interviews and observations, she created a four-fold typology of congregations, which she labeled "House of Worship," "Leader," "Family," and "Community."

"Houses of Worship" are congregations whose mission is narrowly defined to include worship, religious education, and the celebration of lifecycle rituals, but not much more. Though they have official greeters at services and offer programs for new and potential members, "Houses of Worship" do not concern themselves with promoting a sense of community. What congregants value most is "a place to worship and to express or explore their belief in God."[29] Few expect to do much socializing at their congregation.

"Leader" congregations tend to be large and to have a significant public presence in the town. Each holds well-publicized positions on certain religious or social issues—positions that have been set by historical precedent or articulated by the clergy. People join a "Leader" congregation because they identify with these positions and because they want to be in the forefront of the effort to promote them. Like "Houses of Worship," "Leader" congregations are not particularly interested in fostering intimacy or personal connections among their members. They see community as adherence to a common doctrine or devotion to a common cause.

As noted earlier, the "Family" congregations are small and intimate; in these congregations, a sense of community evolved organically.

> The phrases "a sense of belonging" and "I feel like I really belong here" recurred in many interviews. The most common adjectives people used to describe their congregation were "warm," "caring," and friendly.". . .This closeness seems to occur without a great deal of discussion or conscious effort. People refer to the congregation as a family, but there is no elaborated discourse on what it means to be a family. There are no sermons or pastor's columns in the newsletter devoted to the topic. People do not lead Sunday School classes on "community-building" or "what is our family like?" However, they do drop by on a snowy day and see if an elderly church member needs a ride or any errands run or if a new mother is feeling overwhelmed. They do this on an informal, ad hoc basis, without a formal committee structure and without relying on the pastor.[30]

As discussed above, "Family" congregations pay a price for the closeness of their communities. Debates of substantive issues are either avoided altogether or reduced to personal conflicts.

In contrast to congregations that fell into the first three categories, six of the congregations were distinguished by their conscious efforts to create a sense of community. These "Community" congregations are both inward and outward looking, attempting to create a warm supportive place for their members while also challenging them spiritually and morally. Like "Houses of Worship," they pay a great deal of attention to the worship service itself; but rather than seeing worship as the sole province of the clergy (as "Houses of Worship" do), they expect their membership to participate in both its planning and performance. The result is a worship service that is more eclectic than that found in the other types of congregations and that places greater emphasis on self-expression and creativity.

Like "Leader" congregations (and unlike the other two types), "Community" congregations see their role as going beyond nurturing faith, to taking moral and political stands which are informed by one's faith. But unlike "Leader" congregations, in which the denomination or the clergy set the social and political agenda, these congregations are acutely sensitive to the balance that must be struck between engagement in social issues and maintaining a community.

> ["Community"] congregations are concerned with social issues, but they actively resist activity that might be deemed radical, and overtly political language or rhetoric is not well received. Compassionate outreach, about which there is no disagreement, is a favorite way to engage with social issues but not cause division.[31]

"Community" congregations do not assume that connections among their members will arise naturally and spontaneously. Acutely aware of the fact that their members are diverse, highly mobile, and very busy, these congregations foster a sense of community by forming small fellowship groups and by encouraging people to "plug in" to a range of organized activities. In short, "Community" congregations seek to create a sense of shared meaning through active engagement with their faith tradition and with one another.

> [T]here is a sense of members discovering and implementing together a local and negotiated application of the core values of their religious heritage. They figure out, together, in an ongoing way, what it means to be a Conservative Jew or a Biblical Christian or a Lutheran. Members can spark congregation-wide debate on things that matter deeply to them. Disagreements arise and must be addressed in a way that is compatible with their emphasis on being a loving and affirmative community, where everyone's needs are met. Members

find this exciting, frustrating, and challenging, and to them
that is what authentic religious community means.[32]

Congregations are not the only organizations that find themselves in
need of articulating their goals and evolving among their members a shared
purpose. Businesses and civic organizations of all sorts have discovered the
value of a self-conscious, inclusive process of goal setting. The following
exercise is adapted from one created by Tim Lucas and Bryan Smith for use
in the public school of Ridgewood, New Jersey.[33] It is designed to engage
a large group of congregants in an extended discussion of their vision of
congregational life, and thereby begin to forge a shared sense of purpose.

The visioning exercises and text study handouts in chapter 3 can also
be used for engaging congregants in discussions of the purpose of synagogue life. The following text study was designed to sharpen congregants'
ideological focus, encouraging people to think about what it means to them
to be Jewish, why they joined the synagogue, and what the congregation
can do to accommodate members with different ideological leanings.

Creating a Shared Sense of Purpose

This exercise is designed for a large, diverse group of congregants to share their common concerns and evolve a shared vision. The presence of so many congregants in the same room focusing on the goals and future of the congregation can be very energizing, but since participants will only interact with those at their table, it might be good to add a short text study and/or some group singing at either the beginning or the end, to give everyone a common experience. This exercise can be repeated annually, serving as a vehicle for raising issues and taking stock of the congregation's progress on the issues of greatest concern.

Grouping of Participants

Participants should be assigned to tables of seven to ten, with each table representing as diverse a group as possible, including members of the staff. Designate a team leader for each table.

Time

1 to 1½ hours

Facilitation

Step 1: (5 minutes) Participants introduce themselves by responding to these questions: How long have I been a member of the synagogue? What aspects of congregational life do I participate in most frequently or find most appealing?

Step 2: (10 to 15 minutes) Brainstorm a list of participants' issues, questions, and concerns about synagogue life. The result will be a long list of twenty to forty items, some as concrete as "the parking lot" and others as abstract as "prayer" or "God." These should be listed on large pieces of newsprint. Since this is a brainstorming activity, there are no wrong answers, nor should there be any discussion of the individual items until Step 4.

Step 3: (5 minutes) When the brainstorming has run its course, give everyone in the group five stickers to place next to the five items they think most merit further discussion. This voting should take place without any discussion of why one item is more important than others. If all goes well, there will be some consensus, and the list of twenty to forty will be reduced to five to ten items that receive many more votes than the others. Bring a list of the top six or seven issues to the front of the room, where a facilitator will consolidate the lists from every group and compile a combined tally of the issues that have generated the most concern.

Step 4: (30 to 45 minutes) Continuing to work in small groups, discuss each issue in turn, beginning with the one that received the most votes. Ask:

- What questions does this issue raise?
- What aspects of synagogue life does this issue or concept impinge on?
- Who should be concerned with this issue?
- What should be the role of (fill in the blank: the professional staff, the board, a particular committee, all congregants) in dealing with this issue?

The team leaders should watch the time and keep the conversation moving. They should assign members of the groups to keep a record of the important points that are made.

Step 5: (10 to 20 minutes) Post the issues and the answers to the questions around the room. Allow time for people to walk around and get a sense of the group.

Record Keeping

The list of issues should be kept, and distributed to appropriate committees. The in-depth look at the issues should be consolidated, written up, and also distributed to appropriate staff and lay leaders. The "common concerns" could be discussed from the pulpit, in the bulletin, and at various study sessions. Repeating the exercise annually will enable leaders to "take the temperature" of the congregation.

Why Be Jewish?

This exercise was inspired by Barry Holtz's monograph "Why Be Jewish?"[34] Holtz offers nine different reasons why contemporary Jews, who could easily deny or ignore their Jewishness, might choose to identify Jewishly. These reasons run the gamut from religious obligation ("I am Jewish because I feel commanded by God") to spiritual fulfillment ("because it satisfies a spiritual yearning") to a variety of secular considerations ("because it connects me to the Jewish people, Jewish history, the Jewish textual tradition," etc.). To make a discussion of these differences more manageable, Holtz's nine options have been narrowed down to four. In reality, most Jews will find themselves in partial agreement with more than one position, and perhaps even with all four. But looking at these positions separately can make congregants aware of the differences between them, and serve as the jumping-off point for a more extended discussion of what the congregation might do to accommodate these differences.

Time Required

Step 1: Introduction and division into groups: 10 to 15 minutes
Step 2: Small groups: 30 minutes
Step 3: Concluding discussion: 15 to 20 minutes

Facilitation

Step 1: Introduce the exercise. Distribute Handout 1 (which outlines four different reasons for being Jewish), and review the options briefly. Ask people to think about the statement that best articulates their reason for being Jewish. Based on this, divide up into four groups. The groups need not be of equal size, but each group should have at least four or five people in it. If any group is smaller than four, ask for volunteers who are sympathetic to this view (even though it might not be their first choice) to join; if any group is larger than eight, it should divide into two subgroups.

Step 2: Small groups use handouts 2A through 2D, which contain one or two quotations and some questions for discussion.

Step 3: The entire group reconvenes. Each small group summarizes its answers very briefly. Then the entire group discusses the following questions:

- Thinking about all of the programs and activities our congregation sponsors, which of the four types of Jews does our synagogue accommodate the best?

- Should we be doing more to support people who have other reasons for being Jewish and for belonging to our congregation?

- What might our congregation do to bring together people with different reasons for being Jewish, to have them learn from one another?

Four Different Reasons for Being Jewish

If you had to choose among the following four options, which would you say is, for you, the most compelling reason for being Jewish?

1. Being Jewish links me to my ancestors. It gives me a sense of belonging to an ethnic and/or religious group.

2. Being Jewish gives personal and spiritual meaning to my life. It helps me figure out who I am and what my place in the world is.

3. Being Jewish strengthens my commitment to behave ethically and to work toward *tikun olam,* the repair of the world.

4. Being Jewish brings me into a conversation with generations of scholars and commentators. It allows me to learn from them but also to add my own voice to their conversation.

Being Jewish Gives Me
a Sense of Belonging

It was the genius of Mordecai Kaplan to capture the sense of Jewish collectivity. Jews, he claimed, are interconnected through a common history, experience, and destiny; they are linked together as a group by their shared past, their mutual concern in the present, and their shared future destiny.

By redefining Jewishness in terms of belonging rather than believing, Kaplan sought to recapture some of the flavor of Jewish living before the modern era. Before the political emancipation of the Jews, a Jewish person acquired Jewish identity by virtue of membership in the community, not just because of theological or political commitments. One came to one's Jewishness because one had been brought up in the Jewish community and culture.

Because of the nature of contemporary society, our lives are fragmented into many pieces—family, work, and leisure activities fall into separate compartments. In the process, we lose the sense that our lives are a unified whole.... When we feel a sense of belonging to the Jewish civilization, we can begin to see ourselves as elements in a greater scheme of things, and thus achieve a greater sense of wholeness.

Exploring Judaism by Rebecca Alpert and Jacob Staub[35]

- Why might it be important to define (or redefine) Jewishness in terms of belonging rather than believing?

- What problems of being Jewish in the modern world does this definition solve? What problems does it create?

If we think of being Jewish as belonging to the Jewish people,

- Which of our current congregational activities would we consider most important?

- What additional things might our congregation do to encourage people to feel more Jewish? What additional activities might we sponsor? What new policies might we put into place?

Being Jewish Helps Me
Find Personal and Spiritual Meaning

[A]bove all, the need Judaism can answer is the spiritual one—a dimension of life that continues to have great and perhaps even increasing significance in American life....

Spirituality is a view of religion that sees its primary task as cultivating the human soul or spirit. Each person, according to this view, has an inner life that he or she may choose to develop. [In this view,] "being religious" is not a faith in a particular set of principles but an openness to a deep well of inner experiences—experiences in nature, in solitude, or in prayer....

We are not talking about an easy push-a-button or drop-a-pill experience-craving pseudospirituality, one that seeks only "highs" and takes no responsibility for the deep valleys that lie between the peak experiences.... Being a spiritual seeker means understanding that there is work to do.... When asked what Hasidism was all about, Rabbi Mendel of Kotsk replied: "to work on yourself..."

"Why do it through Judaism?" the seeker often asks. My answer comes not in absolutist terms; it cannot. Judaism is a hard path, but one toward which we have a special obligation. If you were born a Jew, or if you are drawn to Judaism, perhaps it is not just by chance. Perhaps what the human future seeks of you is your reading of, your encounter with, this great portion of our shared spiritual legacy. You can raise up sparks that belong to your soul alone, reveal worlds that can be found by no other. The tradition waits for you to discover it.

Restoring the Aleph: Judaism for the Contemporary Seeker
by Arthur Green[36]

- Why might it be important to emphasize the spiritual dimension of Jewishness?

- What problems of being Jewish in the modern world does this definition solve? What problems does it create?

If we think of being Jewish as a matter of seeking and finding spiritual meaning,

- Which of our current congregational activities would we consider most important?

- What additional things might our congregation do to encourage people to feel more Jewish? What additional activities might we sponsor? What new policies might we put into place?

Being Jewish Deepens My Commitment to Social Justice

A passionate belief in and concern for justice for all men is inherent in Judaism. Judaism conceives as its function and its mission the teaching of mankind to obey God's moral law, committing man to a way of life consistent with God's will, impelling them to dedicate their lives to bringing about on earth the kind of perfection in human affairs which is implicit in the universe.

In the words of Bible scholar Harry Orlinsky: "The ringing words of the prophets have carried from age to age the belief that justice was for the weak as well as the strong; that its fulfillment was as much the spirit as the letter of the law; that one could not serve God at the same time that he mistreated his fellow man; that to love God was to love justice, and that the love of justice placed within the conscience of each human being the ultimate inescapable obligation to denounce evil where he saw it, to defy a ruler who commanded him to break the covenant, and to live in the law and the love of God no matter what the cost."

Social action is of the essence of the Jewish religion. By working for the advancement of social justice, we bring a sense of greater reality to our faith, and we fulfill ourselves as Jews.

Justice and Judaism by Albert Vorspan and Eugene Lipman[37]

- Why might it be important to emphasize the Jewish imperative to make the world a better place to live?

- What problems of being Jewish in the modern world does this definition solve? What problems does it create?

If we think of being Jewish as working to create a better world,

- Which of our current congregational activities would we consider most important?

- What additional things might our congregation do to encourage people to feel more Jewish? What additional activities might we sponsor? What new policies might we put into place?

Being Jewish Brings Me into a Conversation with a Long Tradition of Jewish Learning

The specific and unique trademark of Jewish life is *talmud torah* (the study of Torah), if not in the sense that one is duty-bound to learn God's Will and Word, then in the sense that it is desirable to be knowledgeable in the literature and immersed in the wisdom of the Jewish people. The Bible, Talmud and *Midrash*, as well as the philosophy and poetry of the Jewish heritage, are as worthy of intensive devotion as any literature in the world, but for the Jew they are more than that. They are the sources which fashioned the soul of our people. To speak the language of Judaism is to be at home in that literature and in communion with its spirit. Torah, in this large literary sense, furnishes the Jew with culture and calls upon him to continue it creatively.

Teaching Jewish Values by Michael Rosenak[38]

The heart of Torah learning is a kind of special dialogue. The text is read slowly, word by word. As we read, questions emerge. We struggle to solve these questions. Along the way, other voices, other Jews who have looked at these words before, join the discussion with their commentaries. They point out problems, they share their personal solutions. The conversation continues. Between students, between teachers and students, the perceptions differ, the inferred meanings conflict, and the quest continues. In the end, the learner is left staring in his/her own text, the voices and insights of many others are heard, but for each learner the passage has yielded a personal understanding. Jewish text study is a wondrous combination of learning from others and finding out about yourself.

Learning Torah by Joel Grishaver[39]

- Why might it be important to emphasize learning as a key component of Jewish living?

- What problems of being Jewish in the modern world does this definition solve? What problems does it create?

If we think of being Jewish as being engaged in a centuries-old conversation with Jewish scholars and commentators,

- Which of our current congregational activities would we consider most important?

- What additional things might our congregation do to encourage people to feel more Jewish? What additional activities might we sponsor? What new policies might we put into place?

Bringing Tensions to the Surface

Becker found that "Community" congregations succeeded in engaging their large and diverse memberships through careful attention to process. In this they differed markedly from "Family" congregations and "Houses of Worship," which, because they shied away from conflict, kept the discussion of issues at a more superficial level. Because "Community" congregations were committed to a deeper exploration of values and issues, they found ways to engage their members in debates that were substantive but not deeply divisive. Leaders of these congregations reported that they cared less about the outcome of specific controversies than about the honesty and care invested in the discussions. Rather than staking out positions of their own, they cast themselves as facilitators whose role was to make sure that discussions of important religious and social issues remained both open and respectful.

An example of how attention to process can elevate a discussion that might otherwise lead to a rift appears in Samuel Freedman's book *Jew vs. Jew,* which recounts five controversies within various contemporary American Jewish communities.[40] All but one of these conflicts were bitterly contentious and, in the end, insurmountable. The exception is Freedman's account of a *minyan's* deliberation over whether to expand the traditional liturgy to include the *imahot* (literally, "the mothers")—Sara, Rebecca, Rachel, and Leah—in the *Amidah,* the central prayer of the Shabbat service. Leaders of the Library Minyan crafted a careful process in which members from diverse backgrounds were invited to give *divrei torah* (literally, "words of Torah") on this issue, and on the issue of prayer in general, over the course of several months. Only after these *divrei torah* were given were members of the congregation sent written ballots to indicate their preference. This painstaking process enabled the *minyan* to deepen its sense of community without obscuring or papering over significant issues related to prayer and liturgy, feminism and change.

The debate on the *imahot* falls into the category of *machloket leshem shamayim*—a controversy for the sake of heaven, which is to say a controversy that has a higher purpose. In the case of the *imahot* discussions, the higher purpose was deepening the membership's understanding of prayer and affirming the *minyan's* commitment to both Tradition and innovation.

The way in which a conflict can deepen and reaffirm communal commitments is further illuminated in the work of Joseph Reimer, who notes that some of the disagreements he witnessed in his year of ethnographic research at Temple Akiva had a ritualized quality. Though these debates were often angry and accusatory in tone, their outcome was rarely in doubt. Rather than being a forum for making decisions, Reimer argues, the debates served as "cultural performances"—opportunities for congregants to restate their values and acknowledge the potential for contradiction among these values. Drawing on the work of anthropologists Victor Turner and Barbara Meyerhoff, Reimer terms these controversies "social dramas."

One such social drama was enacted at a family education program for sixth-graders and their parents. The theme of the program was death and dying, a topic that the students were studying in their Judaica class on Sunday mornings. Part of the program was devoted to an explanation of traditional mourning rituals and customs. Parents and children asked the rabbi many questions, including ones about which relatives were responsible to sit *shiva* (the seven days of mourning) and recite kaddish (the mourner's prayer). Since the topic at hand related to traditional practice, the rabbi offered traditional answers to these questions. The session ended calmly, but in the evaluation that followed, several parents "started to accuse the rabbi of insensitivity to the needs of children from nontraditional families, in which someone might want to sit *shiva* for a stepparent or their parent's lover."[41] The rabbi defended his answers:

> It's really important to do both things, to say what is traditional Judaism and what we [the synagogue] represent.... When I do my work as a rabbi with a family, I immediately

expand the definition of mourner and family.... But you do have to say what tradition says. I can't put "significant other" in the mouth of tradition.[42]

Temple Akiva affirms two values that regularly come into conflict: the value of preserving the Tradition and the value of accommodating diversity. Because this conflict will never be fully resolved, the synagogue can expect that social dramas, large and small, will erupt rather frequently. Because the outcome of any particular debate is less important than the affirmation of both values, the inevitable conflict can be seen as a ritual enactment. Allowing these issue to be debated publicly affirms the congregation's overriding value: the value of genuine community, in which significant differences are acknowledged but never allowed to split the congregation.

While social dramas are an effective way of acknowledging and releasing tensions, they have the potential to hurt people's feelings in ways that cannot be fully healed. Rather than relying on spontaneous eruptions of this sort, congregations would do well to raise potentially divisive issues more deliberately, in an atmosphere that encourages open, calm, and thoughtful discussion. The exercise following on pages 173–175, adapted from one created by Synagogue 2000, aims to give congregants a deeper understanding of conflicts (both actual and potential) related to synagogue music.

Text study is another excellent vehicle for discussing tensions more abstractly and hence more dispassionately. The text study on pages 180–181 provides an occasion for members of a congregation to reflect on the issue of how much discretion should be given to a congregation's leaders in making a difficult decision.

Discussing Issues of Taste in Liturgical Music

The purpose of this exercise is twofold: to give members of a ritual or worship care committee an opportunity to learn about the range of different tastes in synagogue music among congregants and to give them a vocabulary for discussing these differences. Though issues of taste can never be fully resolved, this exercise creates a forum for people to articulate and examine their own preferences and to gain a greater appreciation of the preferences of others. If members of the ritual committee know in advance that they share many of the same views on synagogue music, they should invite other congregants, who are known to have divergent views, to participate.

Taken together, all four parts of the exercise can easily take 3 hours or more. One alternative is to do parts 1 and 2 at one meeting, and devote either one or two additional meetings to parts 3 and 4. Another alternative is to choose either part 3 or part 4.

Facilitation

PART 1: INTRODUCTION (20 to 30 minutes)

Distribute Handout 3. Read the quotations together, and discuss the questions at the end. The goals of part 1 are to help participants:

- Understand that differences in taste in liturgical music are quite common among Jews, and indeed among Christians as well.

- Understand what lies behind these differences, and develop some empathy for those with different views.

- Begin thinking about how these differences might be discussed in a productive manner.

PART 2: INTRODUCING THE 5 M's (20 to 30 minutes)

Distribute Handout 4. This handout introduces a vocabulary that describes five different moods conveyed by synagogue music, and it invites participants to reflect on the differences between them. The optimal number of participants for this discussion is six to ten; break into smaller groups if necessary. Each group should include participants with a range of preferences.

PART 3: EXPLORING THE MOODS OF A SINGLE PRAYER SET TO A VARIETY OF MELODIES (1 hour or more)

In advance, the cantor or musical director prepares a series of examples of a single prayer that has been set to music in a variety of different ways. A live performance of each example is best, but a tape could also work well. The *mi khamokha* of the Shabbat morning service and the *v'shamru* of the Friday night service are two good examples, but there are many other prayers that could be used.

Step 1: (If this part is being done in a separate session) Review the handout with the 5 M's, and explain that the purpose of this session is to explore the extent to which people agree or disagree about the moods that different musical settings convey.

Step 2: Study the prayer in translation. Ask participants to describe the mood of the prayer; there may be differences of opinion, and these should be noted. Note any Hebrew words that recur. Consider whether some words or phrases should be emphasized or highlighted.

Step 3: Listen to five to eight musical settings of the prayer. After each selection, have participants make notes to themselves about which of the 5 M's is expressed by the music (as noted in the handout, it might be more than one). Then discuss each musical setting separately; which of the five moods does this tune create?

Step 4: Are different musical settings appropriate for different services in the congregation? For different occasions? Should there be a balance of different moods in each service? Are some of the moods more important than others?

PART 4: AN ENTIRE SERVICE, SEEN THROUGH THE LENS OF THE 5 M's (1 hour or more)

Step 1: Referring back to Handout 4, have participants recall their answer to the question about whether the musical mood should be varied through a service, and whether any one mood should be represented more than the others.

Step 2: One of the professional leaders or a knowledgeable layperson presents an overview of the service that will be explored. (The Friday night service is probably preferable, since it is shorter; but this exercise can be done with any of the other services on Shabbat morning or on various holidays.) What are the main prayers, and what are the most important ideas behind each?

Step 3: The cantor sings (or a tape is played with) excerpts from the main prayers of an entire service. Participants should be given pencil and paper to note to themselves the different moods created by the different prayers.

Step 4: Participants compare notes about the variation in mood over the course of the service. Do the musical settings seem appropriate to the individual prayers? Does the service give full expression to the moods that participants considered most important? Should alternative services be offered to accommodate different tastes and expectations of different congregants?

Why Do We Feel So Strongly about Synagogue Music?

Rabbi Jeffrey Summit is an ethnomusicologist who has studied synagogue music. Here are some excerpts from his book *The Lord's Song in a Strange Land: Music and Identity in Contemporary Jewish Worship:*[43]

> Melodic choice and the proper role of music in synagogue worship have been topics of discussion from the talmudic period to the present, but its present realization is in certain ways unique. American Jewish communities now enjoy unprecedented social and religious freedom. They draw from an increasingly larger range of musical resources when "building a service." Each community works hard to find a style of worship that properly expresses who its members are as Jews and as Americans.... For example, worshippers have strong feelings about the vocal style chosen by a cantor or lay prayer leader, and will associate certain values and attitudes with that musical style. [In the 1900s] a leader who sang in a bel canto, operatic vocal style was seen as cultured and artistic—an American. Now this approach can brand a leader as being formal, egotistical, and oriented toward performance. A leader's vocal style, a cantor's use of a guitar, an Israeli folk song in the liturgy all convey symbolic meanings to the listener. Many Jews take the pulse of a congregation very quickly by noting the style of music used in worship....
>
> [Many synagogue goers] do not feel they have been to services unless they hear their favorite tunes for certain prayers. The tune, separate from the words, serves as a portal to the past, a

connection with ancestors, real and imagined. The "right" tune grounds one in history and becomes an assurance of authenticity. The tune is a vehicle for transcendence. For many Jews who do not understand much Hebrew, the tune *is* the prayer.

Not only Jews, but Christians as well, are acutely sensitive to variations in musical styles:

> The Christians with whom I spoke addressed many of the same issues that Jews did when choosing music in prayer. They discussed their struggle to establish traditions that they felt both modern and at the same time in touch with the past. They described their search for music that seemed historically authentic yet spoke to the contemporary soul.... Both Catholic and Protestant worshippers wanted to affirm the unity of their church by the simple act of singing together, yet congregants brought very different ideas of what they should sing, how it should be orchestrated, and who should sing it. In the words of an Episcopal priest, "People don't like to change or be challenged that much. These days discussions about music and liturgy always seem to be contentious."

- Do you sometimes feel that "the tune is the prayer?" Which tunes seem particularly prayerful to you?

- What do you think makes these melodies so powerful?

- Have you ever had a discussion about synagogue music with a person who had very different tastes from yours? Describe the conversation. Was it contentious, as the Episcopal minister states? If so, what made it contentious?

- How might two people who have different musical preferences have a calm, productive conversation about their differences?

- To what extent should our synagogue offer different worship opportunities to people with different musical sensibilities? To what extent should we compromise, and try to accommodate a variety of tastes within the same service?

A Language for Discussing Synagogue Music

Cantor Benjie-Ellen Schiller, professor of sacred music at Hebrew Union College in New York, has developed a vocabulary to help synagogue members discuss their views about liturgical music. She writes:

> We need to understand clearly what occurs within music itself that creates a sense of prayerfulness. If we could scientifically break down sacred music to isolate various moods of prayer, perhaps we could perceive how certain prayer experiences directly relate to particular musical expressions. We have spent too much energy defending particular music styles, as if the music were an end to itself. Let us instead develop a new vocabulary of sacred music that will focus on the unique phenomena at the intersection of prayer and music.[44]

In her unpublished article, "The Many Faces of Jewish Sacred Music," Professor Schiller uses five words to describe the different moods of synagogue music. Conveniently, each word begins with the letter M:

- *Majestic* refers to music that "evokes within us a sense of awe and wonder."[45]

- *Meditative* describes music that "leads us inward, toward reflective, contemplative prayer."[46]

- *Meeting* characterizes music that makes us "aware of the larger community.... When all voices join to create a resounding chorus of prayer, when every voice contributes its sound to the whole...we sense both a personal and a spiritual connection with those with whom we pray."[47]

- *Momentum* is the name Schiller uses for music that "functions as the 'connective tissue' of the liturgy, carrying the worship from one section to another." An example of this kind of music is the traditional chant of the kaddish, which separates one segment of the service from the next. "Its familiarity is comforting; its specific melody, chant or prayer mode is a reminder of where we are in Jewish sacred time."[48]

- *Memory* is a recent addition to Schiller's list. "Sometimes it is the associative connection that one's memory makes to a particular melody that moves people the most.... The music of memory creates continuity with our communal past. In Jewish tradition, particular musical themes serve as leitmotifs for corresponding Holy Days; imagine Yom Kippur without the *Kol Nidre* melody!"[49]

There are no definitive or objective measures of these five musical moods; a melody that sounds *majestic* to one person may sound *meditative* to another. Nor are the five characterizations mutually exclusive. A liturgical piece can create *momentum,* provide an opportunity for *meeting,* and be embedded in our *memory* at the same time. Despite these caveats, many have found that the language of the 5 M's helps them identify and explain their preference for certain types of synagogue music.

- Think about a particular prayer that, for you, is one of the high points of the service. Which of the 5 M's describes the mood of that prayer? (It could be more than one.)

- Should each of the 5 M's be represented in every worship service? In your opinion, are any of the M's more important than the others?

- In many congregations, there is considerable disagreement about which of the M's is most important. What might account for these differences? What might your congregation do to accommodate congregants with different views?

The Power of a Few Good Leaders

Economic ups and downs were experienced in ancient times, as well as modern ones. In this text, the rabbis of the Talmud consider situations in which a synagogue, or items within it, might have to be sold. The text focuses on a debate about how the sale should proceed: Should there be a hierarchy of items to be sold? Alternatively, should the leaders of the town be given discretion in making the decision?

> The townspeople who sold the town plaza may use the funds to buy a synagogue. [If they sold] a synagogue, they may buy an ark; if an ark, wrappings [for the holy scrolls]; if wrappings, they may buy books [of Scripture]; if books, they may buy a Torah scroll. But if they sold a Torah scroll, they may not buy books; if books, they may not buy wrappings; if wrappings, they may not buy an ark; if an ark, they may not buy a synagogue; if a synagogue, they may not buy a plaza. The same applies even to a surplus.
>
> *Mishnah Megillah* 3:1

> Rava said: [The mishnah's prohibition] applies only when the sale was not executed by the seven good men of the town in the presence of the townspeople. If, however, the sale was [so] executed…the funds may be used even to drink beer.
>
> *Babylonian Talmud Megillah* 26b

- What is the logic behind the hierarchy prescribed in the *Mishnah*? Why is the scroll assigned higher priority than the book, the book seen as higher than the wrapping, and so on?

- Does this hierarchy teach us anything about the relative value of other synagogue accouterments? Where, for example, might you place the synagogue's classrooms, sanctuary, and social hall?

- What might the reasoning be behind Rava's assertion, in the Talmud, that seven good men, acting in the presence of the townspeople, can set their own priorities?

- The Talmud doesn't specify the "goodness" of these men any further. What qualifications do you think these "good men" might possess? Why is the presence of the townspeople important?

- Think of a difficult decision our congregation has had to face, now or in its past. Would it have been useful to have a prescribed solution to this controversy? Alternatively, would it have been better to have the decision made "by seven good men in the presence of the townspeople?" What might this look like in practice?

A Perennial Challenge

Some observers of congregational life have argued that synagogues that aspire to become true communities must remain small and homogeneous, but the research presented in this chapter offers a different perspective. It suggests that community is a function of intent and effort, rather than size. By articulating a shared sense of purpose and creating opportunities for meaningful interactions, a congregation can move its members beyond the "service center" mentality to a sense of mutual obligation. By acknowledging the diversity of its members and celebrating, rather than obscuring, the differences between them, it can deepen their appreciation of the complexities of religious life.

The challenge of creating community amid a diverse collectivity of individuals is not new. It may, in fact, go back as far as biblical times. The last third of the Book of Exodus is devoted to the planning, building, and dedication of the tabernacle (in Hebrew, the *mishkan*), the portable sanctuary that accompanied the Israelites on their journey through the wilderness. In describing the voluntary contributions of precious metals and jewels that the Israelites made to the building of this magnificent structure, the text repeatedly uses a distinctive phrase: "every person whose heart so moved him."

> Exodus 25:2: Tell the Israelite people to bring Me gifts; you shall accept gifts for Me from *every person whose heart so moves him.*
>
> Exodus 35:5: Take from among you gifts to the Lord, *everyone whose heart so moves him shall bring them.*
>
> Exodus 35:22: Men and women, *all whose hearts moved them,* all who would make a wave-offering of gold to the Lord, came bringing brooches, earrings, rings, and pendants—gold objects of all kinds.
>
> Exodus 35:29: Thus the Israelites, *all the men and women, whose*

hearts moved them to bring anything for the work that the Lord, through Moses, had commanded to be done, brought it as a freewill offering to the Lord.

The phrase seems deliberately ambiguous: Did every man and woman contribute to the building of the *mishkan,* and did they all do so whole-heartedly? Or did only those who felt they could contribute wholeheart-edly do so while the others refrained from participating?

The ambiguity in the text suggests that even the building of the *mishkan,* the physical manifestation of the presence of God, may not have inspired universal, wholehearted participation. No surprise, then, that the synagogue, descendant of the *mishkan,* faces a similar challenge as it aspires to broaden its membership and deepen its members' commitments at the same time. The challenge is perennial, and the tension will never be fully resolved.

A Hasidic commentary adds another dimension to our appreciation of this text:

> Mordechai Yosef Leiner of Izbica taught: In the building of the tabernacle, all Israel were joined in their hearts; no one felt superior to his fellow. At first, each skilled individual did his own part of the construction, and it seemed to each one that his own work was extraordinary. Afterward, they saw how their several contributions to the "service" of the tabernacle were integrated—all the boards, the sockets, the curtains, and loops fit together as if one person had done it all. Then they realized how each of them had depended on the other. Then they understood that what they had accomplished was not by virtue of their own skill alone, but that the Holy One had guided the hands of everyone who had worked on the taber-nacle. They had merely joined in completing its master build-ing plans, so that "It came to pass that the tabernacle was one" (Exodus 36:13). Moreover, the one who made the holy ark itself was unable to feel superior to the one who had made only the courtyard tent pegs.[51]

Rabbi Leiner's teaching reinforces our notion of the *mishkan* as the ideal prototype for the synagogue. Not only was the *product* beautiful; the *process* of building it brought its own reward. Each individual made a unique contribution; but when the separate parts were combined, everyone saw how much s/he depended on the others. In their joint effort, the Israelites created not only the *mishkan,* but a strong sense of community.

6

Honoring the Past
While Anticipating the Future:
Balancing Tradition and Change

Each of the capacities discussed in chapters 3 through 5 entails a balancing act for the leadership of a congregation—being both reflective and proactive, leading in a collaborative way, and creating community while preserving diversity. The fourth capacity—promoting change while honoring traditions—is the most complex and the most demanding. Synagogues are bound by their own traditions, and they are resistant to change. But the low level of synagogue affiliation throughout the United States, and the even lower rate of actual participation in most congregations (as evidenced in attendance at services, enrollment in adult education, and so on) are indications that change is needed.

People join congregations because they seek to connect (or reconnect) with their Jewish heritage. Too often, however, their ability to forge a strong and durable connection is, in some way, hampered. There are numerous reasons for this failure to connect. People may find the congregation cold and unfriendly; they may find its programs irrelevant or boring; not knowing how to read Hebrew or recite prayers, they may feel intimidated at services or in study sessions. It may well be that the emotional baggage people carry with them from childhood, rather than anything that the congregation does, is what prevents them from appreciating the many good things a congregation has to offer. Nonetheless, the responsibility to reach out to these people lies squarely with the congregation. Synagogues must keep searching for new ways to bring Jews back to Judaism, and to do so, they must change. But as they change they run two risks: alienating those members who are currently satisfied, and failing to uphold core Jewish values and principles.

Thus, the need to balance tradition and change, which can be broken down into three separate, though related, abilities:

- the ability to distinguish between eternal Tradition and ephemeral traditions
- the ability to understand the different dimensions of change, in order to choose which types of change will work best
- the ability to lay the groundwork for change to succeed

This chapter considers each of these in turn.

Integrity in Change: Distinguishing between Tradition and Traditions

Rabbi Lawrence Hoffman, professor of liturgy at Hebrew Union College and the co-developer of Synagogue 2000, cites the following story about a tradition run amok:

> Professor Janet Walton, the liturgist at Union Theological Seminary, tells a tale about a Buddhist monk who used to take his pet cat to worship. The worshippers complained that the cat disturbed their contemplation. So the monk tied the cat down. When the monk died, his disciples insisted on bringing the cat every day and tying it down, as before, to a tether post now known as the "cat stand." When the cat died, a new

cat was purchased for the purpose of being tied to the cat stand. In later centuries, learned treatises were written on cats, and masters of the sacred arts designed cat stands with hidden meanings. Professor Walton uses that tale to challenge her students to separate what is essential for worship from the accumulated debris of cats that may have been necessary, but are not now.[1]

Thinking about how these quaint but inauthentic embellishments of the worship service took hold, one might say that the latter generations of monks mistook traditions (practices that related to the original cat) for Tradition (the essential ingredients of their worship service).

Throughout this chapter, I use the term "Tradition" with a capital T to denote rituals and practices that are essential to religion. In Judaism this Tradition consists of mitzvot (commandments), which derive from the written or oral Torah. By contrast, "traditions" with a small t are folk customs which surround and enhance the Tradition. To hold a Passover seder (the Passover ritual meal), and to end that meal with the *afikomen* (a part of the middle matzoh that is set aside) is to adhere to Tradition; to have children steal the *afikomen* and bargain for its return is to follow a tradition. Likewise, the Tradition is to light a *hanukiah* in observance of Hanukah; by contrast, giving presents, playing dreidle, and eating latkes on this holiday are traditions.

Tradition is what binds Jews together through space and time. Though Jews have lived on six different continents for over 3,000 years, the core of our liturgy and many of our rituals have remained relatively unchanged. A visitor to a Shabbat service in a foreign city may find the melodies strange and the sermon unintelligible, but the basic structure of the service and many of the prayers will be identical to those of his or her home congregation.

The distinction between Tradition and traditions is not hard and fast. Over time, as Jews faced the neverending dilemmas of adaptation and preservation described in chapter 2, some core Traditions, such as offering sacrifices at the Temple, have ceased, and some traditions, such as calling a child to the Torah at the age of 13, have been elevated to the status of Tradition. Nonetheless, Tradition is, appropriately, much more stable than traditions and more difficult to change. For example, in the late nineteenth and early twentieth centuries, when many Americans routinely worked a six-day week, some Reform congregations began to celebrate Shabbat on Sundays rather than Saturdays. Though there was a certain logic to this change, it did not last, perhaps because it was such a radical departure from Tradition, or perhaps because a five-day work week became the norm. On the other hand, the ordination of women as rabbis, which also signified a dramatic break from Tradition, seems to be a more permanent change—at least among liberal Jews. Today, even Orthodox synagogues that would not hire a female rabbi have begun to carve out leadership positions specifically designated for women.

In times such as our own, when Jews can assimilate so easily into the surrounding culture, the task of preserving and transmitting the Tradition has fallen in large part to synagogues. Thus, it is critical for synagogue leaders to distinguish between elements of Tradition that are core and traditions that are more peripheral and therefore more amenable to change. This is not an easy task, because Jews often become even more attached to traditions than to Tradition. For example, giving presents on *Hanukah* (a tradition that developed in America, where *Hanukah* became known as the Jewish equivalent of Christmas) often overshadows the Tradition of lighting the *hanukiah*. In synagogues, the Traditional liturgy is at times dwarfed by the traditional musical settings for this liturgy, as exemplified in this story by Rabbi Jeffrey Summit:

> Every year, freshmen who come to services for the first time at our Hillel Foundation tentatively approach me and say, "Rabbi, I enjoyed services, but you know, you sing all the wrong tunes here." "What are the right tunes?" I ask. "The ones we sing at home!"[2]

These students, Summit argues, are typical of many congregants, especially during the High Holidays; for these congregants, Summit observes, the tune *is* the prayer.[3]

When the tune becomes the prayer, what unites the Jew from Syria, whose preferred tune is decidedly Middle Eastern, to the Jew of Polish extraction, whose preferred tune is Hasidic? Closer to home, if the tune is mistaken for the prayer, what connects the older congregants who favor stately, formal choral music to the younger congregants who prefer participatory folklike melodies?

Making a clear distinction between traditions and Tradition is what lends integrity to the process of change; it enables us to maintain the unity of the Jewish people while accommodating different aesthetic sensibilities and social conventions. Just as the musical settings for our liturgy have continually changed, so has the architecture of our synagogues. It stands to reason that people would feel more engaged in worship that adheres to the musical idiom of their time and takes place in a setting that conforms to their notions of what is holy. The large, imposing sanctuary with the high *bimah* that seemed so majestic and spiritual to the Jews of the 1920s and 1930s feels cold and alienating to those who grew up in the 1960s and 1970s. The baby boomer generation tends to find spirituality in spaces that are more intimate and more informal. But who knows what architectural style will best suit subsequent generations? The environment in which a worship service takes place can and should be continually modified in response to the needs of the congregation. The service itself may also need to be changed to incorporate translations, new liturgy (such as the prayer for the State of Israel), and—at least for some—gender-inclusive language; but these changes should be made more carefully, ever mindful of the age-old Tradition of *k'lal yisrael,* the larger Jewish community.

One of the most vexing and insidious examples of the confusion between a Tradition and a tradition relates to the place of bar and bat mitzvah in congregational education. The Tradition is very clear that Jewish learning is a mitzvah, incumbent on Jews of all ages. There is no such thing as "graduating" from Jewish study; on the contrary, Jews have an obligation to learn and relearn the same texts repeatedly. That is why we read the Torah on a yearly cycle, and why key Jewish texts from the Bible and *Mishnah* were woven into the formal liturgy to be encountered daily. As Jews assimilated into American society, this Jewish view of learning receded in the face of a more Western view: that learning is primarily for children, and that once you have learned something, you have learned it "for good." Consequently, Jewish learning devolved into attending religious school. The bar mitzvah, which was meant to mark a boy's entry into Jewish adulthood, became instead a kind of graduation ceremony. But when Jewish learning ceases in early adolescence, Jewish adults are left impoverished. Memories that were once fresh become stale, and the rich fabric of knowledge and practice unravels. The fragments that remain are likely to be insufficient and even problematic. A child may be enthralled by a Bible story, but as an adult he or she is likely to wonder why there are contradictions or moral ambiguities in the text. Unaware of the ways in which these textual problems have been addressed by generations of commentators, adults may turn away from the Bible altogether. Children tend to think of God as an old man who sits up in heaven, and prayer as equivalent to making a wish. But to fully appreciate Judaism requires an adult conception of God and prayer. It is no wonder that adults whose Jewish education ended at bar or bat mitzvah often find themselves agnostic and unable to pray.

Thus, congregations that aim to uphold the Tradition of learning must challenge the expectation that undermines it—that learning beyond bar/bat mitzvah is optional. This, in turn, will require some major cultural and structural shifts. In terms of the congregation's culture, it means challenging the expectation that all parents have to do is drop off their children at religious school, and creating a new expectation that everyone learns. In terms of the congregation's structure, it involves the creation of a variety of new learning opportunities, so that a wide variety of interests, needs, and learning styles are accommodated. Later in this chapter, I will describe some of the new initiatives that seek to reintroduce the Traditional conception of Jewish study into congregations, and argue that some of these initiatives are more likely to succeed than others. But first, I want to focus on the second requirement outlined at the beginning of this chapter: that congregations understand and appreciate the different dimensions of change and consider which is most appropriate for them.

Understanding the Different Dimensions of Change

Change is an even more complicated concept than tradition. While it was necessary to distinguish between two kinds of tradition, there seem to be many more kinds of change. The literature on change, which grows exponentially each year, makes some of the following distinctions: planned versus unplanned, evolutionary versus revolutionary, incremental versus transformational, first order versus second order,[4] and continuous versus discontinuous.[5]

It is useful to distinguish between two different dimensions of change. The first dimension refers to the scope of the change, from discrete at one end of the continuum to systemic at the other end. The second dimension relates to the goal of the change, from a change in procedures at one pole to a change in outcomes at the other. Charting a proposed change on a continuum along these dimensions helps one see any particular change as only one among an array of alternatives, and is the first step in evaluating how appropriate that change is.

How Pervasive Is the Change—Discrete or Systemic?

Birkhot hashachar, the morning blessings, include a lovely prayer that reminds us of the wondrous system contained within our bodies:

> Blessed are You, Adonai our God, Ruler of the world, who formed humans with wisdom, and created a system of ducts and conduits within them. It is well-known before Your throne of glory that if one of these should burst or one of these get

blocked, it would be impossible to survive and stand before You. Blessed are You, Adonai, who heals all creatures, doing wonders.[6]

Clearly our ancestors appreciated the complicated interrelated system of organs that makes it possible for each and every one of us to exist. Though we understand this intellectually, we don't always fully grasp it emotionally, and then we treat each part in isolation. So it is with organizations. On close examination, their complexity and intricacy become apparent. But when it comes to change, we often act as though each part of the organization can stand alone.

The simplest, most intuitive notion of change is that it involves nothing more complicated than fixing something that is broken or adding a part that is missing. When we change a flat tire or a burnt-out light bulb, we do not bother to check if there is anything else wrong with the car, or whether the electrical wiring is faulty. In most cases, we are correct; it is just a matter of replacing the defective part or perhaps adding something new, such as antifreeze to an engine or a dimmer feature to the light switch. This notion of change as a relatively straightforward activity involving a discrete, isolated part is often applied to institutions as well. When a corporation's sales are down, it may drop its prices or increase its advertising. When the accounting department gets overloaded, a new computer program is installed.

Underlying this approach to change is an assumption that the problem is self-contained and that the diagnosis is correct. These assumptions can be entirely appropriate; sometimes the problem is no larger than poor marketing or outdated software. On the other hand, sometimes a problem is more pervasive, and replacing or adding a new component may not be sufficient. As Lee Bolman and Terrence Deal explain:

> When we see a problem we expect the solution to be close by. If sales are down, for example, we look at the sales force. In complex systems, though, cause may be nowhere near effect, solutions may be far removed from the problem, and feedback

may be delayed or misleading. At home, you flip the switch and the light goes on. In organizations, you flip the switch and nothing happens. Or nothing happens until long after you leave the room. Or the switch eventually causes a toilet to flush in a building ten miles away, but you are still in the dark, and so is the surprised user of the toilet.[7]

If profits are down because other products on the market are more attractive, or because the distribution of the products is inefficient, then it will take much more than a new advertising campaign to rectify the situation. Similarly, if production costs are spiraling out of control, a new accounting system may help diagnose the problem, but it won't, in and of itself, fix it. In these cases, a systemic approach is required—one that takes into account the totality of the organization, looks at the varied and complex sources of the problem, and approaches change more broadly.

The difference between discrete and systemic approaches to change is analogous to the differences between "medical" and "wellness" approaches to illness and health. The medical model is reactive and specialized. One does not go to see a cardiologist unless one is having a heart problem, and a cardiologist is not expected to treat a patient for cancer, an ear infection, or a broken leg. By contrast, the wellness model is proactive and takes a holistic approach. An individual who is not experiencing any symptoms might still be found to have a low blood count, which might indicate an impaired immune system; in a wellness approach, the practitioner will take care to address this problem before it enters an acute phase. In addition, the wellness approach will look to the interconnections between different systems within the body, such as the way a broken leg might limit one's ability to exercise, which in turn might affect one's blood pressure. As the examples suggest, there is merit to both of these approaches, which are best seen as poles on a continuum rather than as mutually exclusive alternatives. In some cases, a single, targeted treatment (such as an antibiotic for an infection or a cast for a broken bone) may be all that is needed; in other cases, it is critical to consider a variety of possible treatments and their wider effects.

In similar fashion, any organization that is thinking about change would do well to consider a range of possibilities, from isolated and self-contained to more pervasive and sustained. For example, as congregations have considered how to make worship more accessible and appealing, they have come up with a variety of possibilities. Some of these have been more discrete, such as introducing a prayer for healing during the Shabbat morning Torah reading, or holding a monthly healing service. Other changes have been more systemic, such as introducing prayers for healing at all services, offering support groups for both ill people and care givers, and teaching about issues related to healing in a variety of contexts. Still other changes may appear at first to be rather discrete but have the potential to become more systemic. For example, recruiting congregants to be greeters at services might remind all the worshipers to be more welcoming, and might lead the congregation to consider the other ways it can reach out to newcomers.

To take an example from another area of congregational life, discrete changes in synagogue governance are the most common because they are the easiest to accomplish. A typical example would be adding a new committee to address a new concern or an unmet need. While any single new committee is likely to be beneficial, the cumulative effect of adding committee after committee as new needs arise might lead to needless duplication or even outright conflict. Were that to happen, a more systemic change might be needed, such as a consolidation or reorganization of the committee system.[8]

But what if this type of systemic change were not sufficient? What if the problem with the synagogue's governance was deeper than inefficiency or miscommunication? What if the committees themselves were ineffective, and important synagogue functions were left to the professional staff or went entirely unfilled? In that case, the purpose of the committees would have to be reconsidered, and the charter under which they operate might have to be revised. This is where the second dimension of change comes in: Is it enough to find new ways of reaching previously agreed-upon goals? Or must one also think about the validity of the goals themselves?

Change in Procedures or in Goals?

Most changes—in organizational life and elsewhere—modify procedures while leaving the ultimate aim (which may be unstated) intact. For example, the goal of an automobile manufacturer is to produce and sell cars profitably. Toward this end, the company might bring down the costs of production by using more efficient machinery or by changing the way the car is assembled. Alternatively, it might seek to become more profitable by introducing a different kind of vehicle, like an SUV or a gas/electric hybrid. Changes in the first set are changes in procedure; those in the second set are changes in goals.

But clearly these polarities (as with the first set, discussed above) are points on a continuum, rather than mutually exclusive. What begins as a procedural change can, over time, lead to a rethinking of one's goals. The change from a typewriter to a word processor, for example, was a change in procedures, allowing those who create and copy documents to do so more efficiently. The change from word processor to computer was also initially aimed at increasing efficiency. But over time, the capacity of computers to do much more than word processing led to a change in goals, as users who had previously only done typing were now able to do accounting, data analysis, and self-publishing.

Though we all know of dramatic changes in the goals of organizations, our natural tendency is to focus primarily on procedural change. Synagogues, especially, tend to assume that their goals are timeless and to limit themselves to procedural change. For example, congregations don't question whether or not Shabbat services should be held, only what their format (*i.e.,* procedure) should be. But things are not as simple as they might at first appear, and changes in goals are often worth considering. Rethinking the purpose of Shabbat services might remind congregational leaders that the real goal is not to fill the sanctuary but to help people celebrate Shabbat. This might lead to the conclusion that some services are more in keeping with the celebration of Shabbat than others; alternatively, it might lead to a discussion of what the synagogue could do to help people celebrate Shabbat in their homes.[9]

A Matrix for Considering Potential Changes

Laying out the two continua at right angles creates a matrix on which it is possible to plot changes, both actual and potential.

Matrix 1

	SYSTEMIC CHANGE	
CHANGE IN PROCEDURES		CHANGE IN GOALS
	DISCRETE CHANGE	

The reality is, of course, much more dynamic than can be seen in a two-dimensional representation. As discussed in the previous sections, a series of discrete changes can have a multiplier effect that leads to systemic change, and dramatic changes in procedures can serve as catalysts for a rethinking of goals.

Arranging the two continua this way, with systemic change at the top and a change in goals on the right, implies one set of preferences. But it would be a mistake to conclude from looking at this chart that one should always aim for changes that lie in the upper right quadrant. A better use of the chart would be to raise questions about the nature of the change one is planning, the reason one has chosen to make this type of change, and the potential synergy and/or conflict among various changes that are contemplated.

Congregational education is a good place to explore the interplay among changes in each of these quadrants. Most congregational learning takes place in the religious school, which enrolls children in grades kindergarten through seven. Between twenty and eighty percent of adolescents in grades eight through twelve (the percentage varies greatly from one synagogue to another) are also enrolled in a formal or informal program. Beyond adolescence, the picture is considerably more bleak. In only a small number of congregations do more than ten percent of the adults participate in some form of ongoing study, over and above the occasional family education or scholar-in-residence program.

Since woefully little research has been conducted in congregational schools, it is difficult to assess the quality of the learning that occurs there.[10] Anecdotally, what we hear are mostly complaints—that religious school is boring, that discipline problems abound, and that the children don't retain much of what they learn. As early as 1910, attempts were made to improve supplementary Jewish education.[11] Early reforms initiated by Samson Benderly and his disciples were more systemic, such as creating communal Talmud Torah schools and enlarging the scope of supplementary education.[12] But from the 1940s on, as the vast majority of supplementary schooling moved to the congregational setting, most change efforts were limited to producing new textbooks, devising new methods of teaching Hebrew, and improving both preservice and in-service teacher education. As indicated in matrix 2, most of these efforts belong in the lower left-hand quadrant; in other words, they were discrete rather than systemic, and they tended to focus on procedures, rather than goals.

Matrix 2

	SYSTEMIC CHANGE	
new process of teacher evaluation	new curriculum for existing school	new models of religious school
		family education integrated into synagogue
		curricularizing adult learning
	more extensive family education	
CHANGE IN PROCEDURES		**CHANGE IN GOALS**
	recruiting avocational teachers	
new textbooks and teaching methods		
teacher appreciation day		stand-alone adult and family programs
	DISCRETE CHANGE	

Periodically, attempts were made by the denominational movements to introduce new curricula spanning grades kindergarten through twelve.[13] When these curricula reviewed and revised the goals of the school (which they did to varying degrees), and when they looked at the entire course of study rather than focusing on a particular subject or a particular grade, these improvements were more systemic and more goal-oriented. But a new curriculum is only as good as the teachers who use it, and in the absence of effective teachers, these curricula did little to improve the over-all education of children. After the initial fanfare that followed their introduction, most were relegated to the storage closet. Notable exceptions were the Bible, holiday, and Hebrew curricula produced by the Melton Research Center at the Jewish Theological Seminary, which were supported by both initial teacher training and continued professional development.[14] However, even a new curriculum and better-trained teachers were not sufficient to improve most congregational schools, because there was little community support for these schools. As long as parents conveyed to their children (explicitly or implicitly) that religious school was not worth taking seriously, the resultant problems with attendance and discipline undermined the best efforts of curriculum writers and teacher trainers.[15]

It is not surprising, therefore, that beginning in the 1970s, educational professionals latched onto family education as a potential solution. This represented an important advance in people's thinking. No longer were synagogue leaders content to improve the education of children through procedural changes; they now wanted to expand the goal, to include educating their parents as well. Not surprisingly, many of the earliest initiatives in family education tended to be discrete rather than systemic. For example, a 1988 study by the Board of Jewish Education of Greater of New York concluded with a recommendation that a family educator be added to the staff of each school,[16] and projects such as Boston Federation's Sh'arim and the Koret Synagogue Initiative provided funding for family educator positions. But when family education was seen as merely creating a new position in family education, and when the new family educator worked in isolation from the rest of the synagogue staff, family education devolved into a series of one-shot programs and had little impact on the overall ambiance and effectiveness of the school.[17] When, on the other hand, the planning of a new family education program brought lay and professional leaders together and challenged them to think more deeply about how they could transform the lives of the families involved, it served, in the words of researchers Susan Shevitz and Deborah Karpel, as "a catalyst for change" in both the school and the synagogue.[18]

From a more systemic, goal-oriented view of family education, it was but a short step to a more radical rethinking of the congregational school as a whole. By the mid 1990s, some new models of the religious school began to spring up. One of these, the Shabbat Community, in which parents and children come together on Shabbat (in some cases in the morning, in others in the afternoon) to learn and worship, is described in more detail in the case at the end of this chapter. Another model, the Family Havurah, places primary responsibility for Jewish education in the hands of parents, offering them such resources as book lists, study guides, *tikun olam* projects, orientations to worship, holiday workshops, the guidance of a mentor, and family *havurot* to join. Still another model, Congregant-Led Experiential Learning, involves parents (as well as many congregants who do not have children in the religious school) as teachers of a series of hands-on, experiential "happenings" for the entire congregation.[19]

In evaluating these efforts, one would need to consider their impact on the students, their parents, and the synagogue as a whole. Are students sufficiently challenged? Are they engaged in their learning? Are they retaining what they have learned? Does the experience lead parents to become more involved in Jewish life in general and in other synagogue activities in particular? What has been the effect of the program on the congregation as a whole? Has it created a new cadre of lay leaders? Has it led to greater collaboration in other aspects of synagogue life? Has it inspired the congregation to approach any of its other activities differently? While no careful studies have been conducted that would answer the questions about students and their parents, it is clear that each of these new models has had an important effect on the larger congregational system. At Congregation Beth Am in Los Altos Hills, the Shabbaton program sparked an interest in adult learning among the lay leadership, who requested that the staff create a curricular map for lifelong Jewish learning; this, in turn, led to a significant expansion of adult learning opportunities and the hiring of an adult learning coordinator. At Westchester Reform Temple, the success of Sharing Shabbat (another variant of the Shabbat Community) fueled efforts to rethink and reconfigure both worship and the post–b'nai mitzvah program. The following case study tells the story of the way in which one change led to another at Congregation Beth Am Israel.

CASE STUDY
Ongoing Experimentation
at Congregation Beth Am Israel

Congregation Beth Am Israel is a Conservative synagogue in a suburb of Philadelphia. In recent years it has grown rapidly to include 380 households. As it has grown it has evolved from a congregation that was "program-driven" to one that is "focused on establishing Shabbat as a central address for shared Jewish experience."[20] This evolution has been guided by a vision of the synagogue as a "Shabbat-centered community where adult and children's learning is rooted within the context of the day."[21] To achieve this vision, Rabbi Marc Margolius, Director of Education Cyd Weissman, and a team of lay leaders embarked on a series of far-reaching experiments.

They began by moving Shabbat Torah study from after the Torah reading to 9 A.M., so that the increasing numbers of b'nai mitzvah would not interfere with the intensive Torah discussions. This had the added benefit of creating a critical mass of congregants by the beginning of the service, to welcome and absorb b'nai mitzvah guests.

Eager to involve more parents in the life of the congregation, the congregation launched a family education program that met for six Sundays over the course of a year. While the program succeeded on its own terms, it seemed insufficient. As Cyd puts it, "these family education experiences were too sporadic. One here and one there wasn't enough to build true community." Reciting kiddush on Sunday to learn about Shabbat was just not the same as sharing kiddush with one's family and community on Shabbat. "Family education events were memorable, but remained outside real life Jewish context. They happened as stand-out moments within the rhythm of a secular life."

In view of the limitations of family education, the next step was to create an alternative model for the religious school, which they called Beit Midrash (house of study). Designed to integrate religious school families into the Shabbat morning schedule, Beit Midrash combines learning that is in keeping with the spirit of Shabbat with attendance at either the main service or various family *minyanim*. By shifting religious school to Shabbat instead of Sunday, and requiring parents to attend with their children, they hoped to make worship and learning on Shabbat morning the focal point of congregational life for all age groups. And, in the words of Rabbi Margolius: "By naming it Beit Midrash, we tried to reframe the experience for both parents and children from 'religious school on Saturday' to 'going to *shul* together.'"

Beit Midrash exceeded everyone's expectations. Begun as a small experiment for a single grade, it expanded each year, to the point where half of the families with school-aged children are enrolled. Beit Midrash helped build a powerful sense of community in the congregation. For example, the fourth-grade curriculum at both Beit Midrash and Beit Sefer (the congregation's more conventional Sunday school) included a session in which parents were invited to share stories about their children's *menschlich* (ethical and caring) behavior. While the session worked well at Beit Sefer, at Beit Midrash the session was more personal and much more moving. Through their Shabbat learning, the families had formed a community and knew of one another's personal struggles. One mother felt comfortable enough to speak frankly about how strong and courageous her child had been when her husband left them; everyone present knew their pain and understood just how profound the child's behavior was.

Ever mindful of their overarching vision, the rabbi and educator convened a lay committee to discuss the creation of learning opportunities for adults that would complement Beit Midrash. They suggested to the committee that they work towards becoming a congregation of learners. However, despite the congregation's stated commitment to education, the committee rejected the idea, saying that they didn't want to privilege learning over prayer or social action. Members of the committee associated learning with formal classes; they didn't see it as a vehicle for either creating community or encouraging more active participation in Jewish life. As Cyd explains, "We thought we were building on our successes, but we did not anticipate the raw nerve the phrase 'Congregation of Learners' would hit. We continued with the same programming but just didn't use the phrase."

As Rabbi Margolius puts it, "Our goal was to help both adults and children experience learning as a holy activity rather than an academic exercise, and to create as many gateways as possible to 'get people in the door.'" They began offering additional classes at the 9 A.M. slot, beginning with Hebrew and Prophets and eventually expanding to more diverse offerings such as "Prayer for Those Who Doubt" and "Women and the Bible." A model evolved in which people would come early for coffee, participate in *psukei d'zimrah* (the morning blessings), spend an hour learning, and, more often than not, stay for the rest of services and even Shabbat lunch.

One experiment led to another. One day a new member offered to teach a new Hebrew course. The class was a great success, and the rabbi realized that the sense of community would be enhanced by having congregants as teachers, as well as learners. He calculated that there were at least forty additional congregants who might make excellent teachers. A Learning Council was created to identify and promote lay-led adult Jewish learning, to nurture new lay teachers within the congregation, and to integrate the learning opportunities for children and adults. There are now four or five simultaneous learning alternatives for adults to choose from as part of the Shabbat morning experience, many of which are led by congregants who had never before been Jewish teachers.

In retrospect, Cyd believes, their experiments were successful because they proceeded slowly and deliberately, and continually solicited people's feedback. "In the early days of our pilot for Beit Midrash, we created lots of opportunities for feedback, such as surveys and meetings. This built ownership of, and willingness to experiment with, the program. After having the experience of trying and owning a small step, there was a group of people willing to try another, more risky step the next time. This created a culture of experimentation." Another reason the experiments succeeded was that people were involved in discussions of the ultimate vision. "Everyone gets on board by reading the research, so they have a framework and language for trying this new thing."

But experiments create new challenges. Beit Midrash is now filled to capacity, and there is no physical space to add another class in each grade. Even the new building currently under construction will not have enough space. Some new families who want to join Beit Midrash have been turned away. This problem is linked to the larger issue of how to help families who are not in Beit Midrash feel that they are part of the Shabbat community. Not many Beit Sefer families come on Shabbat, because parents are generally unwilling to dedicate two weekend days to the synagogue. Can the congregation find other ways to involve these families so that all their education revolves around Shabbat? Would a Shabbat program oriented around *Havdalah* meet the needs of these families and accomplish the same goal?

Another problem is that day school families who once formed the core of the Shabbat community have become more peripheral, since they are not part of Beit Midrash. The staff is exploring ways to integrate day school students into the Shabbat program, such as creating leadership roles for them in the service and inviting the older students to be mentors or *madrikhim* (teaching assistants).

So when professional and lay leaders ask themselves, "Are we there yet?" the honest answer is "No, we have a way to go." Although they have taken huge strides in creating their Shabbat community, it has not yet grown to include the entire congregation. But it helps, says Cyd, "to see these challenges as simply the next step in the ongoing process of experimentation, a natural part of the life cycle of change."

Keeping both the successes and the failures of an experiment in clear view at the same time, without letting one overshadow the other, is important. As Rabbi Margolius puts it, "If on one Shabbat morning there are a hundred people here at 9 A.M., I could think to myself, 'Wow! A hundred people at 9 A.M. on Shabbat morning!' Or I could think that there should be two hundred people here, and wonder where the other hundred are. It's a matter of seeing the glass half empty and half full at the same time, and being willing to always say 'this is a success, but, how can we make it better?'"

As the case suggests, systemic, goal-oriented change is contagious. New thinking in one aspect of congregational life inspires new thinking in other areas, and the involvement of a range of stakeholders who are energized by their experience as planners makes it easier to recruit additional people for the next planning effort. In such a climate, changes that are more discrete and procedural can also play an important role as stepping stones to, and harbingers of, the larger changes that are yet to come. This will become evident in the next section.

The Factors That Contribute to Successful Change

What enables a congregation to institute changes that are systemic and goal oriented? Is it simply a matter of serendipity, of the right people being in the right place at the right time? Can one right person go about finding additional people and, by dint of effort, make this the right time? In other words, how can a group of leaders succeed at making holistic and enduring changes?

A partial answer can be found in the previous chapters of this book. First, this group of leaders must become reflective and proactive, able to think incisively about the past and anticipate the future. Second, they must learn to work collaboratively. Third, they must take into account the diversity of needs, interests, and viewpoints within the congregation, and articulate a vision that will unite the various constituencies despite (or perhaps because of) their diversity. All these capacities can be deliberately nurtured, as I have endeavored to explain.

The capacity to change can also be nurtured if one understands the various factors that contribute to its success. These factors can be encapsulated in a formula that I learned from organizational consultant Robert Weinberg, who, in 2001, became the director of the Experiment in Congregational Education:[22]

Perceived cost of change	<	Dissatisfaction with the present state	×	Vision of the future	×	Belief that change is possible	×	Practical first steps

As Weinberg is fond of pointing out, any number multiplied by zero equals zero. In other words, the formula suggests that if there is no dissatisfaction with the present or no vision of the future, or no belief in the possibility of change, or no ideas about practical first steps, the cost of change will always be too great, and the change will fail to take root. That is the bad news. The good news is that one can compensate for the small size of any given factor by increasing the size of the others.

Dissatisfaction with the Present State

A synagogue that is entirely self-satisfied will be unable to change. For such an institution the price of change, however small, will appear too high. But no congregation has a right to be so smug; the goal of enabling congregants to lead an active Jewish life sets a very high standard for success. More commonly, dissatisfaction exists, but the leadership is too defensive to hear or acknowledge it. One of the interesting things about the successful congregations profiled by Sidney Schwarz[23] is how aware they are of their shortcomings, of the work that remains to be done.

Organizational theorist Peter Senge likens the tension between ideals and reality to a rubber band stretched vertically between two hands. "[T]he gap between vision and current reality [can be] a source of energy. If there was no gap, there would be no need for any action to move toward the vision. Indeed, the gap is *the* source of creative energy. We call this gap *creative tension.*"[24]

The tension can be increased by setting one's sights higher or by taking a closer look at the reality. Visiting other congregations or reading about them can broaden one's horizons and raise one's aspirations. So can text study and discussions of Jewish values and principles. Taking a closer look at the congregation's membership and evaluating its programs by distributing a survey and conducting focus groups can serve as a reality check for excessive contentment.

Senge's rubber band metaphor is helpful because it calls our attention to the potential pitfalls of activities designed to increase dissatisfaction. A rubber band that is too taut is liable to break. Similarly, too much dissatisfaction can lead to despair and undermine people's belief in the possibility of change. The trick is to generate just the right amount of dissatisfaction at the right time.

A Vision of the Future

As the Senge analogy suggests, vision is a critical element of the creative tension that motivates change. A vision of what might be possible energizes people and gives them the courage to take risks. This vision need not be crystal clear at the outset, because it will undoubtedly change over time. Various synagogue leaders may be captivated by different visions; this can lead to fruitful discussions and a deeper understanding of everyone's goals and commitments. This is the process of "evolving a shared vision," discussed in chapter 4 (which contains several exercises to guide conversations about vision). But what motivates people to enter into the conversation in the first place, and what gives them the fortitude to stick with a process which may at times be both confusing and conflicted, is their own personal vision of a better state.

Where does this vision come from? Like a sense of dissatisfaction, a vision of a better congregation can come from many places: from reflecting on one's experiences and disappointments, from experiences at other congregations, and from hearing others talk about their own experiences. A group of would-be change agents have a variety of means at their disposal to inspire their fellow congregants to become more visionary. They can invite speakers, circulate articles, and even organize field trips. The more attention they pay to communicating their vision, the more likely it is that others will "catch" it.

Belief That Change Is Possible

However strong the current dissatisfaction, and however compelling the vision of an alternative reality, few will invest in change if they don't see success as likely—or at least possible. To some extent, optimism and pessimism are deeply ingrained personality traits. Some people are simply more inclined than others to see a glass as half full rather than half empty. Beyond people's natural inclinations, a congregation's history can make predictions of future success more or less credible. Previous instances of successful change will incline a congregation to try again. Failed attempts (and there are many ways of failing) should give pause to the initiators of a change. What factors led to the failure of the previous efforts? Are things significantly different this time around? What will persuade the key players that this time will be different?

Practical First Steps

Despite the rhetoric of the visionaries, some people will remain unpersuaded until they have a more concrete sense of the vision in action. Thus, the fourth ingredient of change consists of the "facts on the ground," the steps that can be taken to give people a taste of what the future might be like. These might include new programs and policies or modifications of existing ones. These small, concrete first steps should be *practical* in that they can be easily implemented; they should also be clearly labeled as *preliminary*—the first exemplars of the larger changes that are yet to come. Referring back to the change matrix on page 196, it is likely that these practical first steps will fall in the bottom half of the grid, because discrete changes are easier to plan and to introduce. If possible, they should fall in the lower right quadrant so as to change people's expectations about goals and implant a new vision.

In the change literature, these harbingers of the future are called low-hanging fruit. Low-hanging fruit is the fruit that is most accessible, ready to be picked without much effort. This concept is explored more fully in *Becoming a Congregation of Learners*,[25] where I suggest the following five criteria that might guide the selection of which fruit to pick:

- Does the program or policy exemplify the values that underlie the emerging vision?

- Will it capture people's attention and therefore create a "buzz" for the more ambitious changes that lie ahead?

- Is it something to which people will respond enthusiastically?

- Will it expose people to new ideas and help spread the vision?

- Can it be implemented easily, so that it doesn't draw energy away from the larger change effort?

The Change Formula in Action: Three Brief Vignettes

The four factors on the right side of the change formula do not operate independently. They interact with and affect one another. For example, a vision of the future state can increase satisfaction, and practical first steps can reinforce people's beliefs that change is possible. The following vignettes—of one disappointing change effort and two successful ones— show how these factors play out in actual situations.

A Disappointing Change Effort

Beit Hatmada[26] has much to be proud of: the stability of its leadership, its financial security, an outstanding religious school, and many innovative programs related to worship and *tikun olam*. Privately, several lay and professional leaders acknowledge their concerns, which include a low level of Judaic and Hebrew literacy and a gap between older members, who grew up in the congregation, and newer ones, who have recently moved to the area. Publicly, however, the congregation's leaders take every opportunity to remind their members that "we are the best!"

When "synagogue transformation" became a buzzword in the Jewish community, the congregation's leaders felt that they, as a flagship congregation, should of course be involved in any effort that was new and "cutting edge." With much fanfare, they created a task force which included some key lay leaders. But the task force's ability to engage in visioning was hampered by the absence of (or reluctance to voice) any genuine dissatisfaction and by the insularity and provincialism of its members. Not only were members of the task force reluctant to voice their dissatisfaction, they had difficulty imagining that things might be done differently, and little exposure to other congregations.

Moreover, the leadership had some reason to think that change might not be possible. Several years before, the congregation had participated in a strategic planning process sponsored by its denominational movement. This resulted in some small changes, such as making the building more accessible to the handicapped. But for reasons that remained obscure, the planning process had been terminated prematurely, which left some of its participants feeling as though their time had been wasted. They were now reluctant to put much energy into a similar effort.

The strongest factor in favor of change was the ease with which the synagogue was able to introduce some practical first steps. Within a year, it had mounted a successful adult retreat, expanded its family education offerings, and introduced a new worship service on Friday evenings. Unfortunately, the success of these programs led many to conclude that they had now transformed the congregation. When some members of the task force began to contemplate more ambitious changes, the top leadership began to absent itself from meetings. After a lackluster second year, the task force was disbanded. Several lay leaders were bitterly disappointed. A year later, a key staff member who had been very active in the task force resigned.

Some in the congregation still remember the change effort fondly and are proud of what they achieved. Others see it as having yielded too little to justify the time and energy that was spent. They believe that these small, discrete changes might have been made without the entire task force apparatus. Most seriously affected were those who became disillusioned, increasingly unhappy with the congregation but unclear about how they might work to improve it.

In retrospect, the congregation might have benefited from a close examination of each of the factors in the equation. This might have led them to become more open about their strengths and limitations, and about what went wrong in their past attempt at change. Alternately, it might have led them to the conclusion that they were not ready for an effort aimed at more ambitious changes and did not need to convene a task force.

A Change Effort That Is Succeeding

When it began contemplating change, Westchester Reform Temple, too, had much of which it could be proud. They too had been blessed by stable leadership, financial security, and excellent programs. In addition, the leaders of WRT had two important qualities: They were exceptionally introspective, and they were eager to learn from the experience of others. Thus, when Rabbi Jack Stern announced his plans to retire, the board realized that rather than simply looking for "the next Rabbi Stern," they would need to think carefully about their congregation and the kind of rabbinic leadership it needed. They also realized that great care would need to be taken in the transition, lest the affection people had for Rabbi Stern undermine the chances of his successor. To help them structure the search and ease the transition, they brought in a consultant from the Alban Institute, a resource organization for congregations. They also visited other congregations, which gave them an opportunity to clarify their own vision and, by comparison, see some of the limitations of WRT. Their new rabbi, Rabbi Richard Jacobs, was selected because his vision of the future matched theirs.

Thus, when WRT was invited to join the first cohort of the Experiment in Congregational Education (ECE), it didn't take long for the leadership to decide that this was an appropriate project for them. Their positive experience with the rabbinic transition had helped them articulate some of the challenges they faced and had given them an inkling of what the future might hold. Most importantly, it had confirmed their belief in deliberate, planned change. Within a year, the ECE task force introduced several small but significant innovations, including a high-profile adult-education series and a Shabbat kit for families. They took every opportunity to promote these first steps as "only the beginning." An alternative model of the religious school, "Sharing Shabbat," soon followed, along with plans to create an alternative worship space and to experiment with a different style of worship. By that time, WRT was "hooked" on change. Rabbi Jacobs and others spoke publicly of being "never finished," always mindful of the next aspect of congregational life that could be transformed. A task force on adolescent education was followed by a task force to redesign the "regular" religious school and a task force to examine worship, as part of Synagogue 2000. Change has indeed become a way of life.

It would be a mistake to conclude from the previous vignettes that the factors that promote or inhibit change are always easy to discern in advance. In fact, things are much more unpredictable, as the following vignette demonstrates.

Success, Despite the Odds

Temple Emanuel of Beverly Hills entered the Experiment in Congregational Education (ECE) just three years after it had nearly merged with another congregation because of a lack of funds. A last-ditch effort saved the congregation and enabled it to bring in Rabbi Laura Geller as senior rabbi, but the synagogue was still plagued by debt, a loss of membership, and a turnover in its top personnel.

Though some cautioned against embarking on a change process, given the precarious state of the synagogue, Rabbi Geller believed that many factors strengthened the congregation's ability to succeed at change. Most obvious was the widespread dissatisfaction, which made people open to experimentation. Because Los Angeles is home to three rabbinical schools and many innovative congregations, many members of Temple Emanuel had had an opportunity to see, first-hand, some different models of worship and learning.

Rabbi Geller and her staff were able to fuel people's hope for a renewed congregation by getting small grants to introduce an array of new programs within the space of a few years. These included a Shabbat morning *minyan,* an intergenerational theater project, a mentoring program for b'nai mitzvah students, an artist-in-residence program, and a cross-denominational high school leadership program. Not all of these new programs were completely successful, and some were phased out over time. Cumulatively, however, they served their purpose, which was to inspire veteran members to think differently about congregational life, to attract new members, and to convince lay leaders to invest their own time and energy in a more sustained change effort. Five years after the ECE task force began its work, Temple Emanuel, like Westchester Reform Temple, has accustomed its members to "a permanent state of change." Two worship care committees[27] (one for the Shabbat *minyan,* the other for a Friday night service) actively solicit feedback from members and meet regularly to consider possible changes. A task force on alternative models of the religious school ended with recommendations for an experimental new model and the establishment of a new task force on adolescent education. Though the congregation's initial expectations were low, its early experiments paved the way for a revitalization.

The Other Side of the Equation: Bringing Down the Perceived Cost of Change

No matter how large the product of the four factors that make up the right side of the formula, change will be resisted if its perceived cost is even larger. Some of the costs of change are obvious: Change takes time and energy, which often requires additional staff, which costs money. Any congregation contemplating change must realize that its current staff, which is probably already overburdened, will be unable to implement the proposed change unless its current work load is reduced. Perhaps some of the staff's work can be turned over to volunteers, or perhaps funds can be raised for additional staff. As synagogue revitalization has become a higher priority among foundations and individual donors, funding for change efforts has become more readily available.

In contrast to the tangible costs of change, the perceived costs are more subtle and more difficult to contend with. Proposals for change frequently encounter considerable resistance. In the words of Michael Fullan, "If there is one cardinal rule of change in human condition, it is that you cannot *make* people change. You cannot force them to think differently or compel them to develop new skills."[28] The literature on change is filled with examples of changes that were introduced with great fanfare, only to be sabotaged by key people within the organization who found them threatening. A classic case is that of a suburban school board, which in the 1960s became captivated by the idea of "open education" and built a new state-of-the-art junior high school, designed to facilitate team teaching. In contrast to the school board, the teachers assigned to the school were skeptical about open education and uncomfortable with team teaching. Over the course of the first school year, the teachers built makeshift walls out of bookshelves to create the self-contained classrooms to which they were accustomed.[29]

Bolman's and Deal's four frames for viewing an organization, which were introduced in chapter 3, are helpful tools for understanding the kinds of resistance that can develop in an organization and for suggesting ways to deal with them.[30] The following is an overview of the way each frame would explain resistance to change and attempt to overcome that resistance. After that, all four frames are applied to a well-known case in synagogue change. An additional application of the four frames to a case involving change can be found at the end of chapter 3.

The Perceived Cost of Change As Seen through Bolman's and Deal's Four Frames

THE STRUCTURAL FRAME

Viewing change through the *structural frame* makes us look more closely at the ways in which change upsets established organizational structures and patterns. A change may create a different organizational hierarchy or a revised set of procedures which—however rational and however necessary in addressing old problems—may create new, unanticipated ones. Like a pair of new shoes, new institutional arrangements require a break-in period.

Introducing these changes as preliminary, and making frequent adjustments, will help ensure that the new structural configurations are appropriate.

THE HUMAN RESOURCE FRAME

The *human resource frame* reminds us that change is often unsettling and anxiety-provoking. Organizational consultant William Bridges distinguishes between *change,* which refers to an *objective event,* and a *transition,* which is a *subjective perception.*

> *Change* is situational: the new site, the new boss, the new team roles, the new policy. *Transition* is the psychological process people go through to come to terms with the new situation.... Unless *transition* occurs, *change* will not work.... Psychological *transition* depends on letting go of the old reality and the old identity you had before the change took place.[31]

Bridges likens the transition period to a neutral zone, a kind of psychological no-man's-land between the old and the new.

> One of the most difficult aspects of the neutral zone for most people is that they don't understand it. They expect to be able to move straight from the old to the new. But this isn't a trip from one side of the street to the other. It's a journey from one identity to the other, and that takes time.[32]

Those who initiate change, Bridges counsels, should take care to help people anticipate the transitions and support them in their journeys through the neutral zone.

THE POLITICAL FRAME

Changes often involve shifts in power, status, and the distribution of resources. Though people may understand the need for a change, and even agree with it in principle, they will inevitably view it in terms of what they, personally, stand to gain or lose. The *political frame* calls our attention to this aspect of change. When people have a premonition (justified or unjustified) that the change might not work in their favor, their reaction may be to try to prevent or sabotage it. This kind of power-grab is rarely overt; it can be accomplished through secret maneuvers and private deals, or by avoidance and delays. To minimize this kind of resistance, those who want to bring about change should keep the planning process as open as possible. They should think through in advance who will lose power, status, or a valuable resource, and how those people might be compensated for this loss; they should consider as well the compromises that might be negotiated to win people over.

THE CULTURAL AND SYMBOLIC FRAME

The *cultural and symbolic frame* enables us to understand the power of traditions. A panoply of stories, music, artifacts, patterns of behaviors, and historical precedents form the culture of an organization. When key elements of the culture are modified, people's basic assumptions about the institution may be challenged, and their loyalty to it shaken. Thus, the students at Rabbi Summit's High Holiday services were disappointed that he used the "wrong" melodies; and many congregants are reluctant to give up a historic building, however much of a liability it has become. Those who initiate change must think carefully about how it may be interpreted and what symbolic messages they can send to bolster the interpretations they favor. For example, in an effort to make their worship more participatory, one congregation redesigned its sanctuary, replacing the fixed pews with movable seating. Because the old pews held fond memories for the older members of the congregation, many of them were retained and placed in strategic locations throughout the building. This enabled the synagogue to send the message that though things change, old traditions are honored.[33]

A Case Study Viewed through the Four Frames

A case that reveals the intricacies of synagogue change is found in Joseph Reimer's book *Succeeding at Jewish Education*.[34] It recounts a crisis that developed when a synagogue's board, acting on the recommendation of the religious school committee, decided that all students be required to enroll in a three-day-a-week Hebrew program, which had previously been optional. The decision provoked an angry response from a small but vocal group of parents, even though the program was universally acclaimed, a majority of religious school students were already enrolled in the program, the synagogue's bylaws had been followed in making the decision, and the committee was prepared to make alternative arrangements for students for whom attending three days a week posed a hardship. The committee was stunned by the outcry and came close to backing down on its decision.

Viewing this case through the four frames offers us a better understanding of the sources of resistance to this change. The *structural frame* directs our attention to the process through which the decision was made. The committee had done its job responsibly, gathering the necessary data and discussing the pros and cons of the new policy over a series of meetings before making a recommendation to the board. The board had full authority to make the decision without soliciting the opinions of parents, or even informing them in advance that this change was being considered. But at least one member of the committee felt they had made a "mistake in the process."

> We lost touch with the constituency we represent. We see ourselves more as a committee relating to [the educator]. We need to keep reminding ourselves of what are the ongoing issues for these parents.[35]

Another member of the committee disagreed: "We are a private institution and not a school board. We are not elected.... You don't just vote with the constituency but take a leadership role."[36]

After a long discussion, the consensus among committee members was that they should have involved parents at an earlier stage, not out of concern for "due process" but—as a *human resource* approach would recommend—in order to "invest" them in the change. Many parents felt overlooked and disenfranchised by the way the decision had been made.

While more parental involvement at an earlier stage was not, strictly speaking, required, it might have offered useful input in the process, made the decision more palatable, and eased the transition to the new policy. In retrospect, the committee realized that they might have faced less opposition had they done differently: given parents advance warning that the change was being considered, created opportunities for people to voice their concerns and offer their own suggestions, and put even more emphasis on the accommodations that would be made for families for whom the change posed a problem.

The *political frame* leads us to consider the less overt, more insidious aspects of this case. Opponents of the new policy responded to it with a show of power—bringing their allies to an open meeting, complaining loudly, and threatening to leave the synagogue if the policy were not rescinded. The educator responded in political terms as well, calling these "'blackmail statements' that must be resisted, because it is impossible to run a temple properly if you allow people to do 'anything they want to do.'" From the political perspective, resistance to this particular change was simply another skirmish in an ongoing battle about how much the synagogue would (as one side might put it) "dictate people's religious practices" or (as the other side might put it) "lower its standards and give in to everyone's demands." In his book, Reimer recounts several similar skirmishes of this sort. In his belief, they are the inevitable product of negotiation between Tradition and change.

Considering this case through the *cultural and symbolic frame,* we see that what upset the opponents of the new policy the most was its symbolic subtext. They saw the policy not only as elevating the value of Hebrew (which it did), but also as devaluing those who did not know Hebrew, especially non-Jewish partners. They argued that the mandatory Hebrew requirement as counter to the Reform Movement's principle of "informed choice," an insult to those who had grown up in the Reform movement at a time when Hebrew was not taught, and a slap in the face to intermarried couples and their children.

Reimer concludes his discussion of this case with some advice for those who might attempt a similar change:

> The task of a committee is to try to see its proposal for change through the eyes of those who will likely have problems with it. The committee can open its process to such people in the midst of its deliberations and learn what the concerns of these people are. While the concerns raised may not deter the committee from making the same decision it would have, it can give the members time to think how they might address the concerns and anxieties that will arise.[37]

It would be better to devote time and energy anticipating and preventing potential objections and concerns than to spend what would amount to considerably more time and energy dealing with the resistance after the fact.

Maintaining the Delicate Balance between Tradition, Traditions, and Change

Earlier in this chapter, the creative tension between the ideal and the real was likened to the tension in a rubber band. But imagine, for a moment, a more complicated kind of creative tension, as in the game known as "parachute."

> In "parachute," individuals stand in a circle grasping the edges of a parachute trying to prevent a ball in the center from escaping. When the tension around the circle is balanced, the ball bounds higher and higher. But as people invariably shift positions, loosening and tightening their grasp with sudden pulls and jerks, the ball leaps off the stretched fabric and skips to the ground.[38]

A new group of players is likely to lose the ball quite a few times before it succeeds in hoisting the ball into the air. Having players who differ in height and weight, and in strength and agility, makes the task even more difficult and leads some players to give up. But the elation that accompanies the first success can motivate everyone to try again. With practice, the players can learn how to coordinate their efforts, raising the ball higher and higher.

Working to revitalize a congregation is like playing a game of parachute. In the beginning it may feel strange and difficult. After a while, people begin to grasp, both intuitively and analytically, how to maintain an appropriate tension. Through reflection and collaboration, they learn how to anticipate one another's actions and how to compensate for their differences. They learn how innovation can enhance tradition, and tradition enhance innovation. Like the ball, their progress will have its ups and downs. Over time, both the process itself and the innovations it yields will reward them many times over.

7

Individual Self-Renewal

American synagogues have the potential to connect their members with the Jewish Tradition and with one another in powerful ways. They can respond to spiritual needs people didn't know they had, and create communities that people didn't realize were missing. Too often, however, this potential remains untapped; many synagogues are what sociologists call "limited liability" organizations, in which little is ventured and little is gained. To claim their rightful place as central addresses in the lives of their congregants, synagogues must develop the capacities discussed in this book—capacities that will enable them to become self-renewing.

Throughout the book, these capacities have been described as residing in the congregation as a whole, because the character of a congregation goes beyond the cumulative character of its members. Becoming a reflective congregation takes more than bringing together a group of reflective leaders. And even if those individuals are accustomed to working collaboratively, the congregation's overall leadership will not automatically become more collaborative. Developing these institutional capacities requires concerted effort over time. Similarly, maintaining the appropriate balance between community and diversity and between Tradition and change is a task for the collectivity, not the individuals within it.

While the work of renewing a congregation is painstaking and difficult, it yields many benefits, not just for the congregation as an organization but for individual congregants and professionals as well. The members of a reflective congregation that practices collaborative leadership are often challenged by their experience in the congregation to become more reflective and collaborative in the rest of their lives. Members of a congregation that values both community and diversity develop a deeper appreciation of both those values. And a collective ability to balance Tradition and change will help individuals find their own sense of balance. As they endeavor to renew the congregation, its members and its leaders renew themselves as well.

Thus, it is only fitting to conclude this book with an exploration of the reciprocal relationship between the individual and the congregation. The following case illustrates two kinds of synergy—between the four capacities discussed in this book, and between the congregation as a whole and the individuals within it.

Developing the Capacity for Self-Renewal at the New Emanuel *Minyan*

The "New Emanuel Minyan" at Temple Emanuel of Beverly Hills is not so new anymore, as it was founded in 1994. Yet, every year the *minyan* takes on new challenges and develops in new ways; perhaps that is why its participants have yet to suggest that a change of name is in order.

Creating this Shabbat morning *minyan* was one of Rabbi Laura Geller's first acts when she became the synagogue's senior rabbi. Few people thought it was a good idea at the time. Rabbinic colleagues warned that a *minyan* might divide the congregation. Members of the board wondered whether it was prudent to incur the additional expense of hiring a part-time rabbi and a cantor (since both the rabbi and the cantor were required to lead services for b'nai mitzvah in the main sanctuary every Shabbat). But Geller saw the establishment of an ongoing Shabbat community as essential to revitalizing the congregation. She believed that a true Shabbat community would require more focus and continuity than the weekly b'nai mitzvah services could provide. In addition, she hoped that the *minyan* would serve as an incubator for new prayer experiences, an advance guard for changing the way the entire congregation prayed.

In its first year, the *minyan* met only once a month under the leadership of Rabbis Sheldon and Janet Marder, well known in Los Angeles for their keen intelligence and quiet spirituality. Had the Temple's board taken a close look, they might have decided that the *minyan* was not a worthwhile investment, since two-thirds of the participants (who rarely numbered more than thirty) were not members of the congregation. But Morrie Rosenblatt, an influential lay leader, became a regular participant and a strong advocate; with his support, the *minyan* expanded and began meeting twice a month.

Over time, the *minyan* developed a distinctive personality, becoming known for its meditative atmosphere, participatory *davening,* spirited singing, and thought-provoking text study. It began to attract more congregants, and several of the *minyan* regulars joined the congregation. When Rabbi Jonathan Aaron came on as assistant rabbi, he and Rabbi Geller took turns leading the *minyan,* which began meeting three times a month. The roster of active members reached 120, with attendance on any given Shabbat hovering at about 60. In the *minyan's* sixth year, the worship care committee was formed; under its guidance, the *minyan* expanded to meet every Shabbat.

Reflection was built into the *minyan* from its inception. At the end of each year, a meeting was held to solicit the feedback of participants. The rabbis spent a great deal of time reviewing the service and thinking about ways it might be changed. Because they wanted the *minyan* to become more participatory, they decided to forgo sermons in favor of interactive Torah study. To improve their text teaching, they began meeting every month with an educational consultant, who helped them analyze previous discussions and plan upcoming sessions.[1]

Rabbis Geller and Aaron knew that the *minyan's* success would depend on collaborative leadership, though it took some time for collaboration to develop. From the outset, lay participants read Torah and *haftora;* soon they began taking turns as greeters. Perry Oretzky, a graduate of the Union of American Hebrew Congregation's pararabbinic course, substituted for the rabbis in their absence. He and other *minyan* members also led occasional text study sessions.

But it wasn't until the seventh year, when the worship care committee began holding open meetings every month, that the *minyan* became a truly collaborative venture. The committee now meets over lunch on the first Shabbat of every month. The rabbis and Cantor Judy Greenfeld participate when they are able to do so, but the committee has also met without them. The topics on its agenda have ranged from child care to the creation of a new *siddur* (prayerbook). When members of the *minyan* wanted to hold their own services, first for Tisha Ba'av (the ninth of Av) and then for Purim, they brought their requests to the committee.

A true test of collaboration came when one of the committee's co-chairs, Richard Tell, raised the question of expanding the *minyan* so that it would meet every Shabbat. "I never had a Shabbat community before," Richard said, "but now that I have one, I feel at a loss on that fourth Shabbat. I can go to other synagogues, but it's not the same. The more time I spend at other congregations, the more I want to be here." As the discussion proceeded it became clear that people wanted a trained cantor or cantorial soloist present on that fourth Shabbat, but they saw leading the service and teaching Torah on that day as a collective responsibility to be shouldered by the laity, rather than the rabbis. "After all," one participant said, "the rabbis should have the opportunity to sit and enjoy the service too."

Like every liberal congregation, the *minyan* must strike a balance between Hebrew and English, the fixed liturgy and interpretive readings, traditional *nusach* (chanting) and more contemporary melodies. The *minyan*'s solution is to recite the Hebrew aloud but make line-by-line translations available in the *siddur*, along with commentaries and contemporary poetry. The responsibility for creating a balance between classical and modern music falls to Cantor Judy Greenfeld, who joined the *minyan* in its fourth year. An early experience taught her to tread very carefully:

> I introduced an interpretive song in English before the *Shma*. I had cleared it with the rabbis, had their permission. But people protested loudly afterwards. At first I felt very hurt. But later I realized that they had the right to protest. The important thing is the comfort level of the *kahal* (the group). From this I learned that you have to wait until people are comfortable. Now when I introduce a new piece of music, I teach about it first in the prayer discussion before the service. And now that people are more comfortable with me, they are more open to new music.

Los Angeles is a diverse Jewish community, and the New Emanuel Minyan mirrors this diversity. Among its members are natives of Iran, Iraq, Israel, South Africa, and Argentina as well as the United States. It includes converts to Judaism, Jews raised with no religion, Jews raised in Orthodox homes, and everything in-between. For the most part, members cherish the *minyan*'s diversity—the Iranian women who shower the Torah with kisses; the Iraqis who read Torah with a distinctive chant; the doubters and the believers; the singles, married, widowed and divorced; the graduate students and the retirees; the affluent and the less affluent; those who are fluent in Hebrew and those who rely on transliteration. Despite its diversity, or perhaps because of it, the *minyan* has become an important community for its members. People's absence is noticed. When someone is ill or has suffered a loss, people call and visit. Of particular joy are the four babies born in the *minyan,* who are passed around from one member to another.

But no *minyan* can accommodate everyone, and the New Emanuel Minyan has also had its dropouts—those who preferred sermons to discussions, those who wanted more English or more Hebrew, those who stopped going to services or who found other congregations more to their liking. Differences remain even among the regulars. Some enjoy having services led by their fellow congregants; others are happy only when the rabbis are in charge. Some feel that the *minyan* is getting stale and needs to change; others feel that it has changed too much already.

Though the New Emanuel Minyan is still a work in progress, it has already proved to be a sound investment. It has served as an incubator for new leadership; new mentors for the b'nai mitzvah program, new members of various committees, and new members of the board have all come from the *minyan.* At the same time, the *minyan* is one of the places within the synagogue where existing leaders can go to deepen their Jewish commitments. After becoming active in committees or on the board, many people have begun attending the *minyan* regularly.

As Rabbi Geller had hoped, the *minyan* has been a place to experiment with participatory worship and interactive learning. Innovations first introduced at the *minyan,* such as calling people up for group *aliyot* and allowing time for silent meditation before the *Amidah,* have been successfully incorporated into the service at the main sanctuary. In addition, the *minyan*'s success has encouraged the clergy to introduce other new services, such as a participatory Friday night service called "Shabbat Unplugged" and a monthly healing service.

As the *minyan* has influenced the congregation as a whole, it has also had a profound effect on its individual members. Richard Tell recalls his first experience with leading services:

> I felt honored to have been asked, but also very anxious. Rabbi Geller heard the hesitancy in my voice. "It will be a stretch," she said, "but you're ready to do it." Her trust in me meant a lot; it compelled me to say yes. I spent hours in preparation. I talked to Perry Oretzky (who had led the service before), to Rabbi Geller, and to Cantor Greenfeld. I observed the rabbis leading services, and noticed that they did things differently from one another; so it would be OK if I did things differently too. I realized that the leader does much more than announce pages; I would need to give instructions, set the mood, and provide transitions. I went over the *siddur,* section by section. I scripted parts of it, so I would know just what to say.
>
> At the service, everyone was so encouraging. They smiled, gave me a thumbs up, and mouthed the words "you're doing great!" It was a very satisfying experience.
>
> But the biggest satisfaction came afterwards. Preparing to lead the service taught me a lot about praying, and deepened my own prayer experiences. I look forward to doing this again. The more you do it, the more you are able to bring to it, and the more you get out of it.

Cantor Greenfeld has found the collaborative spirit of the *minyan* transformative:

> The *minyan* has reinforced my interest in being a cantor. In the beginning I thought I had a feel for what would work, but I learned that it's different for every community. This experience has made me set aside my own ego, and realize that it's not about me. I want people to own it with me. You are a strong leader only because you have a strong *kahal* behind you.

Lee Silber, a long-time member of the congregation who had never attended services regularly, started coming after her mother died. She liked it so much that she convinced her husband to come with her; now it is something they do together which enriches them both as individuals and as a couple. "The *minyan* reminds me of my youth and of my family, which is strange, because even as a child I rebelled against going to services. I feel as though I'm returning to a place that I should have been, but never really was."

Yona Sabar, who grew up in a very observant Iraqi family, notes that despite the obvious differences, the *minyan* has captured the essential spirituality of his childhood synagogue in Iraq:

> The Iraqi synagogue in which I grew up was relatively small, and all the congregants knew one another quite well. The synagogue was considered a holy area, and one has to take his shoes off before entering the prayer hall. One felt the *Shekhina* hovering over the congregation, especially when the Torah scroll was raised open. But the American synagogues I tried at first were large and impersonal, and the only thing that attracted me back to them was a good sermon.

The *minyan* was different; the spiritual feeling, the beautiful chanting, the lively discussions, the sky-lighted hall, and the sense of community, drew him back. "It is so welcoming. Each time I come I feel like I am worshipping with an extended family."

The feeling of community was an added bonus for Sandy Silas, "more than I had anticipated, or even hoped for."

> I started attending the *minyan* because I had been very ill and was looking for spiritual renewal. I found, almost from the beginning, that the music and the singing were a vehicle for me to feel connected to God and to Judaism. The *minyan* became an oasis in my week. Because I had originally gone to deal with my own struggle, I didn't expect to find community there. Through my active participation over an extended period of time, I became close to the people around me, and their presence became an important part of the experience. I went there as an individual; now I feel part of a community.

The sense of community is more complicated for Veronica Abney, an African American and a Jew-by-choice.

Sometimes I think this is a very diverse community, with Iranians, Iraqis, Israelis, Argentineans, and so on. It challenges me to overcome my own difficulty understanding other cultures and their way of doing things. And it is sometimes a comfort to me, being a person of color. But sometimes, I feel that even with all the diversity I don't fit in. Some Jews, regardless of ethnicity, are caught off guard when they see someone black (and not Ethiopian) in their synagogue.

Nonetheless, Veronica has become aware of her contribution to the *minyan*, especially on the Shabbat when she was called to the Torah for the first time:

It was an incredible moment for me. I felt so present that day; I was just there and able to take it in. Afterwards, when people came up to me, and later in the week when others called me, they told me how powerful the moment was for them as well. Then I saw that it wasn't just an experience for me; it was also an experience for many others. I was a part of making that happen; if I hadn't been so open and present, that wouldn't have happened. So I helped to create community.

Scott, who is gay, chose to join the *minyan* rather than either of the gay and lesbian congregations nearby. "I have never believed in ghettoizing myself, as a Jew or a gay person. I like belonging to a diverse group." When Scott joined the *minyan,* he had never belonged to a congregation. As the *minyan* became his Jewish community, he felt an obligation to bring the concerns of gays and lesbians to the rest of the congregation and to reach out to gays and lesbians who were considering joining. Like Veronica, he began to see that he had a special contribution to make. When he and his partner, Gary (who is not Jewish), were called to the Torah in anticipation of the birth of their son, Scott says, "I knew how accepting they were of me, but I was unprepared for the warm response our new family received from the members of the *minyan.* I realized how much the *minyan* had become a part of my life and vice versa."

The *minyan* has had a profound effect on the rabbis. Rabbi Aaron has found that the participatory nature of the *minyan* has enabled him to be more open about his doubts and his questions, as well as his beliefs.

> As a rabbinical student I was told that I have to have all the answers, that I can't be ambivalent. But because of the diversity of the group, and the way it has come together, I can be myself and share my questions. When I try something new, people accept it. I don't feel judged, and I don't feel as though I have to have the final word.

Though her original purpose in founding the *minyan* was to revitalize the synagogue, Rabbi Geller finds that she has gained something of great personal value as well. "I am so grateful to have found a *minyan* in which I can pray."

> I now have a standard by which to judge the prayer services I lead: Could I, personally, pray at this service? Were I to resign as the rabbi of the congregation, I would continue to pray at the *minyan*. I don't yet feel that way about all the services at the Temple, but having such a high standard helps keep me focused on my goals.

Individual Self-Renewal

The experiences of Temple Emanuel and its members are not unique. As the cases at the end of chapters 3 through 6 suggest, synagogue renewal and personal renewal go hand in hand. The following observations from some of the people portrayed in those cases illustrate the reciprocal relationship between the individual and the congregation.

Susan Kippur of Congregation B'nai Jeshurun (whom we first met in the case in chapter 4), has found that her work as co-chair of *bikur cholim* has helped her to redefine her personal goals and refine some of her professional practices.

> As a consultant, I had a tremendous amount of responsibility and self-confidence, based on my long-term relationships with successful corporate clients. But BJ felt like more than just a client—it was a religious institution, a source of intimacy and community, and an increasingly important part of my life. And so, the stakes felt higher and more personal, causing me at first to second-guess myself and ultimately to adjust some of my consulting approaches, to make certain that they fit this new and in many ways more compelling work arena.

And, in fact, Susan discovered that there were some important differences between working with a corporation and working with a congregation. She knew that as a corporate consultant she had been accountable to senior managers to make things happen in their organizations quickly and within existing management and leadership structures. Executives would unilaterally announce cultural changes that needed to be made, and Susan would help expedite the transformation process, working one-on-one and in groups. In her work with *bikur cholim* at BJ, however, the mandate for change came not only from the rabbis but from within the committee and the community itself. The structures and leadership positions needed to be created almost from scratch. And the pace of change needed to accommodate the busy lives of the volunteers who agreed to take on leadership positions in addition to their regular work and family commitments.

> As a consultant to a business, I was expected to reinforce mandated change and push things along rather assertively. Working at BJ, I have learned that it is not only appropriate but desirable to be more patient with the process and—while providing direction and guidance—to give our newly identified leaders the time and space to make contributions that fit into their busy lives.

The payoff for Susan has been as much personal as professional.

> The exciting part is how much I'm getting back. While I am doing the things that I do best (supporting change and helping an organization develop new leadership), I am constantly being exposed to a Hebrew vocabulary and Jewish concepts. It's so powerful, learning them in an environment which I am also trying to change. It wouldn't be the same if I were just learning these words in my Hebrew class. There the Hebrew term *kehilah kedoshah* (a sacred community) would be just one new phrase among many. But to learn this term while I am trying to help create a *kehilah kedoshah* adds a whole new dimension. Words like this take on a sacred meaning when you're learning them and helping to make them happen at the same time.

For Sheryl Primakow (the president of Congregation Sinai, whose story was told in the case in chapter 3), the experience of participating in a congregational change initiative was also transformative.

> The reflective process that our synagogue went through, and the Jewish learning (particularly the text study) that was integral to that process, was so stimulating intellectually. It filled a void in me that I hadn't known existed. Seeing that an institution could do things differently made me realize that change was possible. And that led me to enroll in graduate school.

Now, having completed her degree in counseling psychology and embarked on a new career as a school counselor, Sheryl continues to learn from being part of a collaborative leadership team at a reflective congregation.

> I am getting better at understanding what lies behind people's resistance or neediness; and, as a result, I am becoming more patient and less judgmental. In the beginning of my presidency, I was overwhelmed by the demands people made on me and by their need for approval. Now I see that an important part of my role is to be a listener, a facilitator, and a cheerleader.

Not only lay leaders, but professionals too, have grown from their experiences of creating a self-renewing congregation. Rabbi David Cohen, also of Congregation Sinai in Milwaukee, has found that the process of empowering lay leaders and of deliberating together has been good for him as well as for the congregation.

> We have built up the expectation that the lay people, as well as the professionals, will be out there looking for best practices and new ideas. It not only benefits the congregation; it takes a tremendous burden off of my shoulders. I no longer have to be the sole generator of new ideas or the sole source of inspiration.

Rabbi Cohen and his congregation have begun planning for his sabbatical, which is a year away.

> We have entered into our meetings with the conscious awareness that this is an opportunity for the congregation, as well as for the rabbi. We take it as a given that things should move forward in my absence, that my being away shouldn't stifle programmatic initiatives. On the other hand, some issues shouldn't be decided without me. We are trying to determine which issues these are.

The entire process has been both fascinating and rejuvenating. "I had always known that a healthy congregation is one in which professionals and lay leaders shared tasks. I have a sense of great pride and satisfaction that we have come this far."

Finally, Cyd Weissman, the educator at Congregation Beth Am Israel (whose story is told in the case in chapter 6), has found that continual experimentation has changed her conception of her job.

> I used to think that my job was to be the most creative, dynamic, and responsive educator I could be. My goal was to ensure that students liked coming to religious school and that they learned about Jewish living. My job is different now because my goals are different. Now I see myself as a weaver, not as a painter. My job is to build Jewish space and meaningful relationships. Together, my colleagues and I engage in "intellectual barn-raising."

This collaborative work has changed her relationship to her colleagues and to the congregants in her synagogue.

> The experience has been the vehicle to build deep and meaningful relationships with coworkers and congregants. Instead of knowing people by what they look like, what they do, or who their children are, this experimental process lets you know people by how they think and what they value. I've gotten to know how people take their disappointments and challenges. And because you are all sharing in the experiment, the I becomes a *we*. You begin to say, "we were disappointed," "we were so excited," "we have to rework this." It is an intimate experience.

A Final Text about Self-Renewal

The book of Lamentations, after depicting the horrors of the destruction of the Temple, the sacking of Jerusalem, and the exile of the people, ends with a plea to God: "Take us back, O Lord, to Yourself, and let us come back; renew our days as of old." In the context of this national disaster, this plea makes perfect sense. A bereft, exiled people yearns for a return to their land and to the peace and placidity of their former lives.

The verse seems a bit more puzzling when it is recited in synagogue as the Torah scroll is returned to the ark. The circumstances in which we live are, in many ways, much better than those of previous generations of Jews. Many of our ancestors lived in poverty and faced various forms of persecution. Do we really want to renew our days as of old? Yet, as we stand before the ark, the plea seems appropriate. For, despite our freedom and despite our relative comfort, we long for the simplicity and wholeness of Jewish life as it was lived in "days of old." We are not really asking to *return* to the past, but for something more paradoxical: to be re*new*ed as of *old*.

Today, this prayer seems particularly appropriate as a prayer for the *congregation as a whole*. If the synagogue is to succeed at preserving and transmitting the Jewish Tradition, it must help its members see the Tradition as both vibrant and relevant. To do this, it too must be "renewed as in days of old," bringing a fresh perspective and a fresh energy to what is old, and the resonance of age-old norms and values to what is new. By developing the capacities of self-renewal, a synagogue can begin to answer its own prayer.

NOTES

CHAPTER ONE

1. Jack Wertheimer, "Introduction," in *Jews in the Center: Conservative Synagogues and their Members,* ed. by Jack Wertheimer (New Brunswick, N.J.: Rutgers University Press, 2000), 1.
2. Isa Aron, *Becoming a Congregation of Learners: Learning as a Key to Revitalizing Synagogue Life* (Woodstock, Vt.: Jewish Lights, 2000).
3. Noam Zion, Jo Milgrom, and Gary Tishkoff, *A Help Mate? The Art of Living Together in the Stories of Adam and Eve* (Jerusalem: Shalom Hartman Institute, 2000), 28.
4. Lawrence Kushner, *God Was In This Place and I, i Did Not Know* (Woodstock, Vt.: Jewish Lights, 1991), 75. I would like to thank Cheri Ellowitz for pointing me to Kushner's interpretation.
5. Michael Fullan, *Change Forces* (London: Falmer Press, 1993), 26.
6. Peter Senge, *The Fifth Discipline: The Art and Practice of the Learning Organization* (New York: Doubleday, 1990), 14.
7. See, for example, Thomas Hawkins, *The Learning Congregation* (Louisville, Ky.: Westminster John Knox Press, 1997).
8. I would like to thank Miriam Heller Stern for suggesting the term "capacity."

CHAPTER TWO

1. Numbers Rabah, *Naso* 11:2.
2. Babylonian Talmud, *Megilot* 31b.
3. Since there was no public schooling for children at the time, colonial synagogues offered secular as well as religious instruction for children whose families could not afford private tutors.
4. Abraham Karp, "Overview: The Synagogue in America," in *The American Synagogue: A Sanctuary Transformed,* ed. by Jack Wertheimer (Hanover, N.H.: University Press of New England, 1987), 2.
5. Quoted in Karp, ibid.
6. See Riv-Ellen Prell, *Prayer and Community: The Havurah in American Judaism* (Detroit: Wayne State University Press, 1989), 38–39. I would like to thank David Kaufman for framing these issues so succinctly in a personal communication.

7. David Kaufman, *Shul with a Pool: The "Synagogue-Center" in American Jewish History* (Waltham, Mass.: Brandeis University Press, 1999), 13.

8. Quoted in Kaufman, *Shul with A Pool,* 247.

9. Ibid., 2.

10. Herbert Gans, "Park Forest, Birth of a Jewish Community," *Commentary,* April 1951, 331.

11. Ibid., 335.

12. Samuel Heilman, *Portrait of American Jews* (Seattle: University of Washington Press, 1995), 28–29.

13. Ibid., 282. This observation was originally made by Marshall Sklare.

14. Ibid., 29.

15. Ibid.

16. Ibid., 30.

17. This is documented at length in Riv-Ellen Prell's *Prayer and Community.*

18. Sidney Schwarz, *Finding a Spiritual Home,* (San Francisco: Jossey-Bass, 2000), 39–40.

19. Ibid., 47–48.

20. Donald E. Miller and Arpi Misha Miller, "Understanding Generation X: Values, Politics and Religious Commitments," in *GenX Religion,* ed. by Richard W. Flory and Donald E. Miller (New York: Routledge, 2000), 3.

21. Ibid.

22. Data from the 1990 National Jewish Population Study show that although 66 percent claim to have been members of a synagogue at some point, only 45 percent were members at the time the survey was conducted. See Bernard Lazerwitz et. al. *Jewish Choices: American Jewish Denominationalism* (Albany: SUNY Press, 1998), 125.

23. This observation is not offered as a critique; there may be good reasons for limiting attendance at High Holiday services. Nonetheless, the juxtaposition of the membership cycle with the services that are most popular clearly exacerbates this "service center" orientation.

24. Steven M. Cohen and Arnold M. Eisen, *The Jew Within: Self, Family and Community in America* (Bloomington: Indiana University Press, 2000), 2.

25. Ibid., 205.

CHAPTER THREE

1. Gilbert Rendle, *Leading Change in the Congregation* (Bethesda, Md.: Alban Institute, 1998), 35–36.

2. Ibid., 36.

3. I would like to thank Rachel Adler for her wonderful teaching of this text, which made me realize its relevance to congregational leadership, and Miriam Heller Stern and Lynne Heller for pointing me to some interesting commentaries.

4. Joel Rosenberg, *King and Kin: Political Allegory in the Hebrew Bible* (Bloomington: Indiana University Press, 1986), 149.

5. I would like to thank Sue Huntting for this insight.

6. Emanuel Rackman, *Studies in Torah Judaism*. Cited in David Zisenwine and Karen Abramovitz, *The Sabbath: Time and Existence* (Tel Aviv: Everyman's University Publishing House, 1982).

7. Diane Schuster and Isa Aron, "Becoming a Learning Congregation," paper presented at the Conference on Research in Jewish Education, June 2000, New York, N.Y.

8. Rabbi Block told this story at a lecture at HUC–JIR, Los Angeles, in the fall of 1998.

9. For advice on how to plan and facilitate text study sessions that appeal to a variety of participants, see my chapter in *Becoming a Congregation of Learners* (Woodstock, Vt.: Jewish Lights, 2000).

10. Ibid., 77.

11. Riv-Ellen Prell, "Communities of Choice and Memory," in *Jews at the Center*, ed. by Jack Wertheimer (New Brunswick, N.J.: Rutgers University Press, 2000), 283.

12. Union of American Hebrew Congregations, *Go and Study: A Packet for Ongoing Text Study for Congregational Leaders*.

13. Sheryl Primakow, of Congregation Sinai of Milwaukee. Quoted in *Becoming a Congregation of Learners*, 190.

14. Dan Judson and Peter S. Levi, "*Kedusha*—Holiness, Separation, Dedication," in *Theological Terms in the Talmud*, ed. by Eugene Borowitz (New York: The Samek Institute at Hebrew Union College, 1998), 122.

15. Ronald Heifetz, *Leadership Without Easy Answers* (Cambridge, Mass.: Harvard University Press, 1994), 252–253.

16. Ibid., 258.

17. This brief summary barely scratches the surface of this important book.

18. Dennis Campbell, *Congregations as Learning Communities* (Bethesda, Md.: Alban Institute, 2000), chapter 3. Campbell's version of this exercise, derived from David Cooperrider of Western Reserve University, calls on members of the board or committee to conduct interviews with the entire congregation.

19. This exercise is adapted from a similar one that appeared in *Becoming a Congregation of Learners*, 152–153.

20. Riv-Ellen Prell, "Communities of Choice and Memory," 319.

21. Ibid., 321.

22. The exercise follows the pattern of inquiry first elaborated by John Dewey, who held that all thinking (and indeed all human activity) follows the same basic pattern: an indeterminate situation, followed by a definition of the problem, the generation of alternative solutions, and the evaluation of these alternatives as a prelude to selecting the one that feels best. The exercise takes a group through each of these stages. My thanks to Sara Lee for helping me formulate and refine this exercise.

23. See Alice Mann, *The In-Between Church: Navigating Size Transitions in Congregations* (Bethesda, Md.: Alban Institute, 1998).

24. Edgar Schein, *The Corporate Culture Survival Guide* (San Francisco: Jossey-Bass, 1999), 131.

25. See *Becoming a Congregation of Learners* for suggestions about who to put on the task force.

26. See especially the case studies in Donna Muncey and Patrick McQuillan, *Reform and Resistance in Schools and Classrooms* (New Haven: Yale University Press, 1996).

27. For more on this, see *Becoming a Congregation of Learners,* 95–99.

28. *Temple Sinai Governance Study,* unpublished document, January 14, 2002.

29. Paul Wilkes, *And They Shall Be My People* (New York: Atlantic Monthly Press, 1994), 336.

30. Prell, "Communities of Choice and Memory," 315.

31. For a discussion of the effects of this initiative on the congregation, see ibid., 314–315.

CHAPTER FOUR

1. A synagogue in which the rabbi serves as a halakhic authority might have a more collaborative leadership structure for non-halakhic decisions, related to its administration and budget, but the rabbi's role as the *mara d'atra* tends to extend to these other realms as well.

2. George Parsons and Spead Leas, *Understanding Your Congregation as a System* (Bethesda, Md.: Alban Institute, 1993), 32.

3. Ibid.

4. Sidney Schwarz, *Finding a Spiritual Home* (San Francisco: Jossey-Bass, 2000), 243.

5. Edwin Friedman, *Generation to Generation: Family Process in Church and Synagogue* (New York: Guilford Press, 1985), 226.

6. David Teutsch, "The Rabbinic Role in Organizational Decision-Making," in *The Director Had a Heart Attack and the President Resigned: Board-Staff Relations for the 21st Century,* ed. by Gerald Bubis (Jerusalem Center for Public Affairs, 1999), 166.

7. Ibid.

8. Ronald Heifetz, *Leadership Without Easy Answers* (Cambridge, Mass.: Harvard University Press, 1994), 268.

9. Anthony DiBella and Edwin Nevis, *How Organizations Learn* (San Francisco: Jossey-Bass, 1998), 75.

10. David Conley and Paul Goldman, "Ten Propositions for Facilitative Leadership," in *Reshaping the Principalship,* ed. by Joseph Murphy and Karen Seashore Louis (Thousand Oaks, Calif.: Corwin Press, 1994).

11. Linda Lambert et al., *The Constructivist Leader* (New York: Teachers College Press, 1995).

12. Heifetz, *Leadership.*

13. Ibid., 20.

14. Drath and Palus, 13.

15. Ibid., 15.

16. Ibid., 18.

17. This quotation is taken from a transcript of a presentation by Rabbi David Stern at the 1999 Biennial of the Union of American Hebrew Congregations in Boston (11–12).

18. Interview with Felicia Sol, July 3, 2001, 3.

19. Tamara Cohn Eskenazi, *In an Age of Prose: A Literary Approach to Ezra-Nehemiah* (Atlanta: Scholars Press, 1988), 137.

20. Ibid., 138. See, for example, Ezra's handling of the issue of mixed marriage (Ez 9:1–15) and the fact that he lets the people discover the commandments for themselves through their own reading of the Torah (Neh 8: 8–16).

21. Because history records two kings named Artaxerxes, but the Bible does not indicate whether the monarch in question was first or second, it is impossible to know precisely whether Ezra's arrival predated Nehemiah's, or the other way around.

22. Ibid., 142.

23. Eugene Borowitz, "Tzimtzum: A Mystic Model for Contemporary Leadership." Reprinted in *What We Know About Jewish Education,* ed. by Stuart Kelman (Los Angeles: Torah Aura, 1992), 334.

24. Ibid., 337.

25. David Stern transcript, 10.

26. Sam Leonard, "The Spirit Is A-Movin': Helping Worshipers Find their Voice," *Congregations* 27 (July/August 2001), 15.

27. See, for example, Gaylord Noyce, *Church Meetings that Work* (Bethesda, Md.: Alban Institute, 1994), which contains many additional references.

28. David Stern presentation, 14.

29. Laura Samuels and Isa Aron, "Shared Leadership in a Congregational Change Effort," Jewish Education 65 (Summer 1999), 29.

30. See for example, Burt Nanus, *Visionary Leadership* (San Francisco: Jossey-Bass, 1992) and Michael Fullan, *Change Forces* (Bristol, Pa.: Taylor and Francis, 1993).

31. Sidney Schwarz, *Finding a Spiritual Home* (San Francisco: Jossey-Bass, 2000).

32. Lawrence A. Hoffman, *The Art of Public Prayer: Not for Clergy Only* (Woodstock, Vt.: SkyLight Paths, 1999), 251.

33. This quotation is taken from a transcript of a presentation by Congregation President Suzi Greenman at the 1999 Biennial of the Union of American Hebrew Congregations in Boston, 7.

34. This technique was originally described in J. R. Galbraith, *Organization Design* (Reading, Mass.: Addison-Wesley, 1977).

35. Riv-Ellen Prell, "Communities of Choice and Memory," in *Jews at the Center,* ed. by Jack Wertheimer (New Brunswick, N.J.: Rutgers University Press, 2000), 276.

36. Ibid., 277.

37. Samuels and Aron, "Shared Leadership," 40.

38. Ibid.

39. B. W. Tuckman and M. A. C. Jensen. "Stages of Small Group Development Revisited." *Group and Organizational Studies* 2 (1977): 419–427.

40. Linda Lambert, "Toward a Theory of Constructivist Leadership," in Lambert, *The Constructivist Leader,* 37–38.

41. Samuels and Aron, "Shared Leadership," 39.

42. Anita Farber-Robinson, *Learning While Leading* (Bethesda, Md.: Alban Institute, 2000), 40–41.

43. Farber Robinson, *Learning While Leading* and chapter 5 of Gaylord Noyce, *Church Meetings that Work*.

44. B.W. Tuckman and M. A. C. Jensen, "Stages of Small Group Development Revisited," *Group and Organizational Studies* 2 (1977), 419–427.

45. Parsons and Leas, *Understanding Your Congregation,* 106.

46. Ibid.

CHAPTER FIVE

1. Robert Wuthnow, *Sharing the Journey: Support Groups and America's New Quest for Community* (New York: The Free Press, 1994), 35.

2. Barry Schwartz, "Forming a New Congregation: The Uneasy Tension Between Freedom and Community," *The Reconstructionist* 60 (Spring, 1995): 55.

3. Ibid.

4. John Westerhoff, *Will Our Children Have Faith?*

5. Lawrence Kushner, "Arbitrarily Small Synagogues or Sacred Commons," *Sh'ma* 30 (September, 1999): 11.

6. Penny Edgell Becker, *Congregations in Conflict: Cultural Models of Local Religious Life* (Cambridge: Cambridge University Press, 1999), 85.

7. Ibid., 94–95.

8. Schwartz, "Forming a New Congregation," 55.

9. Riv-Ellen Prell, "Communities of Choice and Memory," in *Jews at the Center,* ed. by Jack Wertheimer (New Brunswick, N.J.: Rutgers University Press, 2000), 291–293.

10. Herbert Gans, "Park Forest, Birth of a Jewish Community," *Commentary,* April 1951.

11. Mordecai Kaplan, *Judaism as a Civilization* (Philadelphia: Jewish Publication Society, 1981), 195.

12. This version is told in Sheryl Lewart Stewart, "An Outreach Vision," *The Reconstructionist,* 60 (Spring, 1995): 22.

13. Steven Cohen and Arnold Eisen, *The Jew Within: Self, Family and Community in America* (Bloomington: Indiana University Press, 2000), 179.

14. Ibid., 179–180.

15. Jeffrey Summit, *The Lord's Song in a Strange Land: Music and Identity in Contemporary Jewish Worship* (Oxford: Oxford University Press, 2000), 59.

16. Ibid., 147.

17. James Wind, "The Main Thing: Finding Diversity and Joy in 'the Work of the People,'" *Congregations,* July/August, 2001, 17.

18. Samuel Heilman, "Holding Firmly with an Open Hand: Life in Two Conservative Synagogues," in *Jews at the Center,* ed. by Jack Wertheimer (New Brunswick, N.J.: Rutgers University Press, 2000), 182.

19. Ibid., 186.

20. Ibid.

21. Joseph Reimer, *Succeeding at Jewish Education* (Philadelphia: Jewish Publication Society, 1997), 49.

22. B. Becker, *Congregations in Conflict,* 112.

23. Taken from an article in Temple Emanuel's Bulletin, *Temple Topics* January, 2002.

24. Ibid.

25. Robert Wuthnow, *Sharing the Journey,* 34.

26. Research conducted in 1975 by The Center For Jewish Community Studies found that only 95 congregations (20 percent of those surveyed) had created *havurot* but that these congregations had, between them, a total of 376 *havurot.* See Daniel Elazar, Rela Geffen Monson, and Gerald Bubis, "The Synagogue *Havurah:* An Experiment in Restoring Adult Fellowship to the Jewish Community," in *Growing Jews: Selected Writings* by Professor Gerald Bubis, ed. by Michelle Wolf with Ellen Rabin (Cincinnati: Hebrew Union College, 2001), 122. We know little of how synagogue *havurot* have changed in the two decades that have elapsed since the Bubis and Wasserman study. While many *havurot* created in the 1970s remain alive and well today, and while new *havurot* continue to be formed, we can only speculate on how *havurot* conduct themselves and the ways in which they contribute to a synagogue-wide sense of community.

27. Fred Rosenbaum, *Visions of Reform: Congregation Emanu-El and the Jews of San Francisco 1849–1999* (Berkeley, Calif.: Magnes Museum, 2000), 411.

28. Gerald Bubis and Harry Wasserman, *Synagogue Havurot: A Comparative Study* (Washington, D.C.: University Press of America, 1983), 51.

29. Becker, *Congregations in Conflict,* 57.

30. Ibid., 83.

31. Ibid., 113.

32. Ibid., 124.

33. Tim Lucas and Bryan Smith, "Community Vision Meetings," in *Schools That Learn: A Fifth Discipline Fieldbook for Educators, Parents, and Everyone who Cares about Education,* ed. by Peter Senge, et al. (New York: Doubleday, 2000), 297–299.

34. Barry Holtz, "Why Be Jewish?" (New York: American Jewish Committee, 1993).

35. Rebecca Alpert and Jacob Staub, *Exploring Judaism: A Reconstructionist Approach* (Elkins Park, Pa.: Reconstructionist Press, 2000), excerpts from 12–14.

36. Arthur Green, *Restoring the Aleph: Judaism for the Contemporary Seeker* (New York: Council for Initiatives in Jewish Education, 1995), excerpts from 5–6 and 14–15.

37. Albert Vorspan and Eugene Lipman, *Justice and Judaism* (New York: Union of American Hebrew Congregations, 1959), excerpts from 6 and 9.

38. Michael Rosenak, *Teaching Jewish Values* (Jerusalem: Melton Center for Jewish Education).

39. Joel Grishaver, *Learning Torah* (New York: UAHC Press, 1990), 11.

40. Samuel Freedman, *Jew vs. Jew* (New York: Simon and Schuster, 2000). The case in question is discussed in chapter 3, 124–161.

41. Reimer, *Succeeding at Jewish Education,* 64.

42. Ibid., 64–65.

43. Jeffrey Summit, *The Lord's Song in a Strange Land: Music and Identity in Contemporary Jewish Worship* (Oxford University Press, 2000). These excerpts are from 19, 20, 33, and 147.

44. Benjie-Ellen Schiller, "The Many Faces of Jewish Sacred Music," unpublished paper in the Synagogue 2000 prayer curriculum, 8–19.

45. Ibid.

46. Ibid., 8–20.

47. Ibid.

48. Ibid.

49. Ibid.

50. The translation of these passages is taken from *The Jewish Political Tradition*, Volume 1, edited by Michael Walzer, et al. (New Haven: Yale University Press, 2000), 390–391.

51. Ituray Torah, Vol. IV. Cited in Lawrence Kushner and Kerry Olitzky, *Sparks Beneath the Surface* (Northvale, N.J.: Jason Aronson, 1994), 109–110.

CHAPTER SIX

1. Lawrence Hoffman, "Beyond the Cat Stand," *Reform Judaism* (Winter, 1990), 26.

2. Jeffrey Summit, *The Lord's Song in a Strange Land: Music and Identity in Contemporary Jewish Worship* (Oxford University Press, 2000), 33.

3. Ibid. For a further explanation of this point, see chapter 5 Handout 3, on pages 173–174.

4. See Larry Cuban, "Changing Public Schools and Changing Congregational Schools," in *A Congregation of Learners,* ed. by Isa Aron et al., (New York: UAHC Press, 1995); and Robert Evans, *The Human Side of School Change* (San Francisco: Jossey-Bass, 1996).

5. David Nadler, et al., *Discontinuous Change* (San Francisco: Jossey-Bass, 1995).

6. This translation is from volume 5 of *My People's Prayerbook,* edited by Lawrence Hoffman (Woodstock, Vt.: Jewish Lights, 2001), 109–110.

7. Lee Bolman and Terrence Deal, *Reframing Organizations* (San Francisco: Jossey-Bass, 1991), 26.

8. See chapter 4, pages 99–102, for an example of how one congregation consolidated its committee structure.

9. See Riv-Ellen Prell, "Communities of Choice and Memory," in *Jews at the Center,* ed. by Jack Wertheimer (New Brunswick, N.J.: Rutgers University Press, 2000) for a discussion of how one synagogue, Congregation Beth El of Minneapolis, helped its congregants celebrate Shabbat; this initiative is referred to, briefly, in chapter 3.

10. The one large-scale evaluation of what is learned in congregational schools, conducted by the New York Board of Jewish Education study, is seriously flawed because it treated cross-sectional data as longitudinal [Board of Jewish Education of Greater New York, *Jewish Supplementary Schooling: A System in Need of Change* (New York: BJE, 1988)]. Only anecdotal evidence of achievement was used to select the schools profiled in The Council for Initiatives' Best Practices project

[Barry Holtz, "Best Practices Project: The Supplementary School" (Cleveland: Council for Initiatives in Jewish Education, 1993)].

11. Mordecai Kaplan and Bernard Cronson, "A Survey of Jewish Education in New York City" in *Jewish Education in the United States: A Documentary History,* ed. by Lloyd Gartner (New York: Teachers College Press, 1909/1969). At the time there were no day schools, but much of Jewish education took place under communal or private auspices. Congregational schooling became the norm after World War II, when Jews moved to suburbs; even today, communal *talmud torahs* remain, though they usually operate in close cooperation with congregations.

12. For more information on these early reforms, see the documents collected in Lloyd Gartner, ed., *Jewish Education in the United States: A Documentary History* (New York: Teachers College Press, 1969).

13. For more information on these efforts, see Isa Aron, "From the Congregational School to the Learning Congregation: Are We Ready for a Paradigm Shift?" in *A Congregation of Learners,* ed. by I. Aron, et al. (New York: UAHC Press, 1995).

14. For a discussion of these curricula, see Ruth Zeilenziger, "The Melton Curriculum and the Melton Hebrew Language Program for Afternoon Hebrew Schools" in *Studies in Jewish Education,* vol. 3, ed. by Janet Aviad (Jerusalem: Magnes Press, 1989) and Joseph Reimer, "Temple Akiba," in *Best Practices Project: The Supplementary School,* ed. by Barry Holtz (Cleveland: Council for Initiatives in Jewish Education, 1993).

15. This point was made most forcefully in three different studies: David Schoem, *Ethnic Survival in America: An Ethnography of a Jewish Afternoon School* (Atlanta: Scholar's Press, 1989); Susan Shevitz, "Communal Responses to the Teacher Shortage in the North American Supplementary School," in *Studies in Jewish Education,* vol. 3, ed. by Janet Aviad (Jerusalem: Magnes Press, 1988); and Joseph Reimer, "The Synagogue as a Context for Jewish Education" (Cleveland: Commission on Jewish Education in North America, 1990).

16. Board of Jewish Education of Greater New York, *Jewish Supplementary Schooling: A System in Need of Change* (New York: BJE, 1988).

17. See Amy Sales, et al., *Sh'arim: Building Gateways to Jewish Life and Communities* (Boston: Commission on Jewish Continuity, 2000); and Joel Streicker, *Program Development and Synagogue Growth: An Assessment of the Koret Synagogue Initiative* (Waltham, Mass.: Brandeis University, 1997).

18. Susan Shevitz and Debbie Karpel, *Sh'arim Family Educator Initiative: An Interim Report of Programs and Populations* (Boston: Bureau of Jewish Education of Greater Boston, 1995).

19. For more information on this model and others, see *Sh'ma* 38/589, March 2002, and the web site of the Experiment in Congregational Education (www.eceonline.edu).

20. Marc Margolius and Cyd Weissman, "Creating a Shabbat-Centered Community," in *Sh'ma,* March 2002, 8.

21. Ibid.

22. The general principles embedded in this formula derive from Richard Beckhard

and Reuben T. Harris, *Organizational Transitions: Managing Complex Change* (Reading, Mass.: Addison-Wesley, 1987).

23. Sidney Schwarz, *Finding a Spiritual Home* (San Francisco: Jossey-Bass, 2000).

24. Peter Senge, *The Fifth Discipline: The Art and Practice of the Learning Organization* (New York: Doubleday, 1990), 150.

25. These are explored more fully in chapter 9 of Isa Aron, *Becoming a Congregation of Learners* (Woodstock, Vt.: Jewish Lights, 2000).

26. This is a fictional name (literally, the hose of inertia) for a composite fictional congregation—a composite portrait based on my observations of many disappointing change efforts.

27. See chapter 4, p. 16, for a more in-depth explanation of what a worship care committee is, and how it functions at Temple Emanuel.

28. Michael Fullan, *Change Forces* (London: Falmer Press, 1993), 22.

29. L. Smith and P. Keith, *Anatomy of an Educational Innovation* (New York: Wiley, 1971).

30. Bolman and Deal, *Reframing Organizations.*

31. William Bridges, *Managing Transitions: Making the Most of Change* (Reading, Mass.: Addison-Wesley, 1991), 3–5.

32. Ibid., 377.

33. This example was given to me by Susan Shevitz.

34. Joseph Reimer, *Succeeding at Jewish Education* (Philadelphia: Jewish Publication Society, 1997), 133–161.

35. Ibid., 145.

36. Ibid.

37. Ibid., 160.

38. Pamela Grossman, et al. "Toward a Theory of Teacher Community," Teachers College Record 103 (2001): 952.

CHAPTER SEVEN

1. For more on this, see the vignette written by Laura Geller in *Becoming a Congregation of Learners* (Woodstock, Vt.: Jewish Lights, 2000), 66–69.

About JEWISH LIGHTS Publishing

People of all faiths and backgrounds yearn for books that attract, engage, educate, and spiritually inspire.

Our principal goal is to stimulate thought and help all people learn about who the Jewish People are, where they come from, and what the future can be made to hold. While people of our diverse Jewish heritage are the primary audience, our books speak to people in the Christian world as well and will broaden their understanding of Judaism and the roots of their own faith.

We bring to you authors who are at the forefront of spiritual thought and experience. While each has something different to say, they all say it in a voice that you can hear.

Our books are designed to welcome you and then to engage, stimulate, and inspire. We judge our success not only by whether or not our books are beautiful and commercially successful, but by whether or not they make a difference in your life.

We at Jewish Lights take great care to produce beautiful books that present meaningful spiritual content in a form that reflects the art of making high quality books. Therefore, we want to acknowledge those who contributed to the production of this book.

Stuart M. Matlins, Publisher

PRODUCTION
Sara Dismukes, Tim Holtz,
Martha McKinney & Bridgett Taylor

EDITORIAL
Rebecca Castellano, Amanda Dupuis, Polly Short Mahoney,
Lauren Seidman & Emily Wichland

COVER DESIGN
Lisa Buckley, San Francisco, California

TEXT DESIGN
Chelsea Cloeter, Chelsea Designs, Tucson, Arizona

COVER / TEXT PRINTING & BINDING
Transcontinental Printing, Louisville, Quebec

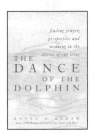 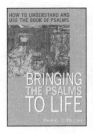   

Spirituality/Jewish Meditation

Aleph-Bet Yoga
Embodying the Hebrew Letters for Physical and Spiritual Well-Being
by *Steven A. Rapp*; Foreword by *Tamar Frankiel* & *Judy Greenfeld*; Preface by *Hart Lazer*

Blends aspects of hatha yoga and the shapes of the Hebrew letters. Connects yoga practice with Jewish spiritual life. Easy-to-follow instructions, b/w photos.
7 x 10, 128 pp, Quality PB, b/w photos, ISBN 1-58023-162-4 **$16.95**

The Rituals & Practices of a Jewish Life
A Handbook for Personal Spiritual Renewal
by *Rabbi Kerry M. Olitzky* and *Rabbi Daniel Judson*; Foreword by *Vanessa L. Ochs*; Illustrated by *Joel Moskowitz*

This easy-to-use handbook explains the why, what, and how of ten specific areas of Jewish ritual and practice: morning and evening blessings, covering the head, blessings throughout the day, daily prayer, tefillin, tallit and *tallit katan*, Torah study, kashrut, *mikvah*, and entering Shabbat.
6 x 9, 272 pp, Quality PB, Illus., ISBN 1-58023-169-1 **$18.95**

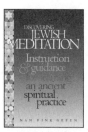 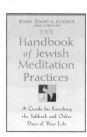   

Discovering Jewish Meditation: *Instruction & Guidance for Learning an Ancient Spiritual Practice* by Nan Fink Gefen 6 x 9, 208 pp, Quality PB, ISBN 1-58023-067-9 **$16.95**

The Handbook of Jewish Meditation Practices: *A Guide for Enriching the Sabbath and Other Days of Your Life* by Rabbi David A. Cooper
6 x 9, 208 pp, Quality PB, ISBN 1-58023-102-0 **$16.95**

Meditation from the Heart of Judaism: *Today's Teachers Share Their Practices, Techniques, and Faith* Ed. by Avram Davis 6 x 9, 256 pp, Quality PB, ISBN 1-58023-049-0 **$16.95**

The Way of Flame: *A Guide to the Forgotten Mystical Tradition of Jewish Meditation* by Avram Davis 4½ x 8, 176 pp, Quality PB, ISBN 1-58023-060-1 **$15.95**

Minding the Temple of the Soul: *Balancing Body, Mind, and Spirit through Traditional Jewish Prayer, Movement, and Meditation* by Tamar Frankiel and Judy Greenfeld
7 x 10, 184 pp, Quality PB, Illus., ISBN 1-879045-64-8 **$16.95**

Entering the Temple of Dreams: *Jewish Prayers, Movements, and Meditations for the End of the Day* by Tamar Frankiel and Judy Greenfeld
7 x 10, 192 pp, Illus., Quality PB, ISBN 1-58023-079-2 **$16.95**

Spirituality—The Kushner Series
Books by Lawrence Kushner

The Way Into Jewish Mystical Tradition
Explains the principles of Jewish mystical thinking, their religious and spiritual significance, and how they relate to our lives. A book that allows us to experience and understand the Jewish mystical approach to our place in the world.
6 x 9, 224 pp, HC, ISBN 1-58023-029-6 **$21.95**

Jewish Spirituality: *A Brief Introduction for Christians*
Addresses Christian's questions, revealing the essence of Judaism in a way that people whose own tradition traces its roots to Judaism can understand and appreciate.
5½ x 8½, 112 pp, Quality PB, ISBN 1-58023-150-0 **$12.95**

Eyes Remade for Wonder: *The Way of Jewish Mysticism and Sacred Living*
A Lawrence Kushner Reader Intro. by *Thomas Moore*

Whether you are new to Kushner or a devoted fan, you'll find inspiration here. With samplings from each of Kushner's works, and a generous amount of new material, this book is to be read and reread, each time discovering deeper layers of meaning in our lives.
6 x 9, 240 pp, Quality PB, ISBN 1-58023-042-3 **$18.95**; HC, ISBN 1-58023-014-8 **$23.95**

   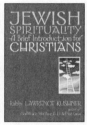 

Invisible Lines of Connection: *Sacred Stories of the Ordinary* **AWARD WINNER!**
5½ x 8½, 160 pp, Quality PB, ISBN 1-879045-98-2 **$15.95**

Honey from the Rock: *An Introduction to Jewish Mysticism* SPECIAL ANNIVERSARY EDITION
6 x 9, 176 pp, Quality PB, ISBN 1-58023-073-3 **$15.95**

The Book of Letters: *A Mystical Hebrew Alphabet* **AWARD WINNER!**
Popular HC Edition, 6 x 9, 80 pp, 2-color text, ISBN 1-879045-00-1 **$24.95**; *Deluxe Gift Edition*, 9 x 12, 80 pp, HC, 4-color text, ornamentation, slipcase, ISBN 1-879045-01-X **$79.95**; *Collector's Limited Edition*, 9 x 12, 80 pp, HC, gold-embossed pages, hand-assembled slipcase. With silkscreened print. Limited to 500 signed and numbered copies, ISBN 1-879045-04-4 **$349.00**

The Book of Words: *Talking Spiritual Life, Living Spiritual Talk* **AWARD WINNER!**
6 x 9, 160 pp, Quality PB, 2-color text, ISBN 1-58023-020-2 **$16.95**; HC, ISBN 1-879045-35-4 **$21.95**

God Was in This Place & I, i Did Not Know: *Finding Self, Spirituality and Ultimate Meaning*
6 x 9, 192 pp, Quality PB, ISBN 1-879045-33-8 **$16.95**

The River of Light: *Jewish Mystical Awareness* SPECIAL ANNIVERSARY EDITION
6 x 9, 192 pp, Quality PB, ISBN 1-58023-096-2 **$16.95**

Because Nothing Looks Like God
by Lawrence and Karen Kushner; Full-color illus. by Dawn W. Majewski
11 x 8½, 32 pp, HC, Full-color illus., ISBN 1-58023-092-X **$16.95** For ages 4 & up

Healing/Wellness/Recovery

Jewish Paths toward Healing and Wholeness
A Personal Guide to Dealing with Suffering
by *Rabbi Kerry M. Olitzky*; Foreword by *Debbie Friedman*

Why me? Why do we suffer? How can we heal? Grounded in personal experience with illness and Jewish spiritual traditions, this book provides healing rituals, psalms and prayers that help readers initiate a dialogue with God, to guide them along the complicated path of healing and wholeness. 6 x 9, 192 pp, Quality PB, ISBN 1-58023-068-7 **$15.95**

Healing of Soul, Healing of Body
Spiritual Leaders Unfold the Strength & Solace in Psalms
Ed. by *Rabbi Simkha Y. Weintraub, CSW*, for The National Center for Jewish Healing

For those who are facing illness and those who care for them. Inspiring commentaries on ten psalms for healing by eminent spiritual leaders reflecting all Jewish movements make the power of the psalms accessible to all.
6 x 9, 128 pp, Quality PB, Illus., 2-color text, ISBN 1-879045-31-1 **$14.95**

Jewish Pastoral Care
A Practical Handbook from Traditional and Contemporary Sources
Ed. by *Rabbi Dayle A. Friedman*

Gives today's Jewish pastoral counselors practical guidelines based in the Jewish tradition.
6 x 9, 464 pp, HC, ISBN 1-58023-078-4 **$35.00**

 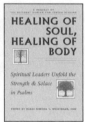   

Twelve Jewish Steps to Recovery: *A Personal Guide to Turning from Alcoholism & Other Addictions . . . Drugs, Food, Gambling, Sex . . .* by Rabbi Kerry M. Olitzky & Stuart A. Copans, M.D. Preface by Abraham J. Twerski, M.D.; "Getting Help" by JACS Foundation 6 x 9, 144 pp, Quality PB, ISBN 1-879045-09-5 **$13.95**

One Hundred Blessings Every Day: *Daily Twelve Step Recovery Affirmations, Exercises for Personal Growth & Renewal Reflecting Seasons of the Jewish Year*
by Rabbi Kerry M. Olitzky 4½ x 6½, 432 pp, Quality PB, ISBN 1-879045-30-3 **$14.95**

Recovery from Codependence: *A Jewish Twelve Steps Guide to Healing Your Soul*
by Rabbi Kerry M. Olitzky 6 x 9, 160 pp, Quality PB, ISBN 1-879045-32-X **$13.95**

Renewed Each Day: *Daily Twelve Step Recovery Meditations Based on the Bible*
by Rabbi Kerry M. Olitzky & Aaron Z. *Vol. I: Genesis & Exodus; Vol. II: Leviticus, Numbers and Deuteronomy*
Vol. I: 6 x 9, 224 pp, Quality PB, ISBN 1-879045-12-5 **$14.95**
Vol. II: 6 x 9, 280 pp, Quality PB, ISBN 1-879045-13-3 **$14.95**

Life Cycle/Grief/Divorce

Divorce Is a Mitzvah: *A Practical Guide to Finding Wholeness and Holiness When Your Marriage Dies*
by *Rabbi Perry Netter;*
Afterword—"Afterwards: New Jewish Divorce Rituals"—by *Rabbi Laura Geller*

What does Judaism tell you about divorce? This first-of-its-kind handbook provides practical wisdom from biblical and rabbinic teachings and modern psychological research, as well as information and strength from a Jewish perspective for those experiencing the challenging life-transition of divorce. 6 x 9, 224 pp, Quality PB, ISBN 1-58023-172-1 **$16.95**

Against the Dying of the Light
A Parent's Story of Love, Loss and Hope
by *Leonard Fein*

The sudden death of a child. A personal tragedy beyond description. Rage and despair deeper than sorrow. What can come from it? Raw wisdom and defiant hope. In this unusual exploration of heartbreak and healing, Fein chronicles the sudden death of his 30-year-old daughter and reveals what the progression of grief can teach each one of us.
5½ x 8½, 176 pp, HC, ISBN 1-58023-110-1 **$19.95**

Mourning & Mitzvah, 2nd Ed.: *A Guided Journal for Walking the Mourner's Path through Grief to Healing* with *Over 60 Guided Exercises*
by *Anne Brener, L.C.S.W.*

For those who mourn a death, for those who would help them, for those who face a loss of any kind, Brener teaches us the power and strength available to us in the fully experienced mourning process. Revised and expanded. 7½ x 9, 304 pp, Quality PB, ISBN 1-58023-113-6 **$19.95**

Grief in Our Seasons: *A Mourner's Kaddish Companion*
by *Rabbi Kerry M. Olitzky*

A wise and inspiring selection of sacred Jewish writings and a simple, powerful ancient ritual for mourners to read each day, to help hold the memory of their loved ones in their hearts. Offers a comforting, step-by-step daily link to saying Kaddish.
4½ x 6½, 448 pp, Quality PB, ISBN 1-879045-55-9 **$15.95**

Tears of Sorrow, Seeds of Hope
A Jewish Spiritual Companion for Infertility and Pregnancy Loss
by Rabbi Nina Beth Cardin   6 x 9, 192 pp, HC, ISBN 1-58023-017-2 **$19.95**

A Time to Mourn, A Time to Comfort
A Guide to Jewish Bereavement and Comfort
by Dr. Ron Wolfson 7 x 9, 336 pp, Quality PB, ISBN 1-879045-96-6 **$18.95**

When a Grandparent Dies
A Kid's Own Remembering Workbook for Dealing with Shiva and the Year Beyond
by Nechama Liss-Levinson, Ph.D.
8 x 10, 48 pp, HC, Illus., 2-color text, ISBN 1-879045-44-3 **$15.95**   **For ages 7–13**

Life Cycle & Holidays

The Jewish Family Fun Book: *Holiday Projects, Everyday Activities, and Travel Ideas with Jewish Themes*
by *Danielle Dardashti* & *Roni Sarig;* Illustrated by *Avi Katz*

With almost 100 easy-to-do activities to re-invigorate age-old Jewish customs and make them fun for the whole family, this complete sourcebook details activities for fun at home and away from home, including meaningful everyday and holiday crafts, recipes, travel guides, enriching entertainment and much, much more. Illustrated.
6 x 9, 288 pp, Quality PB, Illus., ISBN 1-58023-171-3 **$18.95**

The Book of Jewish Sacred Practices
CLAL's Guide to Everyday & Holiday Rituals & Blessings
Ed. by *Rabbi Irwin Kula* & *Vanessa L. Ochs, Ph.D.*

A meditation, blessing, profound Jewish teaching, and ritual for more than one hundred everyday events and holidays. 6 x 9, 368 pp, Quality PB, ISBN 1-58023-152-7 **$18.95**

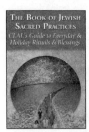    

Celebrating Your New Jewish Daughter: *Creating Jewish Ways to Welcome Baby Girls into the Covenant—New and Traditional Ceremonies*
by Debra Nussbaum Cohen; Foreword by Rabbi Sandy Eisenberg Sasso
6 x 9, 272 pp, Quality PB, ISBN 1-58023-090-3 **$18.95**

The New Jewish Baby Book AWARD WINNER!
Names, Ceremonies & Customs—A Guide for Today's Families
by Anita Diamant 6 x 9, 336 pp, Quality PB, ISBN 1-879045-28-1 **$18.95**

Parenting As a Spiritual Journey
Deepening Ordinary & Extraordinary Events into Sacred Occasions
by Rabbi Nancy Fuchs-Kreimer 6 x 9, 224 pp, Quality PB, ISBN 1-58023-016-4 **$16.95**

Putting God on the Guest List, 2nd Ed. AWARD WINNER!
How to Reclaim the Spiritual Meaning of Your Child's Bar or Bat Mitzvah
by Rabbi Jeffrey K. Salkin 6 x 9, 224 pp, Quality PB, ISBN 1-879045-59-1 **$16.95**

The Bar/Bat Mitzvah Memory Book: *An Album for Treasuring the Spiritual Celebration* by Rabbi Jeffrey K. Salkin and Nina Salkin
8 x 10, 48 pp, Deluxe HC, 2-color text, ribbon marker, ISBN 1-58023-111-X **$19.95**

For Kids—Putting God on Your Guest List
How to Claim the Spiritual Meaning of Your Bar or Bat Mitzvah
by Rabbi Jeffrey K. Salkin 6 x 9, 144 pp, Quality PB, ISBN 1-58023-015-6 **$14.95**

Bar/Bat Mitzvah Basics, 2nd Ed.: *A Practical Family Guide to Coming of Age Together*
Ed. by Cantor Helen Leneman 6 x 9, 240 pp, Quality PB, ISBN 1-58023-151-9 **$18.95**

Hanukkah, 2nd Ed.: *The Family Guide to Spiritual Celebration*—The Art of Jewish Living
by Dr. Ron Wolfson 7 x 9, 240 pp, Quality PB, Illus., ISBN 1-58023-122-5 **$18.95**

Shabbat, 2nd Ed.: *Preparing for and Celebrating the Sabbath*—The Art of Jewish Living
by Dr. Ron Wolfson 7 x 9, 320 pp, Quality PB, Illus., ISBN 1-58023-164-0 **$19.95**

The Passover Seder—The Art of Jewish Living
by Dr. Ron Wolfson 7 x 9, 352 pp, Quality PB, Illus., ISBN 1-879045-93-1 **$16.95**

Children's Spirituality

Cain & Abel AWARD WINNER!
Finding the Fruits of Peace
by *Sandy Eisenberg Sasso*
Full-color illus. by *Joani Keller Rothenberg*

For ages 5 & up

A sensitive recasting of the ancient tale shows we have the power to deal with anger in positive ways. Provides questions for kids and adults to explore together. "Editor's Choice"—American Library Association's *Booklist*

9 x 12, 32 pp, HC, Full-color illus., ISBN 1-58023-123-3 **$16.95**

For Heaven's Sake AWARD WINNER!

For ages 4 & up

by *Sandy Eisenberg Sasso*; Full-color illus. by *Kathryn Kunz Finney*
Everyone talked about heaven, but no one would say what heaven was or how to find it. So Isaiah decides to find out. 9 x 12, 32 pp, HC, Full-color illus., ISBN 1-58023-054-7 **$16.95**

God Said Amen AWARD WINNER!

For ages 4 & up

by *Sandy Eisenberg Sasso*; Full-color illus. by *Avi Katz*
Inspiring tale of two kingdoms: one overflowing with water but without oil to light its lamps; the other blessed with oil but no water to grow its gardens. The kingdoms' rulers ask God for help but are too stubborn to ask each other. Shows that we need only reach out to each other to find God's answer to our prayers. 9 x 12, 32 pp, HC, Full-color illus., ISBN 1-58023-080-6 **$16.95**

God in Between AWARD WINNER!

For ages 4 & up

by *Sandy Eisenberg Sasso*; Full-color illus. by *Sally Sweetland*
If you wanted to find God, where would you look? This magical, mythical tale teaches that God can be found where we are: within all of us and the relationships between us.
9 x 12, 32 pp, HC, Full-color illus., ISBN 1-879045-86-9 **$16.95**

A Prayer for the Earth: *The Story of Naamah, Noah's Wife*

For ages 4 & up

by *Sandy Eisenberg Sasso*; Full-color illus. by *Bethanne Andersen* AWARD WINNER!
Opens religious imaginations to new ideas about the story of the Flood. When God tells Noah to bring the animals onto the ark, God also calls on Naamah, Noah's wife, to save each plant on Earth. 9 x 12, 32 pp, HC, Full-color illus., ISBN 1-879045-60-5 **$16.95**

But God Remembered AWARD WINNER!
Stories of Women from Creation to the Promised Land

For ages 8 & up

by *Sandy Eisenberg Sasso*; Full-color illus. by *Bethanne Andersen*
Vibrantly brings to life four stories of courageous and strong women from ancient tradition; all teach important values through their actions and faith.
9 x 12, 32 pp, HC, Full-color illus., ISBN 1-879045-43-5 **$16.95**

Children's Spirituality

In Our Image
God's First Creatures Award Winner!
by *Nancy Sohn Swartz*
Full-color illus. by *Melanie Hall*

For ages 4 & up

A playful new twist on the Creation story—from the perspective of the animals. Celebrates the interconnectedness of nature and the harmony of all living things. "The vibrantly colored illustrations nearly leap off the page in this delightful interpretation." —*School Library Journal*
9 x 12, 32 pp, HC, Full-color illus., ISBN 1-879045-99-0 **$16.95**

God's Paintbrush Award Winner!

For ages 4 & up

by *Sandy Eisenberg Sasso*; Full-color illus. by *Annette Compton*
Invites children of all faiths and backgrounds to encounter God openly in their own lives. Wonderfully interactive; provides questions adult and child can explore together at the end of each episode. 11 x 8½, 32 pp, HC, Full-color illus., ISBN 1-879045-22-2 **$16.95**

Also available: **A Teacher's Guide: A Guide for Jewish & Christian Educators and Parents**
8½ x 11, 32 pp, PB, ISBN 1-879045-57-5 **$8.95**

God's Paintbrush Celebration Kit 9½ x 12, HC, Includes 5 sessions/40 full-color Activity Sheets and Teacher Folder with complete instructions, ISBN 1-58023-050-4 **$21.95**

In God's Name Award Winner!

For ages 4 & up

by *Sandy Eisenberg Sasso*; Full-color illus. by *Phoebe Stone*
Like an ancient myth in its poetic text and vibrant illustrations, this award-winning modern fable about the search for God's name celebrates the diversity and, at the same time, the unity of all people. 9 x 12, 32 pp, HC, Full-color illus., ISBN 1-879045-26-5 **$16.95**

What Is God's Name? (A Board Book)

For ages 0–4

An abridged board book version of award-winning *In God's Name*.
5 x 5, 24 pp, Board, Full-color illus., ISBN 1-893361-10-1 **$7.95** A SKYLIGHT PATHS Book

The 11th Commandment: *Wisdom from Our Children*

For all ages

by *The Children of America* Award Winner!
"If there were an Eleventh Commandment, what would it be?" Children of many religious denominations across America answer this question—in their own drawings and words. "A rare book of spiritual celebration for all people, of all ages, for all time."—*Bookviews*
8 x 10, 48 pp, HC, Full-color illus., ISBN 1-879045-46-X **$16.95**

Children's Spirituality

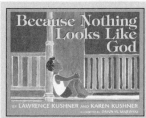

Because Nothing Looks Like God
by *Lawrence and Karen Kushner*
Full-color illus. by *Dawn W. Majewski*

For ages 4 & up

MULTICULTURAL, NONDENOMINATIONAL, NONSECTARIAN

What is God like? The first collaborative work by husband-and-wife team Lawrence and Karen Kushner introduces children to the possibilities of spiritual life. Real-life examples of happiness and sadness—from goodnight stories, to the hope and fear felt the first time at bat, to the closing moments of life—invite us to explore, together with our children, the questions we all have about God, no matter what our age.

11 x 8½, 32 pp, HC, Full-color illus., ISBN 1-58023-092-X **$16.95**

Also available: Teacher's Guide, 8½ x 11, 22 pp, PB, ISBN 1-58023-140-3 **$6.95** For ages 5–8

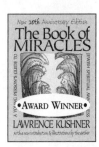

Where Is God?
What Does God Look Like?
How Does God Make Things Happen? (Board Books)

For ages 0–4

by *Lawrence and Karen Kushner*; Full-color illus. by *Dawn W. Majewski*

Gently invites children to become aware of God's presence all around them. Three board books abridged from *Because Nothing Looks Like God* by Lawrence and Karen Kushner.
Each 5 x 5, 24 pp, Board, Full-color illus. **$7.95** SKYLIGHT PATHS Books

Sharing Blessings
Children's Stories for Exploring the Spirit of the Jewish Holidays

For ages 6 & up

by *Rahel Musleah* and *Rabbi Michael Klayman*; Full-color illus.

What is the spiritual message of each of the Jewish holidays? How do we teach it to our children? Through stories about one family's life, *Sharing Blessings* explores ways to get into the *spirit* of thirteen different holidays.
8½ x 11, 64 pp, HC, Full-color illus., ISBN 1-879045-71-0 **$18.95**

The Book of Miracles AWARD WINNER!
A Young Person's Guide to Jewish Spiritual Awareness
by *Lawrence Kushner*

For ages 9 & up

Introduces kids to a way of everyday spiritual thinking to last a lifetime. Kushner, whose award-winning books have brought spirituality to life for countless adults, now shows young people how to use Judaism as a foundation on which to build their lives.
6 x 9, 96 pp, HC, 2-color illus., ISBN 1-879045-78-8 **$16.95**

Theology/Philosophy

Love and Terror in the God Encounter
The Theological Legacy of Rabbi Joseph B. Soloveitchik
by *Dr. David Hartman*

Renowned scholar David Hartman explores the sometimes surprising intersection of Soloveitchik's rootedness in halakhic tradition with his genuine responsiveness to modern Western theology. An engaging look at one of the most important Jewish thinkers of the twentieth century.
6 x 9, 240 pp, HC, ISBN 1-58023-112-8 **$25.00**

These Are the Words: *A Vocabulary of Jewish Spiritual Life*
by *Arthur Green*

What are the most essential ideas, concepts and terms that an educated person needs to know about Judaism? From *Adonai* (My Lord) to *zekhut* (merit), this enlightening and entertaining journey through Judaism teaches us the 149 core Hebrew words that constitute the basic vocabulary of Jewish spiritual life. 6 x 9, 304 pp, Quality PB, ISBN 1-58023-107-1 **$18.95**

Broken Tablets: *Restoring the Ten Commandments and Ourselves*
Ed. by *Rabbi Rachel S. Mikva*; Intro. by *Rabbi Lawrence Kushner* AWARD WINNER!

Twelve outstanding spiritual leaders each share profound and personal thoughts about these biblical commands and why they have such a special hold on us.
6 x 9, 192 pp, Quality PB, ISBN 1-58023-158-6 **$16.95**; HC, ISBN 1-58023-066-0 **$21.95**

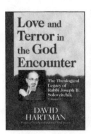 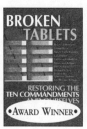 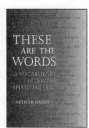 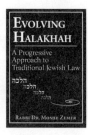 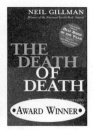

A Heart of Many Rooms: *Celebrating the Many Voices within Judaism* AWARD WINNER!
by Dr. David Hartman 6 x 9, 352 pp, Quality PB, ISBN 1-58023-156-X **$19.95**; HC, ISBN 1-58023-048-2 **$24.95**

A Living Covenant: *The Innovative Spirit in Traditional Judaism* AWARD WINNER!
by Dr. David Hartman 6 x 9, 368 pp, Quality PB, ISBN 1-58023-011-3 **$18.95**

Evolving Halakhah: *A Progressive Approach to Traditional Jewish Law*
by Rabbi Dr. Moshe Zemer 6 x 9, 480 pp, HC, ISBN 1-58023-002-4 **$40.00**

The Death of Death: *Resurrection and Immortality in Jewish Thought* AWARD WINNER!
by Dr. Neil Gillman 6 x 9, 336 pp, Quality PB, ISBN 1-58023-081-4 **$18.95**

The Last Trial: *On the Legends and Lore of the Command to Abraham to Offer Isaac as a Sacrifice* by Shalom Spiegel 6 x 9, 208 pp, Quality PB, ISBN 1-879045-29-X **$17.95**

Tormented Master: *The Life and Spiritual Quest of Rabbi Nahman of Bratslav*
by Dr. Arthur Green 6 x 9, 416 pp, Quality PB, ISBN 1-879045-11-7 **$18.95**

The Earth Is the Lord's: *The Inner World of the Jew in Eastern Europe*
by Abraham Joshua Heschel 5½ x 8, 128 pp, Quality PB, ISBN 1-879045-42-7 **$14.95**

A Passion for Truth: *Despair and Hope in Hasidism* by Abraham Joshua Heschel
5½ x 8, 352 pp, Quality PB, ISBN 1-879045-41-9 **$18.95**

Your Word Is Fire: *The Hasidic Masters on Contemplative Prayer* Ed. by Dr. Arthur Green and Dr. Barry W. Holtz 6 x 9, 160 pp, Quality PB, ISBN 1-879045-25-7 **$15.95**

Women's Spirituality

The Women's Torah Commentary: *New Insights from Women Rabbis on the 54 Weekly Torah Portions* Ed. by *Rabbi Elyse Goldstein*

For the first time, women rabbis provide a commentary on the entire Five Books of Moses. More than twenty-five years after the first woman was ordained a rabbi in America, these inspiring teachers bring their rich perspectives to bear on the biblical text. In a week-by-week format; a perfect gift for others, or for yourself. 6 x 9, 496 pp, HC, ISBN 1-58023-076-8 **$34.95**

Moonbeams: *A Hadassah Rosh Hodesh Guide*
Ed. by *Carol Diament, Ph.D.*

This hands-on "idea book" focuses on *Rosh Hodesh*, the festival of the new moon, as a source of spiritual growth for Jewish women. A complete sourcebook that will initiate or rejuvenate women's study groups, it is also perfect for women preparing for *bat mitzvah*, or for anyone interested in learning more about *Rosh Hodesh* observance and what it has to offer. 8½ x 11, 240 pp, Quality PB, ISBN 1-58023-099-7 **$20.00**

 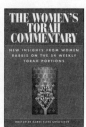   

Lifecycles In Two Volumes **AWARD WINNERS!**
V. 1: *Jewish Women on Life Passages & Personal Milestones*
Ed. and with Intros. by Rabbi Debra Orenstein
V. 2: *Jewish Women on Biblical Themes in Contemporary Life*
Ed. and with Intros. by Rabbi Debra Orenstein and Rabbi Jane Rachel Litman
V. 1: 6 x 9, 480 pp, Quality PB, ISBN 1-58023-018-0 **$19.95**
V. 2: 6 x 9, 464 pp, Quality PB, ISBN 1-58023-019-9 **$19.95**

ReVisions: *Seeing Torah through a Feminist Lens* **AWARD WINNER!**
by Rabbi Elyse Goldstein 5½ x 8½, 224 pp, Quality PB, ISBN 1-58023-117-9 **$16.95**;
208 pp, HC, ISBN 1-58023-047-4 **$19.95**

The Year Mom Got Religion: *One Woman's Midlife Journey into Judaism*
by Lee Meyerhoff Hendler 6 x 9, 208 pp, Quality PB, ISBN 1-58023-070-9 **$15.95**

Ecology

Torah of the Earth: *Exploring 4,000 Years of Ecology in Jewish Thought*
In 2 Volumes Ed. by *Rabbi Arthur Waskow*

An invaluable key to understanding the intersection of ecology and Judaism. Leading scholars provide a guided tour of Jewish ecological thought.
Vol. 1: *Biblical Israel & Rabbinic Judaism*, 6 x 9, 272 pp, Quality PB, ISBN 1-58023-086-5 **$19.95**
Vol. 2: *Zionism & Eco-Judaism*, 6 x 9, 336 pp, Quality PB, ISBN 1-58023-087-3 **$19.95**

Ecology & the Jewish Spirit: *Where Nature & the Sacred Meet* Ed. and with Intros.
by Ellen Bernstein 6 x 9, 288 pp, Quality PB, ISBN 1-58023-082-2 **$16.95**

The Jewish Gardening Cookbook: *Growing Plants & Cooking for Holidays & Festivals*
by Michael Brown 6 x 9, 224 pp, Illus., Quality PB, ISBN 1-58023-116-0 **$16.95**;
HC, ISBN 1-58023-004-0 **$21.95**

Spirituality

My People's Prayer Book: *Traditional Prayers, Modern Commentaries*
Ed. by *Dr. Lawrence A. Hoffman*

Provides a diverse and exciting commentary to the traditional liturgy, helping modern men and women find new wisdom in Jewish prayer, and bring liturgy into their lives. Each book includes Hebrew text, modern translation, and commentaries *from all perspectives* of the Jewish world.

Vol. 1—*The Sh'ma and Its Blessings,* 7 x 10, 168 pp, HC, ISBN 1-879045-79-6 **$23.95**
Vol. 2—*The Amidah,* 7 x 10, 240 pp, HC, ISBN 1-879045-80-X **$23.95**
Vol. 3—*P'sukei D'zimrah* (Morning Psalms), 7 x 10, 240 pp, HC, ISBN 1-879045-81-8 **$24.95**
Vol. 4—*Seder K'riat Hatorah* (The Torah Service), 7 x 10, 264 pp, HC, ISBN 1-879045-82-6 **$23.95**
Vol. 5—*Birkhot Hashachar* (Morning Blessings), 7 x 10, 240 pp, HC, ISBN 1-879045-83-4 **$24.95**
Vol. 6—*Tachanun and Concluding Prayers,* 7 x 10, 240 pp, HC, ISBN 1-879045-84-2 **$24.95**

Six Jewish Spiritual Paths: *A Rationalist Looks at Spirituality*
by Rabbi Rifat Sonsino
6 x 9, 208 pp, Quality PB, ISBN 1-58023-167-5 **$16.95**; HC, ISBN 1-58023-095-4 **$21.95**

Becoming a Congregation of Learners
Learning as a Key to Revitalizing Congregational Life by Isa Aron, Ph.D.;
Foreword by Rabbi Lawrence A. Hoffman, Co-Developer, Synagogue 2000
6 x 9, 304 pp, Quality PB, ISBN 1-58023-089-X **$19.95**

Self, Struggle & Change
Family Conflict Stories in Genesis and Their Healing Insights for Our Lives
by Dr. Norman J. Cohen 6 x 9, 224 pp, Quality PB, ISBN 1-879045-66-4 **$16.95**

Voices from Genesis: *Guiding Us through the Stages of Life*
by Dr. Norman J. Cohen 6 x 9, 192 pp, Quality PB, ISBN 1-58023-118-7 **$16.95**

Ancient Secrets: *Using the Stories of the Bible to Improve Our Everyday Lives*
by Rabbi Levi Meier, Ph.D. 5½ x 8½, 288 pp, Quality PB, ISBN 1-58023-064-4 **$16.95**

The Business Bible: *10 New Commandments for Bringing Spirituality & Ethical Values into the Workplace*
by Rabbi Wayne Dosick 5½ x 8½, 208 pp, Quality PB, ISBN 1-58023-101-2 **$14.95**

Being God's Partner: *How to Find the Hidden Link Between Spirituality and Your Work*
by Rabbi Jeffrey K. Salkin; Intro. by Norman Lear AWARD WINNER!
6 x 9, 192 pp, Quality PB, ISBN 1-879045-65-6 **$16.95**; HC, ISBN 1-879045-37-0 **$19.95**

God & the Big Bang
Discovering Harmony Between Science & Spirituality AWARD WINNER!
by Daniel C. Matt 6 x 9, 224 pp, Quality PB, ISBN 1-879045-89-3 **$16.95**

Soul Judaism: *Dancing with God into a New Era*
by Rabbi Wayne Dosick 5½ x 8½, 304 pp, Quality PB, ISBN 1-58023-053-9 **$16.95**

Finding Joy: *A Practical Spiritual Guide to Happiness* AWARD WINNER!
by Rabbi Dannel I. Schwartz with Mark Hass
6 x 9, 192 pp, Quality PB, ISBN 1-58023-009-1 **$14.95**; HC, ISBN 1-879045-53-2 **$19.95**

Spirituality & More

The Jewish Lights Spirituality Handbook
A Guide to Understanding, Exploring & Living a Spiritual Life
Ed. by *Stuart M. Matlins, Editor in Chief, Jewish Lights Publishing*

Rich, creative material from over fifty spiritual leaders on every aspect of Jewish spirituality today: prayer, meditation, mysticism, study, rituals, special days, the everyday, and more.
6 x 9, 456 pp, Quality PB, ISBN 1-58023-093-8 **$18.95**; HC, ISBN 1-58023-100-4 **$24.95**

The Story of the Jews: *A 4,000-Year Adventure—A Graphic History Book*
Written and illustrated by *Stan Mack*

Through witty cartoons and accurate narrative, illustrates the major characters and events that have shaped the Jewish people and culture. For all ages.
6 x 9, 304 pp, Quality PB, Illus., ISBN 1-58023-155-1 **$16.95**

The Jewish Prophet: *Visionary Words from Moses and Miriam to Henrietta Szold and A. J. Heschel*
by *Rabbi Dr. Michael J. Shire*

This beautifully illustrated collection of Jewish prophecy features the lives and teachings of thirty men and women, from biblical times to modern day. Provides an inspiring and informative description of the role each played in their own time, and an explanation of why we should know about them in our time. Illustrated with illuminations from medieval Hebrew manuscripts.
6½ x 8½, 128 pp, HC, 123 full-color illus., ISBN 1-58023-168-3 **$25.00**

  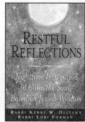  

The Enneagram and Kabbalah: *Reading Your Soul*
by Rabbi Howard A. Addison 6 x 9, 176 pp, Quality PB, ISBN 1-58023-001-6 **$15.95**

Cast in God's Image: *Discover Your Personality Type Using the Enneagram and Kabbalah*
by Rabbi Howard A. Addison 7 x 9, 176 pp, Quality PB, ISBN 1-58023-124-1 **$16.95**

Mystery Midrash: *An Anthology of Jewish Mystery & Detective Fiction* AWARD WINNER!
Ed. by Lawrence W. Raphael 6 x 9, 304 pp, Quality PB, ISBN 1-58023-055-5 **$16.95**

Criminal Kabbalah: *An Intriguing Anthology of Jewish Mystery & Detective Fiction*
Ed. by Lawrence W. Raphael; Foreword by Laurie R. King
6 x 9, 256 pp, Quality PB, ISBN 1-58023-109-8 **$16.95**

Sacred Intentions: *Daily Inspiration to Strengthen the Spirit, Based on Jewish Wisdom*
by Rabbi Kerry M. Olitzky & Rabbi Lori Forman
4½ x 6½, 448 pp, Quality PB, ISBN 1-58023-061-X **$15.95**

Restful Reflections: *Nighttime Inspiration to Calm the Soul, Based on Jewish Wisdom*
by Rabbi Kerry M. Olitzky & Rabbi Lori Forman
4½ x 6½, 448 pp, Quality PB, ISBN 1-58023-091-1 **$15.95**

Embracing the Covenant: *Converts to Judaism Talk About Why & How* Ed. by Rabbi Allan Berkowitz & Patti Moskovitz 6 x 9, 192 pp, Quality PB, ISBN 1-879045-50-8 **$16.95**

Wandering Stars: *An Anthology of Jewish Fantasy & Science Fiction* Ed. by Jack Dann; Intro. by Isaac Asimov 6 x 9, 272 pp, Quality PB, ISBN 1-58023-005-9 **$16.95**

Israel—A Spiritual Travel Guide: *A Companion for the Modern Jewish Pilgrim* AWARD WINNER!
by Rabbi Lawrence A. Hoffman 4¾ x 10, 256 pp, Quality PB, ISBN 1-879045-56-7 **$18.95**

The Way Into... Series

A major multi-volume series to be completed over the next several years, **The Way Into... provides an accessible and usable "guided tour" of the Jewish faith, its people, its history and beliefs—in total, an introduction to Judaism for adults that will enable them to understand and interact with sacred texts.** Each volume is written by a major modern scholar and teacher, and is organized around an important concept of Judaism.

The Way Into... will enable all readers to achieve a real sense of Jewish cultural literacy through guided study. Available volumes:

The Way Into Torah
by *Dr. Norman J. Cohen*

What is "Torah"? What are the different approaches to studying Torah? What are the different levels of understanding Torah? For whom is study intended? Explores the origins and development of Torah, why it should be studied and how to do it. An easy-to-use, easy-to-understand introduction to an ancient subject.
6 x 9, 176 pp, HC, ISBN 1-58023-028-8 **$21.95**

The Way Into Jewish Prayer
by *Dr. Lawrence A. Hoffman*

Opens the door to 3,000 years of the Jewish way to God by making available all you need to feel at home in Jewish worship. Provides basic definitions of the terms you need to know as well as thoughtful analysis of the depth that lies beneath Jewish prayer.
6 x 9, 224 pp, HC, ISBN 1-58023-027-X **$21.95**

The Way Into Encountering God in Judaism
by *Dr. Neil Gillman*

Explains how Jews have encountered God throughout history—and today—by exploring the many metaphors for God in Jewish tradition. Explores the Jewish tradition's passionate but also conflicting ways of relating to God as Creator, relational partner, and a force in history and nature.
6 x 9, 240 pp, HC, ISBN 1-58023-025-3 **$21.95**

The Way Into Jewish Mystical Tradition
by *Rabbi Lawrence Kushner*

Explains the principles of Jewish mystical thinking, their religious and spiritual significance, and how they relate to our lives. A book that allows us to experience and understand the Jewish mystical approach to our place in the world.
6 x 9, 224 pp, HC, ISBN 1-58023-029-6 **$21.95**

Or phone, fax, mail or e-mail to: **JEWISH LIGHTS Publishing**
Sunset Farm Offices, Route 4 • P.O. Box 237 • Woodstock, Vermont 05091
Tel: (802) 457-4000 • Fax: (802) 457-4004 • www.jewishlights.com
Credit card orders: **(800) 962-4544** (8:30AM–5:30PM ET Monday–Friday)
Generous discounts on quantity orders. SATISFACTION GUARANTEED. Prices subject to change.